EMANCIPATION AND EMPOWERMENT OF WOMEN

EMANCIPATION AND EMPOWERMENT OF WOMEN

Dr. (Mrs.) V. Mohini Giri

Foreword by
V.R. Krishna Iyer

GYAN PUBLISHING HOUSE
New Delhi-110002

Emancipation and Empowerment of Women

ISBN: 81-212-0598-0

Published in 2005 in India by
Gyan Publishing House
5, Ansari Road, Darya Ganj, New Delhi-110002
Phones : 23282060, 23261060, Fax : (011) 23285914
E-mail : gyanbook@vsnl.com
Website : http://www.gyanbooks.com

Laser Typesetting at : Shree Vaishnavi Creations, Delhi
Printed at : Chawla Offset Press, Delhi

To

Amma

VANI RAM

who taught me the ABC

of human relations

CONTENTS

FOREWORD

An institution, however well-structured, cannot gain locomotion and fulfil its founding mission unless its chemistry is catalysed by leaders with vision and passion. Sometimes, even an instrument, if its limbs hang limp or its teeth do not bite, may achieve functional success if its engineers operate with devotion to the cause and determination to get things done. An obvious Indian illustration of this general proposition is the National Commission for Women. After long internal struggle and pressure of international voices, the Government of India and Parliament, with dominant masculine ethos, enacted a law good in parts but leaving gaps in critical spaces. And the halting history of women's battle for justice did gain momentum when the Commission went into action led by committed women of stature. The ability to radiate inspiration makes all the difference between success and failure. When the story of the Indian Women's Commission comes to be written one name will shine, one figure will stand tall, one voice will be stridently heard—that person is Dr. Mohini Giri.

Liberation of womanhood to gain her personhood is a fundamental of humanity's human rights. That idea is indefeasible and mounts to new heights of battle-readiness with each passing day. But the male gender, with genetic arrogance and cultural confrontation, resists it with pathological myopia. But Victor Hugo, with far-sighted perception, had said: "A stand can be taken against invasion by an army; no stand can be made against invasion by an idea." The idea of womanhood's gender justice demand is invincible. But ideas need leaders to lend them elan and Mohini Giri has been chosen by current history to play that role—not singly, but ably aided by sisters like Padma Seth, a seasoned soldier and intellectual adviser with wisdom and courage. Today, Mohini Giri is no mere Chairperson of a Commission, from which office she is retiring because of tenurial efflux of time; she is a tempest, a bugle, a marching order personified. Proof? Her speeches and thoughts, collected together and published. If Emerson's observation is valid: "Words are also actions, and actions are a kind of words."

The incendiary impact of the spoken word and the long acting effect of the written word are combined in the book of Mohini Giri, because it is a text of the speeches delivered from various places on various fiery facets of women's grievances. The area covered by the various lectures is immense and the pages sometimes poignant, sometimes indignant. I do not wish to go into the details except to state that she touched none which she did not adorn. Anyone interested in Gender Justice in its dynamics must read Dr. Mohini Giri from Beijing and Nairobi and other parts of the world and within India. Numerous conferences have been addressed by her. New techniques of ventilating women's grievances have been innovated by the Women's Commission and to a large extent there has been an awakening among men and women, politicians and social activists who operate on the urgency of restoring the egalitarian status of women. Let me quote some passages from one of her speeches:

"Thinking together we can move forward. Ideas don't need any legs to stride but they need institutions to translate all the promises to real life. Likewise, cooperation must emerge. We must all cooperate to free women and children from the deplorable human violations.

I know the path is not at all smooth. I know there is no easy way to solutions. There is no magic wand which can be twirled to remove this blot. I know, too, that no matter how many conferences we have, how many laws we make, the truth is that we cannot wipe off the tears from the face of every girl who has been hurt, abused and traumatized. There are not choices. A bold beginning has to be made. We are far from achieving our goals, but for as long as we keep the struggle alive, we can continue to give hope to our children, and vindicate all those who perished as victims.

Let all our voices resound as we commit to restore to the children their dignity, their humanity, their childhood and their bright future."

Principled pragmatism is valiant prudence in issues where society is hesitant and resistant. So she carefully observes:

"In spite of several laws, women have not been able to get justice. There has been constant increase in the number of crimes against women. Harassment of women at work places is also on the increase. It is because women do not come forward and raise their voices. Increasing participation of women in political processes and trade union activities is one of the major ways in which the traditional male dominated value system can be challenged.

In the modern world, the role of the women goes much beyond the home and the bringing up of children. She is now adopting a career of her own and sharing equally with man the responsibility for the development of society in all its aspects. This is the direction in which we shall have to move and move fast."

Practical measures, not idealistic illusions are the road to success. So she argues:

"I believe that we do not suffer from the lack of theoretical formulations and planning strategies. It seems that our weakness lies in the lack of sincerity in execution and vigour in implementation. Dissemination of education cannot be achieved by mere desk work. One has to get down to the field to work among people through measures of confidence-building. It is in this spirit that we suggest here the strategy of sustained application of extension work particularly in geographic pockets identified as low literacy pockets. It is in this context that my suggestion to the corporate sector to launch education projects for women has to be seen."

"We should seriously look at the problem in which many more women will be enabled to become a part of the political process starting from the lowest level. We have now reservation for women in Panchayati Raj institutions and urban local bodies. Unless adequate steps are taken to educate women on the essentials of local administration, the revolutionary steps we have taken towards political empowerment of women may not yield the desired results, particularly when we are in the process of presenting reservation for women in State Legislatures and Lok Sabha. During the first fifty years of this century, women's literacy rose from 0.69 to 8.86% and later during the fifty years of independence 8.86 to 39.29%. These figures are revealing. The pace of progress is too slow which calls for policy level changes and operational techniques. We may have to adopt result yielding techniques in the field of education for women so that we have in the next decade more literate women than the illiterate women."

Sex workers, usually despised as sub-human, have received serious attention from the Commission led by Mrs. Giri. Public hearings have been held and amendments to the Laws have been suggested; rehabilitation of the rape victims has been seriously undertaken, especially when they come from remote areas of Himachal Pradesh and other neighbouring countries.

Inevitably, the Commission, particularly Dr. Mohini Giri, has turned its focus on the Reservation question, proposing 33.1/3rd per cent for women in the legislatures. The widespread and vibrant women's movement has owed its speed and sensitising success to Dr. Mohini Giri and her companion Padma Seth.

The volume is long and the pages many; the subjects are widespread and the concern shown is deep. The progress of the nation is integrally linked with the advance of women. Therefore, we have to take the Commission as a powerful instrument which needs substantial changes so that those who operate the Commission prove victorious in the war against women's injustice. Dr. Giri and her companions, I am sure, will continue to function with great radicalism, even if they retire from the Commission. What we need is cadres and leaders for the job to be completed; and here we have such a team in the Commission and such a leader in Dr. Mohini Giri.

21.5.1998 **V.R. Krishna Iyer**

PREFACE

During my three-decade involvement with social and family issues affecting women in their day-to-day life, personal involvement in tackling the problems enabled me to further inquire and participate in meaningful deliberations. Over the years, befitting particular occasions, it has been the practice to record in some detail the philosophy, the pros and cons of the matters, possible strategies to solve the human problems and so on. The search for solutions is a continuous process. In a humble way, some of the possible approaches are discussed in this volume.

It has been observed that "Social science affirms that a woman's place in society marks the level of civilisation". While it is acknowledged that during the 50 years since Independence, the status of women in India has improved in many respects, yet there are many areas where progress is negligible.

The main purpose of this effort is to create an awareness, partiality among women, social workers and policy thinkers. It is hoped that this publication would generate enough interest in pondering over the issues and taking steps to initiate specific measures for emancipation and empowerment of women.

The primary responsibility for the empowerment of women is really a societal responsibility... to the extent if I have been able to reach out to the various segments of our society in this task... I consider myself as having contributed. I have no illusions that the road ahead is long and arduous but I remain convinced that our collective efforts would succeed and the women of India would occupy their due and rightful place in society.

To Justice Krishna Iyer I owe special gratitude for his guidance. In the preparation of this book, I have received tremendous encouragement and help from many persons. While it would be difficult to acknowledge each and everyone, I am indebted to Justice V.R. Krishna Iyer for graciously writing a thought-provoking Foreword.

I would also like to express my gratitude to Dr. P.S.K. Menon for assisting me at almost all stages, in bringing out this publication.

Shri Amit Garg, Director Publication of Gyan Publishing House, deserves sincere thanks for printing and publishing this book in an excellent manner in record time.

New Delhi **Dr. (Mrs.) V. Mohini Giri**

1

VOLUNTARY EFFORTS IN WOMEN UPLIFT

NGOs: KEY PLAYERS IN NATION-BUILDING

The Young Women's Christian Association (YWCA) in India has a long history of its commitment in serving women and girls of our country. You have given me an opportunity of sharing with you my thoughts and impressions of the UN World Conference held in Beijing as Chairperson of the National Commission for Women (NCW).

Some of you may have attended the conference as delegates and some as NGO (Non-Government Organisation) participants. We seriously deliberated and adopted a platform of action for the coming decade; on behalf of the Government of India and the YWCA as a national level autonomous body with vast experience in the field of women's welfare.

Our Government's commitment towards women's issues and concerns have been stated categorically as :

- increasing our investment on education to 6 per cent of the GDP with the major focus on women and the girl child;
- universalizing mother and child-care programmes to reach out to every corner of the country;
- formulating and operationalising a National Policy on women which will continuously guide and inform

action at every level and in every sector;

- setting up a Commissioner for Women's Rights to act as a public defender of women's human rights:
- institutionalizing a national level mechanism which will monitor the implementation of the Platform of Action.

Although contemporary history has witnessed momentous changes in the last two decades, it has to be recognized that gender discrimination still hounds women globally, be it in the West or developing countries such as ours. We discovered that in their protracted struggle for equality, women around the world face some common problems and obstacles.

The Government of India recognizes the significant role that NGOs can play in evolving new strategies for social change, looking beyond and coming up with new thoughts, new modalities of life, new laws and institutions. In many countries they just set the trends which later become national policies and programmes and this is true in the case of women's movements also. Many of us, representatives of the Government and NGOs have had leaders in the struggle for women's equality in society.

At its 39th session held at the UN headquarters, the Commission on the Status of Women acting as the preparatory body for the 4th World Conference on Women prepared a Draft Platform for Action—"Equality, Development and Peace" which was transmitted for consideration. It contained the analysis of the global context and situations of women and presents a dozen or more critical areas of concerns and strategic objectives and action proposals to address these concerns. We struggled with issues, some of relevance to our country, and others that seemed frivolous in the present scenario affecting the status of women in India.

What we discussed at Beijing with regard to strategic objectives and action proposals are in the nature of abhorring, extension and supplement to the Nairobi Forward Looking Strategies for Advancement of Women, but with significant shifts in emphasis—whereas the Nairobi Strategy attached prime value to equal access to basic services such as health and education and employment opportunities, legal and institutional provisions in support of women's equal rights, the plan of action envisages the empowerment of women by way of equality, education, training, equal access to all types of development resources, power sharing in the form of equal participation in national decision-making, including political participation and structural and institutional adjustments to accommodate these requirements.

The Government's commitment is a powerful tool to be used for successful implementation of the action proposal and we are depending on the cooperation of the legislative and judicial establishments, citizens with diverse and mutually competing interests to help us in this task.

I would like to reiterate that the operation of the given mandate is possible if we work with NGOs, the women's movements and activist groups.

You probably know that efforts have been made to form an organizational structure to coordinate efforts to achieve our goals by setting up of a group cavitating of the Central Social Welfare Board, the National Commission for Women, the Rashtriya Mahila Kosh and the Women's Development Division of NIPCCD.

To bridge the gap between the National Commission for Women and NGOs, I have set up in the Commission a Coordination Committee and have invited organizations at national level, yours being one, to meet at regular intervals for interaction and exchange of views, so that our hands are strengthened as partners in our common concern and objectives to serve best interests of women, a task we have undertaken and hope we will accomplish to the best of our abilities.

Role of NGOs in National Development

I was pleasantly surprised when I received a phone call from Brig. M. G. Datar—Secretary of the prestigious training institution for Armed Forces, viz. the National Defence College inviting me to address the gathering of members of the 36th N.D.C. course which, I gather, is presently being conducted here in New Delhi.

My first reaction to Brig. Datar's invitation was that of "surprise" : surprise at a Brigadier in our Armed Forces requesting me—the Chairperson of the National Commission for Women—to address senior personnel from Indian and foreign armed forces on a socially relevant theme—"Role of NGOs in National Development". At first sight, this theme seemed out of "sync" with the normally accepted role of our armed forces!

However, on thinking it over, one couldn't help feeling that the invitation extended to me was, in fact, indicative of the rapid changes that we are seeing today : about a decade or so ago, hardly anyone in India would have thought that Indian women could be pilots in the I.A.F. nor, for that matter, would we be having women entering the armed forces, the police and other professions which were generally reserved strictly for "Men only".

Similarly, the role of voluntary agencies or NGOs is perhaps a theme which not so long ago would hardly have been considered worth discussing, especially in the context of national development; nor, if I might be bold enough to add, for discussion in a military institution like the National Defence College : if I am wrong, I'd be happy to stand corrected!

For the past 25 years or more - I have personally been involved in one way or the other, with various NGOs. I have always been happy to see the way they have been progressing—of these, two NGOs could be of particular interest to you.

In 1971, I was the Founder President of the All India War Widows' Association while in 1982 I was associated with the Air Force Wives' Association.

My association with NGOs operating in diverse fields has given me opportunity to have first hand experience of problems faced by them, in trying to achieve their stated goals and, more important, how they have tried to cope with those problems. It is heartening to know that in the recent past there has been a general recognition of the fact that NGOs can play an active role in national development, and this recognition has been proclaimed through various statements by the Prime Minister and other leaders.

Growth graph of NGOs in India

Looking back, one could broadly categorize the growth pattern of NGOs into different phases, spread over the past four decades:

- In the early stages, NGOs tended to concentrate on reforms involving social issues and providing some form of institutional services for the weaker sections of our society. The mid-70s saw a torsional shift from curative and ameliorative services to preventive and development aspects. This, in turn, initiated the process of improving the awareness and consciousness of people, especially women, about their status and their hitherto, unknown and possibly, hidden rights. Perhaps noticing the work of NGOs, especially the more effective ones, the Government found these NGOs to be useful tools in welfare and development activities, many of whom were involved in organizations for formulating policies and programmes especially for the poor, the downtrodden and women. It is no secret that women NGOs and women activists played an important role in having a statutory body like the National Commission for Women set up in January, 1992.

- To assist NGOs develop a spirit of "joint venture" with the Government in identifying problems and developing need-based solutions, Ministries/ Departments of the Government formulated various schemes involving NGOs. Under this arrangement, policy-making and funding generally lay in the hands of official, government machinery, while for the implementation of projects, NGOs took on a "lead role".
- As part of the spirit of joint venture, NGOs and Government agencies collaborated in organizing workshops, seminars, etc, : the main objective of these efforts were (a) creating awareness of social and development issues and (b) developing appropriate action plans.
- In the 1990s, while NGOs still concentrated on women's issues, health, child-care, employment and similar socially-relevant courses, they also made interesting and welcome entries into new areas such as land afforestation, wasteland development, water resources development, use of appropriate technology (at grass roots level), and finding innovative and experimental measures to suit specific needs of local communities.

In fact, a trend seems to be on development in the direction of :

- attitudinal changes through education or "awareness" type seminars, discussions, workshops, training programmes (especially at grass roots level e.g. newly elected Panchayat members);

- and mobilization of scarce resources : in fact, there are quite a few NGOs manned by dedicated, academically well-qualified persons who are working silently in the field of low-cost housing, developing alternative sources of energy and assisting in national development by adopting and educating people at the village and Block levels as to how to use technology that is appropriate and useful at grass roots level.

The 'Gram Vikas' of Orissa

What I have said so far, could perhaps fall into perspective if we examine a case-study relating to the growth of a specific NGO over the years. It is easy for me to speak about my experience in some of the NGOs I have been personally involved in, but since personal association could bring in undue subjectivity and bias, I'd like to discuss the case of an NGO, which I have heard about. The NGO I have in mind is 'GRAM VIKAS', which is based in Orissa.

Legally, Gram Vikas was formed as a "society" under Indian laws in 1979 as a non-profit, secular, voluntary organization with its headquarters in the Ganjam district of southern Orissa. However, its actual origin goes back much earlier when a group of students of Madras University formed an organization which they called the "Young Students Movement for Development" (YSMD). I would like to emphasize that this students' organization laid considerable emphasis on the last word of their organization's name—"DEVELOPMENT". The idealism of these students motivated them to agree to work for the development of the weaker sections of society and be willing to forget the comforts of living in an urban society.

Even in their student days this group swung into action when coastal Orissa was hit by a devastating cyclone in 1971. I remember vividly that terrible cyclone when thousands were rendered homeless and considerable rehabilitation work was required so as to make life liveable for the poor and unfortunate victims of that cyclone. But regardless of personal risks and physical discomfort, this group of 200 students—along with other official and non-official relief workers—battled on and helped that cyclone-hit coastal area of Orissa recover from a tragic experience.

Thereafter, a few of those Madras University students stayed on in Orissa and decided to work with, and for, the poor. In fact, they moved on to Ganjam district of Orissa—a district known for its poverty and overall backwardness.

In 1979, this small group of students from Madras University formed an NGO which they called "Gram Vikas", as a non-profit and secular, voluntary organization with its main office at Mohuda (near Berhampur) in Ganjam district. Initially, their developmental activities were restricted to 11 villages in the hills near Berhampur. Since then, their activities cover almost all districts of Orissa, except Puri, Balasore and Dhenkanal.

With about 22 per cent of Orissa's population being "tribal", Gram Vikas' priority focus was on tribal community and marginalized people including SCs. In drawing up their objectives and plans of action they adopted what they called an "Intervention Methodology" with regard to rural development. Basically, this methodology centred around:—

- active involvement of all concerned people from different social levels, from problem identification to planning and implementation of a project;
- multi-disciplinary action to create a force for rural development and social change;
- empowerment of people to consolidate gains and to

progress further.

Activities

Over the years Gram Vikas' operations enlarged and now cover an Integrated Tribal Development programme with activities in the field of:

- land afforestation;
- community based activities;
- income generation (through cottage industries producing pottery, pickles, etc. marketed by Gram Vikas);
- bio-gas and alternative sources of energy;
- rural, health and environment;
- training in rural areas;
- disaster management

Funding

Barring a few cash-rich institutions, Gram Vikas faces the same funding problems which most organizations face; like most organizations, NGOs require funds to meet establishment charges and working capital. But, unlike commercial organizations, funds from financial and banking channels are not easily available nor would they be given at affordable rates. Other sources of financing by NGOs such as Gram Vikas had to be identified: these sources included:-

- donations from philanthropic persons and organizations;
- subsidies and grants for specific development activities under various schemes formulated by the Central and State Governments and their agencies;
- Foreign funding agencies (through donations, project funding, and assistance through training, managment

and equipment for office and outdoor purposes).

To be successful in getting funds for NGOs, knowledge of procedures laid down by funding agencies is a must and also laws governing receipts of funds, especially foreign funding.

Crucial observations on NGOs

From the Gram Vikas case and also from ones of which I have personal experience some general observations can be made as follows :

- Perhaps the most important point which stands out is that life and work in NGOs is no "bed of roses". The manpower needs of NGOs can be met by people who are willing to give up material comforts normally associated with today's urban life: in fact working in an NGO requires total dedication to the aims and objectives of the NGO.

- Ability to interact sympathetically with village, rural and tribal people is required.

- Ability to convince donors and funding agencies that requests for funds are consistent with the aims and objectives of the former is a must.

- Staff Recruitment Retention : While the promoters of NGOs are dedicated to their respective objectives recruiting and retaining staff for work in rural and backward areas at very low salary levels is a very difficult task. Young, unmarried and idealistic people could find job satisfaction in work of this type. However, as they grow older, they naturally think of their family needs and perhaps compare themselves with their school and college-mates in other walks of life. This in turn, urges them to think of looking for greener pastures elsewhere. Obviously a high turnover rate follows especially in NGOs operating in backward areas.

- Absence of Professionalism : A few decades ago, perhaps it was possible for NGOs to function in a somewhat amateurish manner. However, with their activities being recognized especially by the Government as positive aids in national development, NGOs roles, have become important. And with NGOs having problem in recruiting professionals dedicated to the organizational goals and at salary levels which they can afford to pay, this problem assumes a degree of importance.
- Ignorance of Documentation Stipulated by Funding Agencies : This problem perhaps arises from the last point I have just mentioned, viz. absence of professionalism. I daresay, this ignorance of required documentation leads to avoidable delays in NGOs receiving project approvals and funds from funding agencies especially government ones.
- Some of these problems have been solved by networking with other NGOs and seeking professional assistance from persons willing to help.

A short while ago, I had mentioned that NGOs generally received funds from philanthropic donors, government funding agencies and foreign donors (individuals, organizations and governments).

As a general rule, funds are made available to NGOs for specific purposes or projects. But, insofar as government funding is concerned, each agency has a detailed form which needs to be filled in before payments are made. Some of the more important Government funding agencies are the Central Social Welfare Board, CAPART, Ministry of Welfare and other Ministries/ Departments of Central and State Governments.

Foreign donor agencies principally include agencies of the UNlike the UNICEF, UNIFEM, UNFPA, ILO, etc, organizations like the Ford Foundation of the USA,

Overseas Development Agency of the U.K., funding agencies registered with the EEC, etc. Apart from convincing foreign agencies to fund Indian NGO projects the Government of India (Home Ministry) and the R.B.I. exercise strict control over remittances of these type. All such donations are governed by the Foreign Contribution (Regulation) Act, 1976. This Act, among other things, makes it mandatory on the part of the NGOs to ensure that before any funds are passed on to any person or association of India, the recipient association is eligible to receive foreign funds and is also registered under this Act or has obtained prior permission from the Government to receive these funds.

While man-made rules and regulations can be drawn up by individual donors and donor organizations for safeguarding respective interests, unfortunately, man's ingenuity can their side track, bend or break rules to suit his selfish needs. I am not suggesting that this is the case with all NGOs but those few, who come into this category, can do a lot of damage to the reputation of NGOs at large.

Rules for functioning

It is a sad commentary of times, when one reads of cases where a Government donor agency like CAPART—an agency which helps NGOs to use appropriate and rural technology at grass roots level had to blacklist last year, a number of about 150 NGOs for misuse of funds allocated by CAPART to them!

Similarly, there are reports of foreign (private and government) agencies who use NGOs to funnel large amounts of money into India for anti-social and anti-national activities. To try and prevent these anti-social and anti-national acts, the Central Government's Home Affairs Ministry has been made the nodal ministry to check, scrutinize and approve all applications under the Foreign Contribution (Regulation) Act, 1976. Other government agencies like the R.B.I. also come into the picture so as to safeguard the country's interests.

As gentlemen involved in the defence of our country, I am sure you would like me to discuss with you as to how some NGOs use foreign funds for nefarious anti-national purposes. I too would like to have done so! Unfortunately, I must disappoint you : my experience and, background in social services leaves me with very little room for manoeuvre. However, during the Question-Answer session which we will be having later, I would try and comment on any issue which I feel I would be competent to do so : I do hope you will appreciate my point of view, especially when I know there are others more knowledgeable than me in the area of security related problems.

Initially at the formative stage of their existence, NGOs face a number of problems involving organization, personnel, infrastructure, even the bureaucracy and in fund-raising. Perhaps it is the idealism and enthusiasm for an NGO's cause that keeps them going-with single minded devotion.

Common areas of operation

As a general rule, NGOs have entered the field of social welfare which include :

- public charities;
- health care;
- poverty alleviation;
- employment generation;
- education and literacy programme.

In the recent past, many NGOs have in a sense upgraded their work indicating their awareness of issues of national importance which includes :-

- AIDs awareness programmes;
- land afforestation;
- wasteland development;
- mother and child welfare;
- low-cost housing;
- energy conservation;
- alternate sources of energy;
- training of panchayat or local government elected members;
- health problems spastics, muscular dystrophy etc.;
- legal awareness programme;
- use of solar energy;
- crimes against women;
- public interest litigation.

This lengthy "short-list" of new activities, in which NGOs have entered, is in line with what our government has been trying to do. And the best part is that there is no clash of interest between NGOs and the Government. It is a happy thought that both sides are not suspicious of each other; and in fact the government looks upon NGOs as a sort of a catalyst in an overall effort for national development. In fact what I had described in the 'Gram Vikas' case study is perhaps being done by innumerable NGOs which have been formed throughout the country and that comprises what may be called a "magnificent achievement".

WOMEN AND SOCIAL SERVICE

I consider it an honour and a privilege to be with you this evening : it certainly is an honour to be among such a distinguished gathering and, it is my privilege to deliver a speech on "Women and Social Service" —a theme which is of great relevance to all of us in today's society.

Women and the cultural divide

Our society has, what could be called, a cultural divide. In this "Divide" we have, at one end, a highly tradition-bound set of mores, while at the other end, lifestyles, attitudes and values are changing at a bewildering pace, thanks to a cultural globalization brought about through satellite television and rapid advances in information technology.

One cannot help having a feeling that this cultural divide has created a host of problems solutions for which are difficult to come by. Take for instance social issues like dowry, sale of minor girls, rape, sati, female infanticide and eve-teasing. These are a few of the many social crimes which Indian women face nowadays, and tackling and preventing them is a herculean task. I wish we had an easy answer but, sad to say, one cannot be too optimistic. We will need a conscious effort on our part—using legal, and persuasive means to eradicate these weaknesses in our society and enhance the strength that is a part of our heritage.

National culture

Culture is a word which seems to convey different meanings to different people. I think it would be useful to view culture on a national basis, bringing into play gender issues and social service.

Not so long ago, the National Commission for Women studied a draft approach paper on "National Cultural Policy" prepared by the Department of Culture. Three specific aspects of this approach paper are of vital importance to women :-

1. Women in India are a great sustaining and preserving force of culture.

2. The cultural fabric in India continues to be enriched by women's contribution.

3. Women must be assigned an important role in all programmes.

And while bringing gender perspective into our cultural policy goals, we should identify action plans as to how we can achieve these goals.

In this context, it is our belief that creative women should be given an equal chance to be seen, heard and have equal access to people in our society. We should not only recognize creative women but also motivate and assist talented girls to achieve levels of national and international excellence. This is one area where those of you who have the power and influence, coupled with the spirit of social service, could play a useful role.

Legal safeguards or "paper tigers"?

It is a sad commentary on our life and times that despite legal safeguards, violence against women goes on in an unabated manner, both inside and outside the home. Women are often terrorized so that they do not assert their rights. All too familiar are cases of rape, molestation, stripping, eve-teasing, kidnapping and abduction, and so also, domestic violence including wife battering, sati, female infanticide, female foeticide, dowry deaths and dowry harassment.

A recent dowry case involving a famous NRI family—a case which hit the headlines throughout the country attracted attention of many. Apparently, crimes of this type exist in different sections of Indian society, despite moderating influences from other cultures and societies.

A peculiar fact is that although violence against women is a global problem, it is yet to be recognized as an issue of human rights abuse. The major instrument for human rights for women is the U.N. Convention on Elimination of All Forms of Discrimination which was adopted by the General Assembly in 1979. This convention had been ratified by India not so long ago.

To make matters worse, crimes against women has been rising rapidly. For example, in 1991 we had approximately 5157 dowry deaths, 20611 molestation cases, 12300 kidnappings and abductions, 10283 cases of eve-teasing, 15949 instances involving cruelty by husbands and relations.

These figures are certainly not something which we can be proud of ! Almost every day our print and electronic media highlight ghastly stories of man's inhumanity to mankind, especially the female variety. I believe, it is the duty of all right thinking people to try and find ways to overcome these social crimes against women.

Unfortunately, the road ahead is a bumpy one and expecting legal equality for women is somewhat a pipe-dream mainly due to :

1. Socio-cultural impediments and tradition-bound customs which shackle women.
2. Ignorance, illiteracy, superstition and self sacrificing attitude of women.
3. Social, economic and financial hurdles faced by women when seeking justice.
4. Biased/discriminatory attitudes and delays by our law enforcement machinery (police and administrators).

For the reasons I have just cited, our legal safeguards tend to be no better than paper tigers.

Culture, women's issues and Rotary Club

Having concentrated on certain aspects of the dark side of Indian society, culture and crimes against women, many Rotarians may be wondering about the relevance of my speech, especially since most of you are successful, and if I may add "hard-nosed" businessmen.

My first reason has already been stated : women and social service is highly relevant to all of us in India today.

Secondly, it is common knowledge that Rotary Clubs are famous for the excellence of their work in social service. Fund raising for deserving socially important causes, organizing medical camps for the poor, the needy and the weaker sections of our society, are some of the examples of the excellent social service done by Rotarians.

I have no doubt that this good work will continue in the future. And in order to assist you in your noble endeavour perhaps my speech could be thought provoking and laced with a few directional pointers.

Where do we go from here?

I have been highlighting some of the horrific aspects of society's crimes against women. I have also mentioned several factors inherent in our society, which tend to make a number of our legal safeguards look like paper tigers.

It would be pointless on my part to conclude on a depressing note. Fortunately, we have amongst us individuals, NGOs and social service organizations like the Rotary Club whose efforts help in minimizing some of the horrendous social evils we find in our society.

Suggestions

At the same time, I am aware, there are limited resources in terms of time, expertise and funds. Social action would, therefore, depend on available resources. However, there are a few suggestions, that I think are worthy of your active consideration :

1. Design and develop educational awareness, grass roots programmes bringing out "cause and effect" aspect of crimes against women.
2. Provide professional training so as to improve relevant skills enabling socially backward women to be more economically viable.
3. Improve work safety standards in factories employing women.
4. Provide health care, nutrition, safe drinking water, fuel and fodder at grass roots level.
5. Support community based welfare activities.
6. Use communication skills in networking NGOs, social service groups like the Rotary Club and Government agencies at grass roots level.
7. Assist socially backward women entrepreneurs to upgrade the quality of their products and find markets for them.
8. Liaise with funding agencies to assist women entrepreneurs with their financial requirements.
9. Train elected women Panchayat members to be more communicative, persuasive and effective members of their Panchayats.
10. Assist in funding and monitoring time bound socially relevant projects concerning women.

12. Consider individual or joint sponsorship of short-duration (one to three minutes) T.V. programmes highlighting women's issues. These could be telecast over Doordarshan on a national and regional basis.

13. Assist in promoting women's adult literacy programmes.

14. Use your personal skills in areas of your influence to minimize disputes affecting women.

15. Try and convert our paper tigers to be effective legal instruments in safeguarding of women and their rights.

---

*A happy marriage is the union of two good forgivers.

2

THE NATIONAL COMMISSION FOR WOMEN

ROLE OF THE NATIONAL COMMISSION FOR WOMEN

The National Commission for Women is a product of the women's movement in the country. Parliamentarians and legislators gave the needed push to the passing of the National Commission for Women Act, 1990. (For the statute refer to Appendix I). The National Commission for Women (NCW) was constituted to perform various functions including investigation and examination of all matters relating to safeguards for women under the Constitution and other laws. The Commission has also to review, from time to time, the existing provisions of the Constitution and laws affecting women and recommend amendments thereto so as to suggest remedial legislative measures to meet the lacunae or shortcomings in such legislation. Through its various expert committees on laws and legislation, the Commission has examined and formulated measures to fill areas where there are no laws, such as domestic crimes and look into the adoption of abandoned and destitute children, the common marriage bill, compulsory registration of marriages, etc. While looking into complaints on violence against women and also violation of legal provisions and safeguards for women, the National Commission could take *suo motu* notice of matters relating to deprivation of women's rights, non-implementation of laws, in order to provide protection to women and also to achieve the objective of equality and development. Besides, it could take action where non-compliance of policy decisions, guidelines or instructions were aimed at mitigating hardship and ensuring welfare and providing relief to women.

Activities

The first and foremost case that of Poonam Baluja, may be cited, where the victim was wrongly confined to jail after sunset and the police officer was persuading her to enter flesh trade to earn adequate riches. Almost a secret investigation made by NCW of this case resulted in dismissal of the police official concerned. It was a rare case, of a type wherein the police was fighting its own police vigilance department for having produced and corroborated the evidence given by the NCW. It is important to mention about this case as our first fight against victory gets gender justice. In spite of the fact that NCW has been especially set up as a statutory autonomous body, it is not to be equated with the role of crime against women's cell or an NGO or any other institution fighting individually and collectively for safeguarding women's rights. However, the NCW being the apex body on whom a lot of confidence has been reposed by the society and especially by the women at large, NCW took upon itself the onus of taking up certain exemplary cases which would have wider impact on maximum number of women in the country. Banwari Devi's gang-rape in Bateri village in Rajasthan has been a case in point. It is because of NCW's investigation and insistence and persuasion, that the Prime Minister came forward to offer an immediate relief to the victim and also through the CBI to thoroughly investigate the case and book the culprit. While one accused was arrested the other two are still absconding.

The NCW's intervention in this case catapulted focus on atrocities against rural women and *Saathins* who are state functionaries. This acted as a deterrent against violence on women—village functionaries like ICDS, the *Saathins*, gram, etc. Another case that needs mention is the timely intervention of NCW in a stripping case of Usha Dhiman, of Saharanpur who was a prey to the unruly elements and land mafia. Strangely, in the presence of police personnel, Usha Dhiman was stripped in public and was not lent a helping hand by anyone including the police. It was at the NCW's behest that an enquiry was conducted, transfers of concerned officials have been effected and due punishment was given. Similarly, in village Kutra, a tribal woman named Basanti Bara was elected as the President of the Panchayat and she has alleged that the State Minister for Tribals and Women Welfare of Orissa, who came to inaugurate the community centre, started molesting her in public. Her complaint reached NCW and the NCW, with its powers of a civil court, could summon the collector, the DSP and various officials, the victim and also the accused minister. These are some instances that could be quoted as NCW's successful fight against gender injustice. There are other instances and cases of grievances that we have received and attended to but the Commission cannot boast of solving all the cases. The Jayashankarpur (Orissa) village gang rape case by the police force was totally subdued by the local politicians, administration and the police. NCW's record has so far shown how party politics, caste or religious affiliations hinder the commitment to help the women who have been afflicted by various crimes. Apart from investigating various cases could investigate and summon witnesses and get the guilty punished through existing judicial delivery system, the NCW could organize a variety of conferences, workshops and seminars, where issues pertaining to gender bias are discussed and recommendations are forwarded to the concerned authorities for implementation. Though the Commission is short of adjudicatory powers, it has the power to persuade and advise the planning process of socio-economic development of women. Its contribution to the reforms in jails and especially in getting non-criminal lunatic convicts and undertrials released is significant. Various jails are inspected and the NCW is organizing sensitization programmes for I.G. Prisons, and prison and police officials.

The Commission could also undertake promotional and educational research to find out ways of ensuring due representation of women in all spheres and identify factors responsible for impeding their advancement and growth such as, lack of access to housing and basic services, inadequate support services and technologies for reducing drudgery and occupational hazards, and in increasing their productivity. About 36-40 reports have been produced and various recommendations have already been sent to the concerned ministries/departments for implementation.

In its crusade against discrimination, violation of women's rights/human rights and the ever continuing gender injustice, the NCW has successfully gained recognition by the Supreme Court and various commissions who advised the Commission to prepare guidelines by which some respite and cheer could be brought to the unfortunate women victims. The Commission also funds, to some extent, litigation involving issues affecting a large body of women and makes periodical reports to the Government, both at the Centre and the State. The Central Government has referred a number of laws that needed amendment and there is constant interaction and consultations with the Ministry of Home Affairs, Ministry of Health, Department of Women and Child Development Ministry of Human Resource Development, Ministry of Welfare, etc.

The Commission has also successfully intervened against the Kerala Christian Bill denying Christian women's right to inheritance to property. Mary Roy's is a case in point. NCW has decided to intervene in the case filed in the Supreme Court by senior citizens of Karnataka against $33_{1/3}$ per cent reservation of women in Panchayati raj and local sabha governments. They proposed to challenge the 73rd and 74th Amendments to the Constitution on ground that the aforesaid Amendments are contrary to the equality provision in the Constitution. (For extracts of 73rd and 74th Amendents of the Constitution refer Appendix II). We requested senior advocates of the Supreme Court in all these cases to represent the NCW including the case of Khartoonisa Begum's on the question of *Futwa*. In spite of the fact that the Commission has been empowered to enter into all areas pertaining to women's issues and problems, the NCW feels that the remote village women still remain outside the precincts of justice.

Status of NCW

I am happy to share with you that we have State Commissions for Women functioning in several States of India and this will be a part of our networking. Now there are twelve Commission for women in the states of, Assam, Delhi, Karnataka, Kerala, Maharashtra, Orissa, Tamil Nadu, Tripura, West Bengal, Goa, Himachal Pradesh and Madhya Pradesh. These Commissions are very enthusiastic in seeking guidelines from the National Commission and also in feeding us with information on the status of women in their respective States. They are free to refer cases which may be beyond their jurisdiction. I wish that each State police system takes notice of this fact and tries to establish contacts with the State Commission so that this becomes a happy alliance in search of justice for women.

Not a day passes, without the headlines in newspapers screaming, murder, mayhem or rape of women, even in the capital city of the country. This is not to say that there are no murders of men and children. The country is facing, as never before a torrent of crime, due to various socio-economic reasons not to speak of infiltration of illegal migrants, besides enemy State sponsored terrorism to strike at innocent victims, be they women and children or other citizens.

However, the worst-affected in this crime scenario are the women, as biologically they are vulnerable to sexual assault, rape, mass rape and gang rape, often committed by ruffians and the criminal factions to settle old scores with their rivals and enemies. Much of this kind of heinous crimes and atrocities have their roots in the drug mafia, foreign patronage and enemy country strategies to destabilize the civilian population, women and children and strike terror in their hearts. Planting of crude bombs, human bombs, exploiting women as suicide bombers have all now become a part of the criminal pattern.

This being briefly the crime pattern where do we go from here. Arresting of further crime and criminals creeping into society in the garb of respectable or even common citizens and devising various ways and strategies for prevention of crime must be made the fundamental base for grappling with this enormous problem, which is indeed a global phenomenon today.

Objectives of NCW

One of the chief objectives of the National Commission for Women is to ensure the safety and security of all women, as a prelude towards their progress and development. We must explore every possibility for prevention of crime and also bring to book the criminals who have perpetrated such crimes as rape, bride-burning and dowry deaths. But this is no easy task.

Statistics tell us that a woman is raped every hour, a dowry death occurs every one-and-a half hours and a woman is molested every hour somewhere or the other in the country. Also, every seven minutes an act of criminal offence against women is committed. There is an alarming increase and rise in crime from year to year, in dowry deaths and marital cruelty. This is indeed a grim situation.

Many factors linked to the growth of crime are, no doubt, beyond the control of police. As far back as in 1970, a United Nations Congress on Prevention of Crime identified some crimogenic factors, these are : urbanization, industrialization, population growth, outpacing the availability of housing, water supply, and other civic services, internal migration, not to speak of illegal migration, rapid technological changes in transport and communication techniques, which aid the international criminals to operate globally under cover of secrecy and thus cover their tracks.

A recent study of the working of the police reveals a considerable number among them are virtually untrained and not able or equipped to grapple or cope with critical situations, particularly due to mass recruitment of constables without fulfilling even the minimum requirements, often due to graft practices. In the process, many recruits with even a shady criminal past and record have managed to get inducted into the police force, both at the Centre and of course in the States, making a mockery of all procedures including routine police character certification. An ordinary citizen has to clear himself at so many levels before even a minor appointment either in the Government or even in the public or private sectors, but the guardians of law often skip these essential and vital formalities looming large over the civilians transcending and transgressing all laws.

In this context the Vohra Committee report of the former Home Secretary, acquires special significance. In this report, he was assisted by the heads of the Intelligence Bureau, Central Bureau of Investigation, and other experts but many of the recommendations, now over two years old are yet to be implemented and are collecting dust. These have not even been debated, mainly because the report has underscored the evils and repercussions of the continual and near perpetual criminal nexus of the unscrupulous politicians with the underworld dons and mafia. Also, over the years the criminals themselves get elected to local bodies and finally attain political stature, with immense evil and destructive powers to use every kind of luxury as perceived by them and mainly young women become pawns in their game.

The vested interests

Resultantly, the criminal-political nexus has acquired and sustained such incredible power that they are able to subvert the country's law and order scenario, jeopardizing the daily lives of the common citizens, worst-affected being women and children. Solutions to this grim scenario of crime and therefore crime prevention are aplenty. But it is only through pressure groups and public opinion that the Government may be expected to act. Justice V.R. Krishna Iyer said:

> A tireless and zealous worker in this field has very often underscored the importance of a separate sophisticated force, with special skills, drills, techniques, technology and aloof from the fossilizing near feudal set-up. A special ethos, ethic and professionalism are absolutely essential to meet the challenge of criminal cunning, the menace of macabre intricacies and the subtle machinations of criminals and this force must of course not resort to vulgarity, violence or any other vice.

The apathy of police stations to accept FIRs brought specially by women, the women undertrials languishing in jails because of police delays in filing reports in the courts, are serious matters to be attended to. There has to be an ongoing sensitization and training programme for the lower levels of police personnel. This is an urgent need since the police personnel have very often been ignoring the special legislation on dowry, sati, etc. A proper understanding by the lower police force that women's rights are human rights is very essential and important.

We are not for once under rating the various disabilities faced by the police as a system. The inadequacy of staff, lack of modern gadgetry, the various laws and procedures inhibiting their functioning are common knowledge.

Moreover the police, which cannot be totally independent of the executive must devise ways and means for a minimum of operational independence particularly in the discharge of statutory duties and responsibilities. The National Police Commission has suggested that this can be ensured by regulating the transfers of officials and giving them a fixed tenure and also fixing specific duties/ responsibilities in a time-bound frame. A suggestion was also made to set up statutory commissions State-wise in order to contain sometimes erratic transfer exercises by the executive, which disrupt the smooth coordinated functioning of the police force.

A band of women constables must be recruited in each district, each town and city, preferably with proximity to the rural areas, to enable them to ensure the security and safety of the women and child population and to check crime and book the criminals. We are proud of women police officers like Kiran Bedi, and a host of others, who while doing a yeoman service in the preservation and sustenance of a smooth and coordinated law and order system, continue to direct their attention to some of the criminal patterns, crucial and peculiar to the women population and provide safety guidelines for custodial-rape and torture, miscarriage of justice and in proven cases of guilt, find ways and means of reformation as also through deterrent policies for the rest of the people.

The police is also in a dilemma, for, if they act effectively, they are charged with excesses. If they do not, they are accused of inaction. We are here today, to exchange views and ideas and sort out the chaotic situation, arising out of a degenerating society, which has lost its moral fibre to a great extent and which in turn has generated an uncontrollable growth of crime and violence. At the risk of repetition, one must stress that it is the common woman who finds it impossible to stir out after dusk, alone, even during an emergency, not to speak of daylight molestations, eve-teasing, rape, robberies and murders, kidnapping, abduction and sometimes bride-burning.

Conclusion

But all is not yet lost. The youth of the country, both women and men seem to be up in arms against crime, lawlessness and violence and this may provide the much-needed base and infrastructure for annihilation of the twin evils of crime and violence.

I look forward to the day when half of the police force consists of women. Also, a continuous interaction between National Commission for Women and the National Police Academy will, I am sure, lend fruitful results in our common quest to eliminate violence against women and help in ushering gender justice.

NCW: THE RAY OF HOPE FOR WOMEN

It is an accepted fact that, even on the threshold of the 21st century, there is no section of our society more oppressed, more exploited and more neglected than women. In every segment, class or community, women suffer all the disabilities inflicted on that group and in addition, suffer the consequences of gender discrimination too. Yet, their contribution in economic life, social well-being, cultural continuity and ethical standards is far greater than their share of the population.

A national daily of Delhi commented on 29th January, 1995 under the caption 'Cries of Oppression' that, "while we progress technologically, earning ourselves a reputation for a world of satellites, missiles and fifth generation computers, we have also acquired the distinction of recording one rape in every 42 minutes, besides increased cases of crimes against women, including molestation, stripping, eve-teasing, kidnapping, dowry deaths, female foeticide, even sati, and the lakhs of women who are abused and battered by their husbands in the privacy of their own homes. The National Commission for Women (NCW) is now in the process of hearing tales of atrocities committed on hapless women across the country, but the women who appeared before the NCW's bench of jurors and social workers cannot be assured of justice as the Commission does not have 'teeth or nails', it can only make recommendations. Most of the cases heard are about dowry deaths, sexual harassment at the workplace, rape, desertion and being refused alimony after divorce. "My only ray of hope is the NCW, said a mother, whose daughter was burnt to death for not giving enough dowry." Such is the confidence, such are the expectations and such are the demands that the women of the country have of the Commission.

On the completion of its tenure of five years, an evaluation of the national forum might be appropriate. A legitimate question that might arise in one's mind would be how well did the NCW fare in its search and endeavour for striving to secure equality, justice and fair treatment in all that matters in the life of women for their honourable existence without oppression, denial of opportunities and deprivation of rights.

Origin

It may be recalled that the NCW was constituted on 31st January, 1992 under the National Commission for Women Act, 1990. NCW Act, 1990 is a statute having the potential to catalyse all the arms of the State under parliamentary democracy, i.e. the legislature, the executive and the judiciary, though much more powers could make the Commission an effective instrument to be of substantive assistance to the aggrieved women. When we sit in judgement to evaluate the work done during its five years existence, we would perhaps be perplexed by the spontaneous and overwhelming response its work has aroused in the shape of hopes and expectations as also that of dissatisfaction in some cases.

Structure, objectives and functions

To mention briefly the structure, objectives and functions of the Commission, it is composed of a permanent national forum of seven full time members consisting of a Chairperson, five members and a member-secretary. The Commission's functions cover every aspect of women's concerns and issues. They range from protective laws and constitutional provisions to empowerment. (To refer to constitutional provisions affecting women refer to Appendix IV). Specifically, these functions are to : (a) take up the cases of violation of the provisions of the Constitution and of other laws relating to women, (b) look into complaints and take suo moto notice of matters relating to : deprivation of women's rights, non-implementation of laws enacted to provide protection to women and also to achieve the objective of equality and development, non-compliance of policy decisions, guidelines or instructions aimed at mitigating hardships and ensuring welfare and providing relief to women and take up the issues arising out of such matter with appropriate authorities.

In addition, the Commission could (a) commission special investigations of specific problems related to discrimination and atrocities against women; (b) undertake promotional research to suggest ways of ensuring due representation of women in all spheres; (c) evaluate the progress of the development of women under the Union and in all States; (d) inspect jails, remand homes, and other institutions and places of custody where women are lodged voluntarily or involuntarily.

While investigating complaints, NCW has the powers of a civil court in trying a suit; it can summon and enforce the attendance of any person, and examine that person under oath, as well as require the production of relevant documents, etc.

While discussing on the theme, one cannot resist quoting Justice V.R. Krishna Iyer. In one of his works he stated that :

> Women's welfare is legislated galore but remain paper tigers since men are to implement it. That compounds the crime, since even policemen are if reports are correct, among criminals who endanger women. Even the laws are so lacunose that the judiciary, if objectively judged, will be found guilty... Women must be awakened as has happened in the anti-arrack campaign of Andhra Pradesh women. Social awareness is the beginning of radical change. A massive campaign involving the vast masses of illiterate women, is necessitous all over India.

Taking full cognizance of Justice Krishna Iyer's observations and also after evaluating the work done during the three year tenure of earlier Commission, I decided on joining as Chairperson in July, 1995 and identified some thrust areas to bring about perceptible results in dealing with women's concerns. These were :

1. Speedy Justice for Women (through Parivarik Mahila Lok Adalats)
2. Legal Awareness Programme for Women Colleges
3. Custodial Justice
4. Steps Towards Rehabilitation of :
5. Women & Children in Prostitution
6. Widows
7. Blind Women

8. Destitutes and

9. Anti-Arrack Campaign

Till the end of July '97, NCW, through the good offices of District Legal Aid Society, the Judiciary and NGOs have held about 100 Parivarik Mahila Lok Adalats. By no means is this a mean achievement in that it has handled about 5700 cases. In the field of legal awareness campaign, we have sponsored through NGOs, 35 training camps/workshops coupled with Panchayati Raj training for women. Further, 180 women's colleges were covered to give legal training to 200 teachers and 5000 girl students and others. This again is an innovative step, the results of which would be sustainable and widespread.

Another important area is that of legal literacy for visually handicapped women. With the cooperation of the Sunanda Bhandare Foundation, 60 blind women were given training during 1997.

We are finalizing a status paper on prohibition and development of women to ensure that anti-arrack movement is taken to its logical conclusion in achieving total prohibition.

We can cite innumerable cases and specific areas handled by NCW recently. These cover the critical concerns, such as,—

(i) Outraging modesty of women, also involving persons in high eminence.

(ii) Atrocities on women, e.g. Uttarakhand

(iii) Dowry harassment, dowry death

(iv) Harassment at workplace

(v) Gender based denial of opportunities

NCW's effort in mobilising support for 81st Constitutional Amendment Bill providing for 33 $_{1/3}$ per cent reservation in Lok Sabha and State legislatures are too well known needing no elaboration.

Processing of complaints, commissioning witnesses where necessary, constituted an important function. The impetus for entertaining a few representative individual complaints came from tales of woes of umpteen harassed women explained in various complaints both written and oral that the Commission were receiving both in office and during tours of Chairperson, Members and the Member Secretary. The harassed women were running from pillar to post to seek justice. During its tenure, it received a total of about 800 complaints relating broadly to dowry, murder and dowry related atrocities, disputes over matrimonial properties, rape and molestation, harassment at work-places, desertions and other atrocities. In most of the cases, it has been possible for the Commission to take up the issues with the concerned authorities and persuade them to set right the wrongs done.

Realizing the intensity, gravity and volume of the work in the complaint cell of NCW, we have added counselling and pre-litigation services round the clock to offer prompt and effective assistance to the aggrieved women.

Assessing NCW's performance, at the end of its three years' term, a Calcutta English daily in its issue of February 2, 1995 commented

> Should one just dismiss it as a weak offspring of the government and an appendage that has disillusioned those who fought for its creation? Or should one give it credit for its first few tottering steps towards getting women a better deal from the government and the society at large? Or perhaps the NCW qualifies for both brickbats and bouquets, if one takes into account its vast but powerful mandate and its list of achievements.

We are confident that when one would make an assessment at the end of NCW's six-year term in 1998, the number of bouquets would heavily outnumber the brickbats. It must be admitted that the issues are so large that NCW would need vastly improved powers, facilities and cooperation from all concerned to make the life of Indian women better than today.

STATUS OF STATE COMMISSIONS

May I extend to you all a hearty welcome. It is appropriate that we meet on this auspicious occasion of celebrating the completion of one year of functioning of the second term of the National Commission for Women. We are utilizing this opportunity to launch a series of programmes and highlight issues of women's concerns spread over all the five days of this week. Participation of the State Commissions in these programmes provides an excellent opportunity for interaction, and avenues for networking, not only among the State Commissions and NGOs and others but also lays a strong foundation for future cooperation and collaboration on all issues concerning women (For list of State Commissions refer to Appendix III).

I take this opportunity to welcome in our midst and congratulate the Women's Commissions of Delhi and Kerala which were constituted after the last conference of States and National Commission which was held in March, 1995. As a matter of fact, the Commission in Kerala was set up only a few days back.

We had been pursuing with various States the question of setting up of Women's Commission and had expected several more State Commissions to have been formed by this time, but most of the States have not found it feasible so far in spite of assurances. We hope that 1996 will witness the constitution of Women's Commission at least in all major States like Uttar Pradesh, Madhya Pradesh, Bihar, Rajasthan, Karnataka, Haryana, Andhra

Pradesh and others.

The three-year term of the first National Commission for Women came to an end on 31st January, 1995 except for one member who had not completed three years. Weeks, and then months, passed by without the vacancies being filled with the result that only one member and the member secretary carried on the Commission work until July, 1995 when the Chairperson and four other members were nominated. The intervening six months were utilized to complete the ongoing projects and other pending work, drawing up future plans, convening a conference of the State Commissions, organizing two or three seminars/ workshops, taking stock of the work done in the preceding years and attending to some other issues like drafting our part for the Country Paper for Beijing Conference. Ms Padma Seth joined us as Member in January, 1996. Last March, two members resigned. Thus, the Commission is now short of two members. A new member secretary, Dr Nisha Sahai Achuttan, joined us only a couple of weeks back.

On assuming charge, I made it a point that the Commission work at a breakneck speed so as to make up for the loss of six months. The achievements of the Commission during this one year period are many and we are satisfied. I would like to specifically mention a few of our activities. In order to bring a quick settlement of women's cases pending in civil courts for long periods, the Commission organized Parivarik Mahila Adalats in various States, taking assistance of the State's Legal Boards and the judiciary, and actively associating the local NGOs in organizing the Adalats. So far, settlement in more than one thousand cases have been reached, with Gujarat taking a lead. I would request the State Commission to give a fillip to the Mahila Lok Adalats in their States. We have taken up seriously with the State Governments, the question of release of undertrial women prisoners who have been languishing in jails for unnecessarily prolonged periods. Similarly, the question of premature release of women life convicts under Article 161 of the Constitution and of term convicts under section 432 of Cr. P.C. is also being pursued. We understand that Andhra Pradesh Government recently issued orders for release all undertrial women who had been in jail for more than a year. I hope you will vigorously pursue the issue of the release of women prisoners in your States with the respective authorities.

The Commission has undertaken a large-scale programme for creating legal awareness among women. For this purpose, we have tied up with the National Law School, Bangalore where selected lady teachers of women's colleges from all over the country are trained in legal matters pertaining to women and they in turn hold legal awareness classes for girl students of their colleges. Another action plan of the Commission has been to give impetus to the anti-arrack movement in the country. Liquor, as we all know, is a major cause of ruin of many poor and middle class homes. Women's groups in several States have started anti-arrack movements, with marked success at a number of places. The Commission aims to bring into a network the various women's groups all over the country engaged in anti-arrack struggle so as to create a strong lobby against the evils of liquor. A workshop to strengthening the movement has been mooted.

The Commission has also been making efforts towards rescue and rehabilitation of children from brothels and of women forced into mental asylums.

The Commission took up cases of injustice done to widows and has initiated, with the help of NGOs, rehabilitation programmes in Mathura and Vrindawan.

With regard to political empowerment, adequate representation of women in Parliament and State Legislatures has been pursued by the Commission and the results are now before you.

In a vast country like ours, with a variety of customs and social values, different languages and different levels of education and economic development, the problems facing women differ from region to region. Many of them are area specific, some others specific to communities and groups. A good number of these problems fall within the domain of respective States and can best be handled by the State Commissions. The National Commission for Women has to look into the issues of wider common interests. It is, therefore, essential that every State should have a Women's Commission.

It is of utmost importance that a close liaison is maintained between the National and State Women's Commissions and a good measure of coordination and collaboration in their activities attained so that the recommendations on the issues are not divergent or conflicting. For instance, there are many women-specific Central laws and also numerous provisions in IPC (For references of constitutional provisions for women refer to Appendix IV). They are all under constant review and examination by the National Commission. In a number of cases, State Commissions have also gone into these issues and recommended amendments according to their own perceptions. In such a situation, the recommendations of various Commissions on the same issue may turn out to be different from each other. We must speak with a united voice, if we are to be effective. The best course would, therefore, be that in legislative matters having national purport, the views of the State Commissions are forwarded to the National Commission for framing recommendations. Networking is thus of great value in avoiding duplication of effort and also for achieving general consensus on crucial issues.

No development process can bear fruit without enlisting the cooperation and support of NGOs, the vital link in connecting people with the administration. It was an excellent idea mooted in the last meeting that the State Commission prepare a directory of NGOs working for women in their States along with brief description of the field of their expertise as also a list of experts in various areas related to women. I hope it has been possible for them to proceed in the matter during the last one year.

Another idea of great value broached last time was to prepare a statewise database on women. Database is the most important input in preparing strategies or programmes for women's welfare and development. I hope the State Commissions have made good progress in this sphere as well.

I thank you all for responding to our invitation and hope our meeting will pave the way for a new era of cooperation between us. We eagerly look forward to your suggestions.

THE SCOPE AND REACH OF NCW

On behalf of the national commission for women, state commissions for women, NGOs, women activists, social scientists and millions of those women who are not assembled here but look towards NCW for wise counselling, support and activism, I extend to you, Hon'ble Prime Minister, a hearty, warm welcome. It was so gracious of you to have accepted our request to be present here today to address this vast gathering in the occasion of the commission completing one year of its second term of office.

I know that you are aware of the particular circumstances and the goals with which the national commission for women was established. However, I hope you will bear with me if I recall a few of the most critical aspects of the birth of the NCW.

NCW is just four years old. It has been a ray of hope and inspiration to our women and NCWA it is significant that the National Commission for Women Act, a product of sustained and committed women's movement in our country, was enacted during the Janata Dal government headed by Shri V.P. Singh. We all know that your enlightened leadership is committed to uphold social justice and we women can except more than a fair deal in matters of deprivation, injustice and inequality. The evidence is not far to seek. The announcement by your government of one-third reservation for women in state legislatures and parliament augurs well and speaks volumes regarding your concern for empowerment of women.

While we welcome your government's commitments we also would urge that in all structures of governance—economic, social and political—expert groups and policy making positions should include women.

NCW was set up specifically to be an autonomous statutory body, an independent commission which would have the "independence" to interact with the government,—the state as well as society accountable for women's condition. It was even thought at one time to model it on the concept of the *Lok Ayukt* so that it would be particularly directed to redress discrimination against women, the inequality between men and women across all barriers.

In order for it to perform this role of acting as a guardian of women's rights, to prevent as well as to make amends for injustice done to women, by definition it had to be genuinely independent both in its constitutional construction as well as in its operational instruments and process. The NCW Act is a welcome legislation. It would be more effective if it is vested with some more investigating, prosecuting and implementing powers within the broad framework of our constitutional scheme of judiciary and executive and parliamentary system of democracy.

With your blessings, we would like to review the constitution and procedures of NCW and the administrative linkage of the commission with the ministry and reformulate the act and the procedures of the commission such that it can truly be a monitoring body, provide annual reports to the government, scruntinize and advise on recommendations on policy made by the government on behalf of all those groups in India who have, with such courage and wisdom, safeguarded and moved forward women's rights in India.

We would like it to be a bridge between what is called the civic society, the non-governmental sector and women's voluntary organizations who are deeply in touch with the daily lives of the women, their problems, and their abilities and viewpoints. The commission was designed to be a bridge between this lively broad-based constituency of women's organizations and the government.

This particular moment in the Indian political evolution is of interest and significance to the Indian women's participation in national development. A coalition government which brings together regional parties and national parties provides for women the kind of opportunity that they have always sought. Women, as you know, tend to come together as 'women' which is more important to them than their identities as people belonging to a political party or a religion or a caste. There is a bonding amongst women which provides a natural platform of solidarity. With the formation of the coalition government, women see two great opportunities—first, they can come together as 'women' and know that the government being a coalition provides a unified platform for them. Secondly, a coalition government is seeking a common minimum programme, a consensus and a direction. Women are a natural coalition across class, caste and political parties and can provide this mechanism for a coalition government to implement its policies.

At this venue today, there are representatives from nine states where state commission for women have been formed and I am proud to say that they come from all the political parties that have formed the UF government. The common minimum programme that you have placed before the country and which has been translated into national economic policy through the budget is close to the vision and priorities of the Indian Women's Movement. We agree that providing basic amenities like water, sanitation, housing, primary education, health to the poor is in fact a package that is crucial for the poor women of India—rural as well as urban. We would like to be a strong route or instrument through which to ensure that these packages in fact reach the poor.

To enable us to perform this role of expressing the woman citizen's voice and holding the State society accountable, we ae developing a monitoring framework, some new indices of measurement which would indicate effective utilization of programme as well as its impact on reduction of poverty and inequality. The Commission and the State level Commissions with the help of women's movement namely the voluntary organizations would like to build up the capability to be able to ensure that the delivery arrangements for this programme are efficient and they reach those for whom they are meant. We would also like to develop mechanisms of accountability where we can monitor the delivery, draw attention of the public and the elected bodies to what is right and what is wrong and make sure that this objective gets fulfilled with the best use of the resources.

To enable us to perform this function, it would be very important for your government to invest in the women's movement funds and political support—funds and independence to the National Commission and the State Commissions.

We have now twelve State Commissions for Women. May I plead for the use of your good offices to get established Commissions for Women in each of the remaining States.

Although it might look a little odd because as a Chairperson I am suggesting that the NCW Member and Chairperson as also the State Commissions for Women must be accorded a status commensurate with functions, decorum, protocol and expectations that the government and the people have of NCW, still it is common knowledge that when dealing with men and matters the status counts a lot and its absence has many a time created embarrassment and lack of results. I am sure that this matter pending with the government would receive benevolent consideration.

In the past nine days, we have had gatherings of women networking with NGOs and State level Commissions for Women, those working with custodial justice, in prostitution, codification of criminal law, of those who are looking at the empowerment of women through credit or though labour legislations. We have also had discussions with the State Commissions and with other women's groups. Through these discussions several proposals have come up which we would like to place before you.

We would like to call attention to some of the major concerns and responses that have emerged in our discussions with the women's organizations. You have always called attention to not only the poverty in this country but the deprivation in the sense that there are villages without drinking water, people without homes, children without schools and so forth. Therefore, we do not have to tell you about destitution, especially that which faces women and girls and female infants.

Poor women are successful in providing and

managing financial services for themselves through innovative structures like chit fund, self help group co-operatives, etc. These efforts need to be taken note of in designing financial committees at all levels and their experience should be included in the formulation of policy.

However, within this category there are some women such as widows, prostitutes and women prisoners. We have in the last one year visited prisons, met widows, gone to red-light areas and with a great deal of intimate interaction have come up with specific ways in which we could relieve these women from what can be called the atrocities committed against them. In a nutshell we will be presenting to you the reports of these discussions and our study as well as our recommendations for action and indeed I know that it is we—the women's organizations, the Commissions on women in partnership with the government that are to redress and respond to these atrocities.

However, there are some key points on which we need to have your directions. A whole package of needs is required for those who are in prostitution ranging from children, to their health that requires the attention of the government. Amongst many of the things the prostitutes have asked for is that raids should not be made in red-light areas, and you can understand it because these raids are usually made to further worsen the situation. We were able to have the Hon'ble home minister with us during a discussion with prison officers and I am happy to tell you that we were able to get his attention to this issue. Similarly on prostitutes we have had the attention of the Hon'ble minsiter for human resource development Mr. S.R. Bommai, who has very ably and clearly told us about the action he would take.

Another deep concern of women is the tremendous violence which they experience when the men in their families are drunk. The anti-arrack movement which is primarily associated with Andhra Pradesh, is not only in

Andhra Pradesh. It has spread like wild fire in all the States in India. The National Commission for Women called a meeting of women engaged in anti-arrack struggles and found that it was flooded with requests to attend from groups starting from Uttarakhand going all the way to Kanyakumari. On the West, from Goa, Maharashtra to Orissa in the East, all wanted to belong to what they call a "Mukti Manch", they want freedom for their village from the violence of alcohol. They asked for 'Gram Swaraj', the word that Gandhiji used. They wanted the *gram* to have Swaraj from arrack. Freedom from liquor is the slogan they coined. Women have led the battle against bottle. In Andhra Pradesh, neo-literate women used broomsticks and chilli powder to force the closure of liquor shops. The stories they told were gruesome; husbands raping daughters, because they could not distinguish them from their wives. And one woman said only when prohibition came in Andhra Pradesh were we able to sleep soundly. Earlier in 1992, women activists in Haryana torched a liquor shop sparking off a State wide movement. Almost similar tactics, as in Haryana were adopted by women in Kochi, Kerala. Today, there is a ban on sale of arrack in Kerala.

On the reverse side, I must point out to you that the economic argument that there is a loss in excise is not true. In Andhra Pradesh, according to the officials, household incomes of poor households has gone up by Rs. 500 as a result of non-consumption of alcohol. In turn these household are now buying rice, vegetables, cloth and generate a demand in the market which adds to the economies buoyancy. They have also, for example, saved seven crores in one district as savings from this additional income. It is well-known that what is lost in excise revenue is more than made up in sales tax revenue by the amount of goods that are purchased with the money saved form liquor. What is less recorded but is equally important is the fact that the health of men, women and children improves because of the food that is available with the increased income. And this, I am sure, saves money on health services. There will also be money for them to be spent on children's education and so forth. Therefore, there is an additional increase in revenue which is invisible but which saves money for the exchequer.

We know of your great concern for rural areas of India and for the poor. From the women's point of view it is removal of arrack, namely implementation of prohibition in a more widespread way that is even more important than providing employment. Because the money saved from liquor is income for women and children. We eagerly look forward to hearing your response to our ideas and hopes.

One of the most important issues of discrimination against women is the wages that women receive notwithstanding Equal Remuneration Act. Women's wages are always lower than men very unjustly because they work hard if not harder than men, whether it is on roads, farms, fields, etc. Thus, we would like to safeguard and implement the Equal Remuneration Act and also make sure that the valuation of women's work is reflected in their wages. We welcome the commitment made in the budget that within four months a paper would be presented on the implementation of the minimum social programme on basic amenities. The district *taluka* and village are the most important theatres for action and redressal for women. Women like those engaged in anti-arrack or *chipko* have found the need for district committee with some legal and statutory powers to direct the administration. We, at the Commission would like to be deeply involved in all the discussions and plans for development.

Your government's most important unifying platforms is secularism. Women, more than any other category of people have a bonding and identity which goes beyond caste, religion and class. We would like to offer the large and widespread network of women's organizations as those who will make the most earnest efforts to build communal harmony. We would like to have consultations with women from different religious groups and build with them a platform of a common minimum programme.

I have spelt out here before you some urgent matters deserving your attention. As we are all eagerly looking forward to a few words of encourgement and assurances from you we will be submitting a detailed memorandum listing out immediate concerns of women needing urgent attention. I refrain from referring to them now and delay your wise counsel and valuable advice.

*A happy home is heaven in advance.

3

SENSITIZATION PROCESS

CUSTODIAL CARE FOR WOMEN

First of all, I would like to congratulate Ms. Kamala Kumar and the faculty members of the Institute of Social and Psychological Research to have chosen the important topic of "custodial care for women" as the theme of this workshop. The deviant or criminal woman constitutes an insignificant phenomenon than male. In proportional terms, women's share in crime, in comparison to men is negligible. Therefore, in penal thinking and literature, women have figured very little. Traditionally, the dividing lines in crime-coping approaches and mechanisms have been adult and juvenile, rather than male and female.

It is interesting to note that until the year 1975, for instance, which was adopted by UN as the International Women's Year, a full-fledged report on the status of women had never been compiled in many countries, including India. The appearance of women's liberation movement in the West in the past '60s helped give a considerable jolt to this apathy.

Non-prison custody

In contrast to prisons, custodial reform and handling of persons, particularly women in institutions other than prisons have evoked only meagre and sporadic attention. Non-prison state custody consists of:

(a) police custody;

(b) custody in social welfare institutions; and

(c) custody in mental health institutions.

Of the three principal forms of state custody, viz. prisons, police and welfare (including social welfare and mental health institutions), the third form of custody is institutionally least prone to high visibility and public accountability and consequently also to reform. The origin of state managed custodial welfare lies in the well-meaning intent of the state to come to the rescue of women in distress and in need of any kind of protection from acts of desperation, deviance or immorality. Although the legislative mandate for state social welfare custody goes back further, in free India, the *locus standi* for social welfare custodial institutions is traceable to the Women's and Children's Institutions (Licensing) Act, 1956, which was repealed by the Orphanages and other Charitable Homes Supervision and Control Act, 1960. Examples of additional legislation which have a bearing on custodial institutions for women are the different Children Acts, the erstwhile Suppression of Immoral Traffic in Women and Girls Act, 1956, Indian Lunacy Act, 1912 and Acts preventing beggary, etc. Women's and Children's Institutions Licensing Act, 1956 referred to the large number of "bogus" institutions existing in the country and exploiting destitute women and children. Inhuman conditions prevail in these institutions. In order to protect women from such exploitation, legislation is necessary to regulate and licence institutions caring for women and children under eighteen years of age, and to provide for the proper custody, care and training for their inmates. The current information indicates that the situation has not improved very much as revealed from the Smt. Krishnalekha Sood High Powered Committee appointed by the Delhi Government in 1995, to oversee the functioning of the custodial institutions/homes run by the Department of Social Welfare of the

Government of NCT, Delhi.

Custodial care and human rights

Custodial care and human rights have become an abiding concern of the social justice community. In recent times, international and national organizations, e.g. the National Human Rights Commission, the National Commission for Women, State Commissions on the conditions of jails, and expert committees on custodial violence, have all scrutinized the working of the police and prisons and social welfare institutions of custodial care for women.

This concern is based on the strong realisation that citizens live in places under closed regimes and that the reluctance of authorities toward transparency of functioning is itself a symptom of unseen and unheard violations especially against women inmates.

In a study sponsored by NCW, the Tata Institute of Social Sciences, Mumbai had suggested, *inter alia*, that, —

1. All categories of women who can be taken into penal custody should be included in the preview of a policy for women in custody. This includes suspects, undertrials, fine-sentence and other short-term prisoners, long-termers and women presently taken into custody under the Immoral Traffic Prevention Act, Beggars Acts, Police Acts, etc. Suitable guidelines may then be issued to the judiciary, police and prison administration with respect to arrest, bail, sentencing practice, degree of security in custody, etc.
2. Prevention, reformation rehabilitation must be considered an integral part of penal policy for women.
3. Prostitution *per se* and begging should be de-criminalized. Women engaging in such occupations should be perceived as victims rather than offenders. Hence, the concerned laws should be amended to

debar the arrest and imprisonment of women prostitutes and beggars barring those involved in trafficking.

4. Legal aid and advice must be made available to every woman taken into custody. It should be the responsibility of the police to inform the legal aid authorities that a woman has been arrested. Likewise, the concerned magistrate should also ensure that the woman is adequately represented.
5. There should be no discrimination between men and women with respect to facilities and programmes.
6. A clear distinction should be made between penal custody and institutionalization for welfare and protection. The former is compulsory, whereas the latter must be voluntary.

I would like to conclude by referring to some of the highly relevant observations of Justice Krishna lyer report on women prisoners. In the Indian environment, destitution and exploitation are embryonically linked. Together they can serve as a launching pad for crimes. The causes of destitution are themselves linked to the socio-cultural and economic disabilities whose cutting edge operates more sharply for women than men. The inequity of the socio-economic status inherited by women compounds their inability to benefit equitably from the development process. "Struggling for equality from a position of disadvantage" reinforces the vulnerability of the distressed women making them more culpable to social maladjustment, abuse and exploitation. It is in such a context that offences against women can experience a spurt as much as offences by her.

It is this process of actual or impending victimization and of the induction of women into criminality that makes women in distress and women victims of crime the subject of correctional welfare and custody. In pursuit of the objectives of protecting women and making women less vulnerable to exploitation as well as to deviant behaviour, the state has adopted the modality of taking the distressed, needy and victim women into its custody. The legal support for such custody is derived from a host of social and other legislations. Let us endeavour to make the institutions for custodial care for women a decent place for reform and rehabilitation and nothing else.

I have great pleasure in inaugurating the convention and hope the deliberations would pave the way for a better deal for women in custody.

Vande Mataram!

GENDER BIAS IN POPULATION CONTROL MEASURES

"While the world is rightly worried about 1.8 billion Indians in the next century, are we also similarly concerned?"

India is not only the second most populous country in the world, but is also in the process of becoming number one in the next century! A disturbing thought, indeed keeping in view the fact that India became aware of the implications of uncontrolled population more than 50 years ago and was the first country to launch a major fully State-funded family planning programme.

In spite of massive efforts to improve the quality of life, poverty and backwardness haunt fairly large sections of the population. We are confronted with a host of problems in almost all spheres of life, specially those relating to management of natural resources like food, forests, land, water and the environment. As a result, serious apprehensions arise about our desire to eliminate poverty which is the critical factor for the success of any development strategy. Speaking in Stockholm, the late Mrs. Indira Gandhi had said that "Poverty is the worst pollutant". It is time we asked how far we have succeeded in banishing it.

India's population stabilization programme has been giving increasing attention to factors beyond family planning and urging an interdisciplinary approach and an integrated population and development strategy. The urgent need to eliminate poverty through global economic cooperation, which would create a favourable environment for family planning as an integrated part of development requires reiteration.

Gender Inequity

The current family planning slogan in India is that the key to population control is female literacy, employment to women, better health care for them and in brief their empowerment in the real sense. But I recall that only some time ago the assertion used to be "Development is the Best Contraceptive". Though, in between, there was a phase when it was said, though feebly-that "Contraception is the Best way for Development", but then this slogan died (or was killed) very soon perhaps because it smelt of the "Chinese way" which we like to hate because of our own complexes.

However, what puzzles me most is that how can female literacy control population growth while male literacy cannot do so. Why after all, women employment can bring down the birth rate, but male employment cannot act that way? In brief, why development of women alone is the key to population control but not the development of men. Certainly women do not procreate all by themselves, nor do they enjoy frequent and repeated maternities and surely they are not pregnancy addicts. Then why is it that while the development of women should help in family planning and not the development of the other sex?

I am afraid, no modern economist would like to, or can explain this puzzle, because it requires the sincerity and compassion towards women, of an intensity no less than that of a Mahatma Gandhi who explained the true reasons for the proliferation of unwanted children which we call population growth. Gandhiji had no hesitation in pointing out that the unwanted maternities are the consequence of male (i.e. husband's) "aggression". He recognized the fact quite clearly that a very large percentage of maternities in India are caused just as a result of sheer and often crude sexual aggression of husbands and not because of any conscious decision of couples to have a child. And that is why Gandhiji in spite of being opposed to contraceptives approved male sterilization.

The whole strategy to control population growth through women's development cannot be but based on the following, though latent, premises

(i) since the pain, risk and burden of maternity are borne by women, it is therefore women's concern and responsibility to protect themselves from the unwanted pregnancies,

(ii) women must discharge this "responsibility" to save this planet Earth from over-crowding; and to enable women to carry out their "responsibility" effectively they should be provided with the required development (e.g., literacy, employment, etc.), facilities (e.g., contraceptives, clinics, etc.) and moral support (e.g., social approval to abortion, etc.) It is for this very reason that our Parliament has recently passed a Maternity (Amendment) Bill to grant six to ten weeks of paid leave to a working woman who undergoes abortion

(iii) men, developed or otherwise, should shun the belief that they have no responsibility or concern to share in matters of conjugal sex and to remain a responsibility-free and careless sex partner, totally unconcerned about birth control.

No wonder, therefore, the Parliament has not put in the Bill any kind of constraint or disincentive on the husband of the working woman who undergoes abortion, and the husband can jolly well "enable" the woman to "earn" the "abortion-leave" again and again.

The whole concept of "Development of women is the best contraceptive" is in fact a subtle example of male chauvinism but if only our women activists could understand this and see the trap in this approach to put the entire burden and responsibility of family planning on women alone. Hence, would it not be desirable that women insist, as Gandhiji did, that since the main cause of population growth is the husbands' "aggression", the onus of birth control ought to be on husbands and vasectomy is the logical solution and ideal too?

The male bias apparent

It is well known that our society is highly male dominant and it is the husband who decides the number and sex of children in the family. It is the reckless male sexual aggression that is the root cause of unwanted maternities. Vasectomy is the best, easiest, cheapest and safest way of family planning and yet, paradoxically and pretentiously, the planners and the intellectuals keep on advocating and pleading for women development to control our population growth. I must say that compelling a man—rich or poor—who has already got two children to undergo vasectomy is in no way atrocious or inhuman. But it is certainly inhuman to let helpless women get inflicted with frequent maternities (or abortions) and to let a large percentage of our children to perpetually live a subhuman life till the nation succeeds economically while empowerment/development of women is achieved to a demographically effective level.

In my opinion, women must not degrade themselves by begging for development in lieu of accepting the full responsibility of family planning being thrust upon them. Development is the birthright of every human being—male or female—irrespective of its role in population control.

It is argued that though any coercion in family planning is bad but what can be said about the husband's "aggression" and the consequential abortion or maternal morbidity/mortality? Or, do we think that it should be a part of womanhood to be on constant guard against the husband's "aggression" throughout the female reproductive life, spanning almost over quarter of a century by using contraceptives months after months and suffering the associated side-effects besides the inconveniences.

Development of women as a strategy to promote family planning is defective and anti women, besides being a degrading and cruel way to control population growth. Besides, this approach liberates men from any share of responsibility in population control, whereas in all fairness the responsibility of family planning must be on men.

We are perhaps not fully aware as to what an extent the Indian democracy has of late been plagued with the politics of vote banks based on caste and community. And the interests of a vote bank demand maximization of its size which in case of vote banks based on caste and community can be achieved mainly by producing more children. Hence, demographically this aspect of the politics of vote banks is an extremely dangerous development and it is for this reason that no political party is taking any initiative to promote family planning or declaring population control measures.

Under these circumstances the only way to check our rapidly increasing population is to delink population control from the political process in India which ironically is promoting population growth; and assign the task of population control to an autonomous constitutional authority like the Election Commission, National Commission for Women or still, it should be left in charge of the Panchayats with greater representation from women. Panchayats should be at the forefront of family planning programme and the bureaucracy and implementing agencies should follow their lead. The programme has to became a peoples' movement—the Panchayati Raj women could influence the couple at the village level for a small family.

Important aspects

Some of the prominent features of our population which need to be noted are as follows :

1. Sex ratio is an indicator of balance between males and females in human population. In a population closed to migration, sex ratio denotes sex differential in mortality. Further, imbalance affects the social, economic and community life. In India, the sex composition is weighted in favour of males. Higher female mortality is said to be one of the important causes of the low female ratio. Though the sex ratio is adverse for the females among tribals also, comparatively speaking the distribution of males and females among Scheduled Tribe population is a little more balanced. Some students of tribal affairs have taken it to mean that the females in tribal societies have been protected through traditional values and mores.

2. Different notions have been afloat about family planning practices among tribal communities. On the whole, tribal system of medicine is either invested with mystery or looked upon as a bundle of superstitions. Prima facie, it seems it is composed of three dominant components—herbal, psychosomatic and magico-religious. They are brought into play by the tribal faith-healers, medicine-men, Shamans et al. But there is need to conduct, through independent and objective

evaluation of the traditional tribal system of health care, particularly the tribal system of medicine. We have also to consider the possibilities of crystallisation of health system or systems which incorporate the positive features of tribal and modern systems.

3. India was the first country to launch an official family planning programme in 1952. Yet the population situation continues to be a matter of great concern. No culture-specific or area-specific assessment or formulation have been made. Literacy of female population is a key factor.
4. It is to be noted that some Indian States also have paid attention to women's and children's programmes with concomitant results in the education and family planning fields. These have been instrumental in arousing their consciousness of family parameters.
5. Research indicates that there is a nexus between family planning and level of health facilities available. This is particularly true in tribal areas. It has been seen that demographic trend among the tribal people on the whole indicates that their rate of growth is not less than that of the non-tribals. But health care services in tribal areas are not only scarce, even their quality is questionable. This has a directly adverse relation with family planning programmes.
6. It has been found that women generally go in for sterilization after they have had the desired number of four or five children. Further, women, particularly tribal women, are cajoled through cash or other incentives into undergoing sterilization operations inopportunely, because it enables attainment of targets of some officials.
7. Since it is being realized more and more that women are the fulcrum of the programmes, their involvement, through Panchayats or otherwise, is essential.

India's developmental efforts in the past have given us the strength to deal with challenges that lie ahead of us. In spite of a cumulative build-up of a diversified base, the growth process stands threatened by exploding population rise. The Eighth Five Year Plan had as a priority objective, "Containing population growth through active peoples' cooperation and an effective scheme of incentives and disincentives". The objective was not achieved for the reason that "peoples' cooperation" was without gender equity and justice in population control measures. It is our fervent hope that in future, there will be a fair deal for all sections of our fellowbeings.

BONDED LABOUR AND CHILD BONDAGE

To cure injustice, you should expose them before the light of human conscience and the bar of public opinion, regardless of what tension that exposure generates. They must be brought into the open where they cannot be evaded.

—Martin Luther King

Slavery, bondage and child abuse are exploitative practices of an extreme nature. It is an expression of arrogant authoritarianism of the feudal system. These are flagrant violations of human dignity and human rights. Indian history is replete with glorious examples of efforts of many right-thinking individuals and groups—the present organizers of this event included—to abolish these inhuman practices.

Article 23 of our Constitution prohibits traffic in human beings and *begar* and other forms of forced labour. The Bonded Labour System (Abolition) Ordinance, 1975 provided the substantive basis for the elimination of bonded labour and was replaced by the Bonded Labour System (Abolition) Act, 1976 which is now two decades old. A real assessment of the implementation of the Act is now called for to verify the authenticity of the claim that within these 20 years many good things have been done.

Operational aspects of the Act

The Act abolishes the bonded labour system (sec. 4); renders any agreement or custom to that effect void (sec. 5); extinguishes liability to repay bonded debt (secs. 6-9); and an overriding effect (sec. 3). It contains several important safeguards for the bonded labour, and importantly in section 15, the burden of proof that the bonded labour debt claimed is not so, is on the creditor, and not for the bonded labour to prove. The Act casts a duty on the District Magistrates and the implementing authorities to take steps to inquire into cases of bonded labour and to promote and secure the welfare and economic interests of the bonded labour (secs 10-12).

The Act is also significant in providing for prosecution and punishment including imprisonment for anyone who compels bonded labour (sec. 16), advances bonded debt (sec. 17), and abets the offence (sec. 20). The Act mandates vigilance committees in each district and each subdivision and lays down its composition (sec. 13), and gives a pivotal role to the committee as an advisory, investigative and coordinating body in tackling the bonded labour system (sec. 14).

The Bonded Labour Act has also to be read alongside with several other enactments which deal with the rights of individuals and workers.

There has been considerable debate over the definition of bonded labour. The Bonded Labour System (Abolition) Act, 1976 under section 2(g) defines the bonded labour system in a comprehensive manner. Briefly put, it means that a person binds himself to the service of his or her creditor for considerations received, to render, by himself or through any member of his family, his labour or service on wages or otherwise, permanently.

There have been very many instances where the definition has been interpreted in a such a manner that many of the instances of bonded labour practices are not booked under the Act. Apart from this, it has been revealed through court cases that, "The dilemma which the judiciary faced in course of enquiry was vividly described when the workman is taken into confidence and is assured of protection he gives out a story of harassment and torture by the contractor but when officially questioned he is afraid of making necessary disclosures".

Instance in the case of Tamil Nadu

This has been corroborated in the Report of the Commission on Bonded Labour in Tamil Nadu in Civil Writ Petition No. 3922 of 1985 of the Supreme Court of India (People's Union for Civil Liberties—Petitioner versus State of Tamil Nadu and other—Respondents). It was stated by the Commission that it encountered numerous cases where the bonded labourers who had been candid with the Commission were almost immediately either physically assaulted, threatened or moved away, and the Commission came across several cases of those who changed their minds overnight on whether to divulge information of their plight, ostensibly on outside pressure. Another difficulty that is faced when dealing with the problem is the task of estimating the extent of bonded labour.

The Tamil Nadu Commission, after visiting twenty-three districts of the State identified 1417 bonded labourers in 20 different occupations. The communitywise break-up (in percentage of the bonded labourer) were :

1. Scheduled Castes 44%
2. Most Backward classes 26%
3. Backward classes 24%
4. Scheduled Tribes 6%

Occupationwise among the Scheduled Castes, 90

per cent belonged to agriculture; among the MBCs and BCs more were in quarrying.

Of the 1417 bonded labourers 1239 were men and 178 women.

The Tamil Nadu Commission found that bonded labour existed in substantial manner in all the districts of the State and that the estimates were that their number in Tamil Nadu may be over 10 lakhs. It found the relevant rehabilitation measures inadequate and incapable of dealing with the problem. It is amazing that the Commission found lack of official acknowledgement of the prevalence of the bonded labour system in the State, which led to both unpreparedness and often attempts to camouflage realities.

The Commission found the employers of bonded labour and their agents are having a free and unrestricted run, in conducting their operations. It was also found that about 10 per cent bonded labour were children of whom majority were girls. The Commission felt that rather than addressing merely the symptoms of the bonded labour system, attempt should be to deal with the underlying factors and root causes that promote the bonded labour system. The Commission observed that women workers, even more so, those in bondage or wives of bonded labourers, are particularly defenceless and exposed to several forms of exploitation including sexual harassment. The Commission observed that, given the complexity and nature of the bonded system, any worthwhile rehabilitation efforts must address the psychological, physical and economic aspects covering several facets such as housing, nutrition, education, employment, health, etc. The Commission recommended the constitution of a National Authority for Bonded Labour.

The findings of the Tamil Nadu Commission, in many respects would also be relevant to other States where bonded labour exists. Various studies have revealed that rehabilitation measures have not helped the bonded labourers in any substantial manner. The will and application to tackle the menace is lacking in majority of the cases. Notwithstanding the efforts of Swami Agnivesh and others like him, neither the child labour nor the bonded labour have found any solace. We need more spirited, dedicated and forceful fora like the one here, to ventilate the grievances of the bonded labourers in order to eliminate the system and cleanse the society and bring human dignity to everyone.

The purpose in explaining in some detail these provisions and findings was to emphasize the fact that there is a big gap between the precept and the practice. In spite of best of intentions it is seen that the system of bonded labour is not so easy to be abolished. The main factors : the affected, the employer and the Government do not seem to work in tandem to achieve the common objective of eliminating this obnoxious practice. It is here that the NGOs and social activists could play a decisive role in bringing about the needed coordination to accelerate the process of release and rehabilitation of bonded labourers.

The movement for the elimination of bonded labour is to be focussed on the root courses of its continuance in spite of legal measures and relevance of assistance packages. To me, it is evident that the enforcement of the Act is weak and implementation of programme tardy. To add to these, there is no societal response to get rid of an inhuman practice and to cap it all, poverty conditions and fear of oppression prevents the affected to seek justice. Let us all resolve to work towards the complete elimination of bonded labour in our country in this Golden Jubilee Year of our Independence.

NATIONAL FORUM FOR BLIND WOMEN

The AICB (All India Confederation of the Blind)

National Forum of Blind Women is an appropriate institution deserving support and encouragement in its endeavours to fulfil the aims and objectives so essential to improve the condition of blind women. We all know that visual disorders threaten an essential means of communication between the individual and her environment. This disability leads to a reduction in personal coping and adaptive functions which causes significant limitations in overall performance in daily living.

Establishing links with like-minded agencies and organizations for setting up institutions and services is the Forum's prime objective for improving the condition of blind women. Hence, it is opportune that the role of the National Commission for Women in protecting and promoting the interests of all sections of women in our country is explained in brief.

The National Commission for Women, a statutory body set up in 1992 under a Central Act, strives to achieve equity, equality and justice for women in all spheres of life. It pursues gender justice through intervention in cases of violation of equality laws, denial of opportunities and deprivation of women's rights. NCW arranges counselling and assistance to women victims of atrocities and women in distress all over the country. A separate Counselling and Pre-litigation Cell has been estabilished in the commission for the purpose. Specific steps have been taken to amend laws inadequate to protect women interests in different areas such as dowry, rape, custody, property rights, marriage, divorce, maintenance, etc. From the beginning of this year, Parivarik Mahila Lok Adalats and legal awareness campaigns have been held in different places of the country, benefitting thousands of women. The active cooperation and assistance of NGOs and the judiciary in these efforts needs special mention. Special focus is laid to solve the problems of girl child, prostitutes, widows, women in custody and backward social groups.

It is significant that the National Commission for Women has decided to observe our 50th Year of Independence as the Year of Gender Equality with Social Justice. It will undertake a series of important activities commencing from 2nd October, 1996 and culminating on the International Women's Day, 8th March, 1997 relating to women of the weaker section, specifically benefitting women of the Scheduled Castes, the Scheduled Tribes and the Backward Classes and minority communities befitting the celebrations of Fiftieth Year of Independence. The Commission proposes to place before them through these programmes a vision of tomorrow's India as a land of equality and justice. Through these efforts, the Commission would help in the integration of the principle of gender equality and the principle of social justice. The programme was launched in Orissa, on Gandhi Jayanti, 1996 when about 20,000 people assembled at Parlakhemundi from the districts of Phulbani, Koraput, Rayagada, Ganjam and Gajapati and resolved unanimously to request the Government of Orissa to introduce prohibition in Orissa and particularly for the benefit of women in the State. I have narrated in some detail these activities of NCW with some purpose. And, that is, we as a Commission are committed to bring about improvement in the life of all women, but with some priority, i.e. for disadvantaged groups of women. We have plans to take up next, the problems of disabled groups of women, that is those women in the category of physically and mentally handicapped (locomotor, visual, hearing and speech).

I had occasion to go through some of the papers presented at this conference. These are extremely useful for evolving an effective strategy to improve the status of blind women. For an enlightened group here, it might not be necessary for me to dwell upon the details of the handicaps that blind women face in day to day life. Nor is it essential to provide statistics to prove that blind women are sufferers on many counts.

The figures

In brief, there are several estimates on the size of the disabled population itself in our country. The Census Organization has collected information on physical disabilities or infirmities in the dicennial census from the very beginning. But it was discontinued from 1941 onwards in view of the doubts expressed about its reliablity. For the first time after Independence, the Census Organization collected information on the physically handicapped in the 1981 census. The census covered three broad categories of disabilities, viz. totally blind, totally dumb, and totally crippled. However, the census provided only a framework for later detailed investigations by other agencies. No information regarding sex, age and other characteristics was collected. According to the census, the total number of disabled persons in the country in 1980 was 11.2 lakhs (excluding Assam where no census could be undertaken); consisting of 4.79 lakh totally blind, 3.64 lakh totally crippled and 2.77 lakh totally dumb. The National Sample Survey conducted a comprehensive survey on disabled persons in 1981, the International Year of the Disabled persons (IYDP). This survey covered 3 types of disabilities viz. visual disabilities, communication disabilities and locomotor disabilities. Mental disability children in the age group 0-4 years were excluded. The survey arrived at an estimate of 1 million persons having at least one or the other disability which constituted about 1.8 per cent of the total population of 680 million (1981 census). About 10 per cent of these suffer from more than one physical disability. Considering each type of disability separately, those having locomotor disabilities constituted the maximum number (5.43 million), followed by those with visual disabilities (3.43 million), hearing disabilities (3.0 million) and speech disabilities (1.75 million). As per one of the papers, presented in this conference, the estimated population (NSSO) of the blind is 40,50,000 and according to the survey conducted by the National Family Health Survey, the population of blind women is 17,77,685 of whom 70 per cent live in the rural areas. It needs to be added that the estimates of the size of the population of visually handicapped would largely depend upon the definition adopted.

It is important to note that more than three-fourths of the visually handicapped persons are in rural areas and that among them the majority are females (59%). When we consider the term 'blind women', various images come before us. Her profile is indeed one of vulnerable character. She could be subjected to any amount of indignities, just because she is handicapped in protecting herself from the viscissitudes of an unkind world. The socio-economic factors play a vital role in attitude formation for and against blind women. The blind person's own self-image is shaped by the responses of family members, her peer group and the community at large.

The problems of blind women are in many ways different from the problem of blind men. Further, as is evident from the information so far available, blind women are more in rural areas. There is, however, no definite information about their educational levels, economic status and skill capabilities. I thought the first task, therefore, would be to concentrate on assessing the problems of blind women in rural areas comprehensively before we could prescribe any remedy.

Efforts of the Government in the direction

In the last fifty years, the Government of India and the State Governments have taken a number of measures to improve the condition of blind persons, especially with regard to imparting education. The traditional approach has been that of segregation in isolated institutions. The effort towards integrated education has not attained enough progress. Of particular significance is that negative attitude towards blindness in general and blind women in particular are strongly prevalent. The urgent need is to mount appropriate awareness and sensitization programmes with specific focus on rural areas. Another important aspect is the absence of social security measures for blind women. The agencies working for blind women are very few and still fewer in rural areas. Another step would be to accelerate skill upgradation and training programmes in a more sustained and demand oriented approach. As blindness in early ages is caused due to nutritional deficiencies, it need hardly be stressed that here, prevention rather than cure would be more welcome.

---

*Wealth sharing mechanisms are a key ingredient in the political stability necessary for rapid growth.

4

WOMEN IN PARTICIPATORY DEVELOPMENT

Arise, awake and not stop till the goal is reached

—Swami Vivekananda

ROLE OF WOMEN IN GROWTH AND DEVELOPMENT IN INDIA

The imperative need of gender partnership in matters of development has been recognized, though belatedly. It is well known that gender equality in economic, social and political fields, as fundamental rights, is guaranteed by our Constitution to the 500 million strong Indian women, who incidentally form about one-sixth of the world's women population. "Growth and Development" is a very general term. Assigning a role, performing a role and deriving the results of such a role in such growth and development, by women could take place only under certain set conditions.

In a country like ours, where parliamentary democracy is in practice, for our women to play a meaningful role would mean that conditions should be created where women's voices are heard and their needs are recognized and participation is unhindered. For such a set of conditions to exist, women should be empowered and, to me, it appears that political empowerment, in a democracy, is the prerequisite. Women in decision-making positions would alone facilitate growth and development on the desired course.

The rural contribution

In a vast country like ours, there are major differences in resource endowment and levels of development among regions and communities. This is also reflected in women's development. For example, backward social groups and hilly and tribal areas and desert areas as also in general, the rural and urban areas pose different problems for which different solutions have to be evolved. To say, in a very simple routine manner, "Role of Women in Growth and Development" is grossly simplifying the theme. Take the case of rural areas where, someone had observed recently that "Entry of women in the rural economy has been a forced one. As a natural law, the green pastures or market-friendly ventures and micro businesses in rural areas would naturally be first saturated by the rural men, more so, by the more potential men of the village. The poorer and men of lesser capability would automatically take the secondary economic activities of the village. When the rural women enters the same rural economy which is by then fully saturated, they would naturally be left with no options which can still have market demand. Besides, as the rural women till date do not have free access to resources, they cannot go in for high investment areas. The rural women cannot afford to have their full time allotted for the economic activities. Thus, they are saddled with a bundle of disadvantages, namely less or no resources, no technical expertise, no experience with outside economy and no demand for the products they make."

When such a situation is prevailing, the planners and development experts would have to reconsider how to make women's role effective for the nation's progress.

No doubt, in recent times, greater attention is being paid by the Central and State Governments to identify inadequacies in the developmental efforts for women and consequently measures have been initiated, *inter alia*, (1) to support sensitization programmes to bring about awareness and gender specific approach, (2) to ensure unhindered access to service, and (3) to facilitate them to function as equal partners and participate in planning, implementing and supervising development programme, particularly in the context of the assigned role of women in Panchayati Raj institutions. In addition, endeavours are reported to be afoot to overcome the socio-cultural and administrative constraints by constant interaction among concerned groups to realize in full measure women's potential. In this task, the role of the media and voluntary agencies would be crucial. What is needed to promote an egalitarian order is a happy blending of "women's uplift" approach and "equal rights" guarantees. This strategy is particularly relevant in the context of prevailing social, economic, political and administrative scenario in our country.

Development is a loaded word. When we address ourselves to the concerns of rural and urban Indian women and of entrusting a role to them, a lot of forbearance on the part of everyone concerned with "development" would be needed. A routine application of "formulae capsules" would be disastrous. We know from our experience that from mere economic growth to growth with equity and justice, from Government initiative to people's involvement and participation, from socio-economic development to human resource development and from endowment to empowerment, the pattern of planning and development has indeed come a long way in our country.

It is a truism that, no country in the world treats its women as well as its men. It is also well known that there cannot be any educated people without educated women. If general education had to be limited to men or to women, the opportunity should be given to women, for then, it would most surely be passed on to the next generation.

And without education, political empowerment and assuming a role in development would be distant goals.

Women by virtue of gender, experience discrimination in terms of denial of equal access to the power structure that controls society and determines development issues. For true equality to become a reality and partnership in growth and development to become a reality, the sharing of power with men on equal terms must be a major strategy.

All the virtues of rural India which brought unique recognition, in fact, are currently being recognized as the issues of gross inequity and wilful subjugation of rural women under the cultural ethos. If development has bypassed some poor pockets and social groups within a nation and women in general, it is rural women in particular who have been utterly bypassed. It is said that the current gender debate itself has become intellectually so sophisticated that in spite of all its vigour and potential to break the gender inequity, the much awaited realization of the need and demand for gender equity is yet to dawn on the horizons of India.

In this era of liberalization, privatization and globalization, in the entire economy, the areas that can be directly intervened by the Government will be very limited. Consequently, the scope to cover substantial portion of women population under government sponsored programmes will be limited. Therefore, the government's intervention can at best be the intent of the modern State only. Thus, the role of women would also get reduced unless alternate strategies are worked out now itself.

May I point out that gender disaggregated data unequivocally proved that our women are yet to access fully any one of the institutions of modern development. Many of the concepts, rules, regulations and procedures of present day developmental institutions are incompatible to the traditional societal values and ethos which confined large majority of women within the frontiers of the family, preventing them access to benefits of developments.

The major concerns of rural women

Basic minimum needs such as drinking water, fuel, etc., by collecting water, and firewood from increasing distances, taking care of the nutritional needs of the children and the old, continue unabated as the main concerns of the rural women. For majority of them, the drudgery still persists notwithstanding the advances our country has made in science and technology. It took Five Year Plans to mount specific plan strategy to meet the minimum needs of rural population in which female members of the family have high stakes. The Minimum Needs Programme (MNP) introduced in the Fifth Plan had eight components : elementary education, rural health, rural water supply, rural roads, rural electrification, rural housing, nutrition and environmental improvement of urban slums. Later, in the Sixth Plan, adult education was added. Subsequently, in the Seventh Plan three more items—rural domestic energy, rural sanitation and public distribution system were added. Reviewing the MNP, the Eighth Plan document records that "in most cases, the physical and financial targets have been achieved satisfactorily except in the area of rural sanitation... However, the quantitative achievements do not mean much in themselves... In the Eighth Plan, the emphasis should shift from mere targeting to achieving qualitative results". We do not know what will happen in the Ninth Plan, or for that matter what will happen to the Ninth Plan itself. In this area, women's role so far has been minimal.

The constitutional hopes

Women could indeed contribute substantially to the nation's growth and development and also improve their own status if the provisions of 73rd and 74th Amendment Acts to the Constitution and particularly the subjects enumerated in the XI and XII Schedules (Appendix II) could be faithfully implemented. But the tragedy is that the State Governments are hesitant to delegate financial and jurisdictional powers to implement programmes. The attitude inherent in the approach of "beneficiary" and "master" prevents development programmes to take off. "Participating" approach has not become a part of our plan implementation notwithstanding populist gimmicks and rhetoric and in all these, the women suffer.

One is reminded that half of the world's population is denied the right to equality in most countries and more so in developing nations like ours. The Constitution of India provides for equal rights and privileges for both men and women and special provisions for women to help them improve their status in society. The five decades of planned development in India through the Eight Five Year Plans have not altered the status of women, very much, especially rural women except in some experimental projects and some sections of urban population or elite rural people. Planning in India is aimed at the empowerment of the people through participation in economic and political processes today. It is confronted with the paradox of women participation without power.

Essentials for full participation

Women could play a pivotal role in the growth and development of the country. It is, however, seen that to the extent that women are part of the population in areas affected by development, they have been mostly associated though the degree of association has been of different scale. In order to effectively involve women to enable them to be real partners in development, the following five major aspects need be considered:

(1) In the transition from subsistence and reproductive

activities to income generating ones, women have to be empowered first educationally and in skill formation and upgradation.

(2) Their role in the household economy needs to be recognized. These economic functions are essential for the preservation and development of the family's and nation's human capital.

(3) Socio-cultural and institutional practices in the ownership of property and/or access to land related resources, credit and technology, etc., must be women friendly.

(4) The women should have the possibility of making alternate choices in the paradigms of development. When shifts in economy take place, women in the agricultural sector should have opportunities in industrial sector occupations.

(5) The grass roots level local government institutions, i.e. the Panchayats and the urban local bodies, where one-third elected members are women must be made functional through adequate delegation of powers.

The world is undergoing tremendous changes affecting every aspect of human development. It is no more possible, nor is it desirable to keep away half the population consisting of women from taking part in the development of a nation. The effort should be to remove all obstacles in the way of their active participation and empower them with all requisites to pave the way for a better life for all.

DEVELOPMENT PARTICIPATION OF WOMEN IN SAARC AND ASIA-PACIFIC REGIONS

The Federation of Indian Women Entrepreneurs deserves congratulations for organizing this two-day conference and two-week long exhibition as a part of India International Trade Fair. Perhaps more than any other region of the world, SAARC and Asia Pacific countries display an outstanding phenomena of economic growth and dynamic political and legal framework. Many of these countries also share some of human deprivations. Poverty, gender inequality and discrimination against certain social groups do persist. Women's participation in national development is not merely a question of providing some special concessions to them. Women's collective action on issues of relevance for their empowerment is the key factor around which women's movement as a whole has to be organized and directed. The region consisting of SAARC countries and Asia Pacific nations have their diverse models of economic success. In India, economic reforms based on globalization, liberalization and empowerment of women by 33 per cent reservation in areas such as Panchayati Raj are opening up new vistas for the development of women and the improvement in their status.

The women entrepreneur

Entrepreneurship is being recognized as a full-fledged new frontier towards which women are turning to fulfil their aspirations economically and socially. Enterprises are attractive to manufacturing, trading or services to women, because of low barriers to entry and the flexible nature of the work, which makes it easy to combine gainful employment with domestic responsibilities.

Entrepreneurs are the real architects of economic life. They are the ones who have shown that genius is sweat and toil and sacrifice and that natural resources gain value only by ingenuity and labour. From their knowledge of failure, they forge success. In accepting risk, they achieve security for all. In embracing change, they ensure social and economic stability.

Entrepreneurship is neither a science nor an art. It is

a practice. But, as in all practices, medicine or engineering for instance, knowledge in entrepreneurship is a means to an end. It is not a 'flash of genius' but purposeful tasks that can be organized into systematic work.

Etymologically, the term entrepreneur has been derived from the French word 'Entrepreneur' which connotes "Undertaker". The dictionary meaning says that an entrepreneur is an organizer of an economic venture, especially one who organizes, owns, manages and assumes the risks of a business.

The centrally planned economies all over the world are becoming increasingly liberalized economies. The economic liberalization implies the progressive transfer of economic and social activities, to private hands. Privatization, in effect means, orientation of economy more and more towards local, regional, national and international market forces. The State would more and more confine itself to public utilities and withdraw from the competitive and commercial activities. The Government will play the role of the enabler and facilitator providing infrastructural facilities appropriate to the section, region and production line. Who can take advantage of these facilities? The answer is clear. Only those who have the entrepreneurial potentiality and achievement propensity.

India, with a developing economy, even after nearly five decades of planning, still has a long way to go to catch up with the leading developed economies of the world. The goal may be distant but surely, the time required to reach it can be cut down by accelerating the pace of development. One way of doing this is by the promotion of industrial and business ventures created by the initiative and enterprise of entrepreneur class. On the whole, thus, there is a positive linkage between an economy of prosperity and the growth of entrepreneurship.

Women entrepreneurs have many challenges to face. They are subjected to discriminations in many areas. It may be recalled that the National Commission for Women co-sponsored a "Regional Policy Consultation on Young Women and Economic Development". The Commonwealth Youth Programme, Asia Centre, organized the meet at Bangalore in 1993. The main concerns identified during the consultation included the following :

1. There were no specialized policies or schemes for providing financial assistance to young women.

2. There was lack of regional networking in terms of change of information, such as publications, newsletters, teaching materials, etc. Besides, market information was also lacking.

3. The need to sensitize the support system towards the needs of young women entrepreneurs and identifying their problems was of critical importance.

4. At national and international levels, networking and coordination were necessary among the agencies involved. Wherever possible at national level, the non-Governmental agencies may form umbrella organizations for coordination of effort and articulation of their views on the subject.

The Federation of Indian Entrepreneurs has as one of its objectives "to facilitate interaction amongst women entrepreneurs of SAARC and Asia Pacific countries and to identify areas of cooperation".

I am confident that the conference would suggest useful practical methods to enhance the professional capabilities of women entrepreneurs of the region to contribute effectively to nations' development empowerment, economic prosperity and the well-being of humanity.

I have great pleasure in inaugurating this conference.

INDIVIDUAL AND SOCIETY : THE CORRELATION

"Adrift on a meaningless voyage"

Man today seems at odds with himself. Serenity is a vanishing quality of life. We live in a tempestuous and troubled world torn apart by political divisions, religious intolerance, racial prejudice, violence and conflict almost in every sphere of our life. The world presses in upon us, insistent, confusing, often tragic. Although there is basic social order in most places and most of the time, it is an order continually disrupted. "Some men form aggressive groups to fight for what they conceive to be their rights. Others, uprooted and drifting on a sea of social change, are buffeted by moral storms, often sinking into crime or vice or trying to save movements" (Robert C. Angell). Although social scientists cannot say with any degree of certainty that there has been a relative increase or decrease of "meaninglessness" during the past century, the condition is nevertheless a pervasive force in all society.

We live in a culture of violence, a world rife with hatred and crime. Human life goes on striving towards excellence, understanding and improvement. In that, I see hope and individual human endeavour to make a difference. However small that difference may be should not matter. Each one of us is capable of performing a modest "act of kindness" towards our fellow human beings. Our conscience is the best guide in such matters.

Society

Society is a collection of individuals, who form groups and act as mediators between individuals and society. This collectivity of interrelated groups share a common location in space and common tradition at a specific point in time. It is a collective unit capable of maintaining itself through reproduction and nurture, motivation of enough segments of the population to perform those tasks that are believed to be necessary to ensure survival.

The definition of society as a relational system of interaction among individuals would direct our attention away from the role of groups as mediating agents. The contribution that any person makes to society is always through a group. The economy is operated through the organized efforts, the group efforts of individuals. Education is provided for groups of children and young adults. In short, because of the division of labour in all societies, we must recognize that they are more complex systems than mere aggregates of individuals as would be.

"Society" in the literature of social science usually refers to one of several concepts. For example, we can speak of society like "Indian Society" or we may use the word to refer to groups, specified or unspecified, such as family, community and culture. Precisely defined concepts of society are found, or usually defined to distinguish between society and culture, or as society and individual.

Societies are characterized by both general and total cultural systems binding on all members and by specific cultural systems to which only certain segments must adhere. It must be kept in mind, however, to avoid confusion that since "both are systems of expectation, each person has a different set of expectations for each cultural context in which he finds himself. Still, it is the system of universal expectation that characterized the cultural system of a given society". (*Success and Opportunity* by Herald Mizruchi)

In each society those who do not conform to a set pattern of the adjusted are called ruleless or ungoverned and some also call those groups maladjusted. Every individual at some point becomes aware of the desire to say that such a thing was good or bad, such an action right or wrong.

Today we are concerned with the apparently increasing process of fragmentation and depersonalization of the individual in complex society.

Ideal society

What is an ideal society?

Every society has a set of moral values and moral problems which have to be solved.

"Life has no meaning, there is no joy, no faith, no reality."

"Everybody is 'happy'—except that he does not feel, does not reason, does not love."—C.V. Wedgewood

At this point, let us turn to the meaning of 'value' and more specifically, success values and the way we have approached them.

A value is a 'group' conception of the desirable. I would like to use care in distinguishing between what we often refer to as values the refined referents of the process of valuation—and the underlying conception that influence our judgements of these values. It is only in the latter case that we are truly dealing with values, while in the former we are focusing on what may, for purposes of convenience, be called value-referents (Williams, 1960 p. 402).

The conception of the desirables, that is, value comes from the family, which is the smallest unit of a society, from educational centres, and copied from parents, teachers, elders and the society.

Family

The family in India was considered an ideal and strong unit as it had remained united and stable over a period of time. However, the family unit and stability can be explained by its patriarchal ideology where roles and responsibilities and control and distribution of resources are strictly determined by a hierarchy of age, gender and generation. As a social institution, family has consisted of more or less formal rules and regulations organized around the fulfilment of societal needs. It has been an integral part of the ethnic community which has promoted patriarchy in the family.

Whatever else the sociological study of society may encompass, it must include family roles and relations. It is one of those central truisms, so obvious, that it is easily overlooked, that each person lives usually for most of his and her life, with the others of his family; that his social character and his individual personality are moulded by them; that shifts in family roles and responsibilities, in their collective and cumulative effect, have a great deal to do with changes in the entire society.

Therefore, the society's oldest and most crucial unit 'family' warrants special attention.

Families assume diverse forms and functions from one country to another, and within each national society. These express the diversity of individual preference and societal conditions, but everywhere it provides the natural framework for the emotional, financial and material support essential for the development of its members. It urges that programmes in society should support family in the discharge of their functions, rather than provide substitutes for such function.

Parenting is the one lifetime profession where no training or qualifications are required. Parents are left to learn and operate by trial and error. The child is the desired outcome, focus and means of sustenance of the family unit.

As the child deals with the reality of life around, it is obvious that the first environment is the family. Relationships with human beings that constitute this family forms the basis of their experiences. This remains true throughout life, as the child grows and enlarges its experiential base into society. Hence, environment to a large extent determines the future of humankind.

At birth, the child does not have a concept of self. The mother, family members, trees and even inanimate objects are seen part of itself. This is a high level of transcendence, indeed—something that mystics and spiritual aspirants thirst for, in their quest. This is accompanied by a high level of "faith" in the world. The child enjoys life and has faith in everything around it as a manifestation of true recognition of concept of God.

Indian family

If we were to do a survey asking people from all walks of life, what they considered to be the most important change that the Indian family has undergone over the years, a large majority will probably point to the disintegration of the traditional Indian "joint family" to form what is called the "elementary" or "nuclear family". This should come as no surprise since, for many decades, scholars and the common people of this country have regarded the "joint family" as being a hallmark of Indian society, an institution whose name indicated close cooperation and support from the family members in all matters, and also evoked ideas of large groups of people living together and sharing in each other's lives. This ideal, it is believed is being steadily eroded with the onset of industrialization, urbanization, modernization and related changes. These trends are also being held responsible for people becoming more selfish, self-centred and hence, less concerned with the welfare of their extended kin.

Expressions of concern about the "threats of the family" and the "disintegration of the family" in modern times tend to focus upon overt symptoms of the disease, rather than on the ailment itself. Opinion leaders call for efforts to preserve and strengthen the structure of "the family" without examining its foundation.

Meanwhile, idealized images of "the family" pervade the mass media, particularly in popular cinema and consumer advertisements. These contribute in different ways towards enhancing the mystique of the "traditional joint family" or glorifying the "we two, our two" family formula, while glossing over unpalatable realities about both. At the same time, soap operas on satellite television lend new meaning to matters like marriage and human relationships.

This is not to say that nurturance, love and affection are totally absent. One has to understand that families are both sites of cooperation and conflict, in which women are specifically disadvantaged. Families can be a source of emotional strength, but are more often sites of women's oppression. While physical abuse of women exists sometimes within the family, the work burden arising out of division of labour are outcome of conflicts.

These problems are perceived as intrafamilial problems, rather than recognizing the interconnection between women's position within families and their position *vis-a-vis* other social institutions, like religion, state, media and markets. For example, in India, the personal laws are formed, based on religious beliefs.

Neither is it correct to view problems like drug abuse, rising criminality and violence solely on the disintegration of families. As Kapur (1993) observes, these are social problems related more to unending poverty, communalism and fundamentalism, racism and other oppressions than to the individual failings of individual family members.

The feeling of instability and insecurity, and the loss of professional pride are consequent to a certain degree of destabilization that comes from break-up of joint family, migration to urban areas which provides a fertile ground for the growth of backward looking ideas. The response to the loss of a "structured, predictable and explicable world" may as well be a throwback to the "safe-haven" of the traditional relationships and value systems, which may lead to a further downgrading of the position of women in society and within the family. But such "restorations" of traditional relationships will not be complete, and are likely to bypass some of the positive aspects of such relationships, like care for the aged. This is because the whole philosophy of liberalization, marketization and commercialization will pervade the value systems also.

The daily life of an Indian in the past was surrounded by ethics and values from the religion. Good health was assumed by way of religious fast like "Ekadasi" and on certain days fast was dedicated to the presiding deity, environment was protected and cared for by religious rituals—worship of neem trees, *tulsi*, etc. If someone in the family erred, the fear of punishment by God was imposed, weekly silence was observed for self discipline; festivals were celebrated with the worship of Gods; the family was the focal point of all this behaviour pattern which was set by religous rituals.

Modernization effect

Modernization in the post independence era in India, has been characterized by the socioeconomy changes which have come about as well as the erosion/undermining/loss of significance of traditional structures. Aspirations of the family and changes thereof have occurred in the background of this loss, and it has tended to affect family ethics. In terms of behaviours of young members, this has given rise to certain rituals or loss of rituals. Most problems of this group, whether academic or motivational, are offshoots of this scenario. Issues of independence and its role in watching television, dressing in a particular manner, choice of friends, spending habits, attitudes, comfort seeking, etc., are also offshoots of this.

No one can deny that family life in India today is in a crisis. This is true about both urban and rural areas and about families at different economic levels, belonging to different communities. Among the many outward symptoms of this is the increasing of violence within the family, wife-beating, dowry deaths and other crimes against women; the widening gap between generations as regards people falling in love and getting married without parental consent and so on.

This means that families need to either deliberately hold on to traditional rituals or alternately develop consistent new rituals to provide their young members a stable base to grow up in. Rituals here do not refer to religious practices but a family's day to day structures and enduring patterns of behaviours, attitudes and so on. Here hierarchy can be maintained.

An alternate position needs to be considered in view of the inevitability of current family movement. It is increasingly obvious that families have shorter lives than earlier. Since the life span caused by migration, nuclearity, quest for higher education, etc., is short, the young members' perception of comfort in a family will be a function of the degree of democratization in that family. This position is non-hierarchal. It seeks to build an entirely new family culture given the current concerns. Most families actively do this but without reflection, self-examination or a deliberate intention or enhancing young members' growth. Since affiliation, routines and family structures in the democratization position require to be voiced and discussed, families would have to make a concerted decision to build a family and not just do it intuitively.

In the ultimate analysis, a healthy family is where the young members have good or healthy family image.

Religion and society

In the name of religion and spirituality, the grill of rites and rituals confuse the child. Even prayer is reduced to a charade of petitioning God—the parental understanding of religion or spirituality is only superficial.

Is it any wonder then that these distortions impress themselves as fundamentalism? How unfortunate it is that children are the victims of the collective indiscretions of humankind?

Some Premises

1. We need to develop attitudes and abilities that permit us to understand our fellow human beings and human diversity. Such a consciousness and spiritual awareness are essential for our living together in the "global village".
2. We need to focus on developing a capacity and an inclination to make peace—peace within ourselves, peace with brothers and sisters and peace with Mother Nature in order to bring about a non-violent and just social order to this planet.
3. We need to face conflicts and difficulties which are inevitable in our modern life in a rational, constructive and realistic way and search for creative solutions to the "material problems" that nurture tension, anger, aggression and violence.
4. Lasting and sustainable peace would require rearrangement of our relationships and priorities in our lives and social structure.
5. We need to abandon the idea or mindset that a certain culture, ideology, way of thinking or life can be imposed on others through the use of force or violence.

These premises clearly suggest the need for peace,

education and training in conflict resolution.

WOMEN AND RELIGION

What seems fascinating to me is the combination of several factors. The first and perhaps most important one—is the fact that this university is celebrating its 40th year of existence. Prof. Dahiya, may I convey to all of you at the University of Kurukshetra my good wishes on reaching this landmark and hope that it will grow from strength to strength.

The other interesting factor is that your Women's Studies Research Centre has selected "Women and Religion" as the theme for this seminar. This theme is particularly apt, especially in today's world "Women and Religion" have become important issues worldwide.

When thinking about religion, my mind reflects back to the days of the *Mahabharata*. Considering that your university was the scene of epic battles and thought-provoking discourses, as narrated in the *Mahabharata* we could perhaps consider the location to be on auspicious grounds. I hope your seminar will receive divine inspiration from its locale and make your deliberations useful.

In these days of crass materialism, there is a general feeling that religion does not play much of a role in our lives. More often than not religious ceremonies are treated as rituals,—take for instance, visits to temples, mosques or churches. What really happens? I am not being sceptical when I say this, but, if we do a sort of an 'ABC' analysis of the people involved, we'd find that only a small group, the 'A' group in reality are firm believers and fully conscious of what's happening during each part of the ceremony. The next 'B' group would perhaps be marginally larger than the 'A' group. This group would consist of people with some knowledge and awareness of religious rites, while the third 'C' group would be the largest with no knowledge of what's going on, perhaps a motley crowd of fundamentalists, those with blind faith, tourists and even sightseers.

And when we talk of religion, we should also bear in mind the role played by faith. It has been said that faith can move mountains suggesting the great expectations which faith can generate or take something nearer home : not so long ago, our media were full of stories about a miracle surrounding milk-drinking idols of Lord Ganesha. And these stories even received international attention. I am sure you will remember that a number of believers rushed to these temples who really went there out of belief and piety. Although many people tried to find rational explanation for this phenomenon, pious believers remained unconvinced that what happened was not a miracle!

Although religion and festivals, linked with religion do play important roles in our lives, the materialism we have seen during the last few years of the 20th century seems to have overtaken religion as a binding force within the family.

From a contemporary perspective, our attitude, our way of life, our religion, our culture and our civilization, created in the past, are so different from each other that they created divisions rather than unity. In fact, many of these ways of life have been too narrow, too restricting and too inhibiting, and, in turn, lead to a stunting of personal growth and social development.

And while, in the recent past, we have the welcome move towards liberty, equality and freedom—on a worldwide basis—we have a trend, especially in societies and nation-states where there is a one-religion dominancy, for religion to be oppressive, rather than a liberating force. A classic example of this could be found in the universal patriarchal oppression of women having its roots in religion and which are upheld by many religious structures, customs and institutions.

And, although some societies—as in Kerala—follow a matriarchal system where women are supposed to play dominant roles but, when it comes to religion and practices, we have traces of patriarchal dominance : as an example we have an age-old practice banning women between 5 to 50 years of age from entering the sacred temple at Sabarimala, in Kerala.

Apart from religion's patriarchal oppression to women, a peculiar trait in religions is that, they have often been the source of divisions, a source of conflict, bloodshed and war. Examples of these can be found in the Crusades, the wars of religion in Europe, "Ethnic Cleansing" in the former Yugoslavia - and nearer home, we have the Kashmir problem, fuelled from across the border, where the driving force had its links with Islam.

What I have said so far is perhaps in the nature of a general overview of religion since, I am sure, others will make more in-depth presentations; but, in the context of "Women and Religion", perhaps I could make few observations and raise a few questions :-

1. Despite many societies and countries as like ours, legally and constitutionally, providing equality for men and women, in practice there is a big gap between legal guarantees and actual ground realities.
2. Strange as it may seem, there is a worldwide phenomenon where women, are often victims of violence and male dominance.
3. Religion, instead of becoming a force for peace and harmony, has become a source of conflicts, mistrust, jealously and even wars.
4. Although, legally we are all equal (men and women), why then are women regarded as inferior?

Independent women may not feel this way but, unfortunately, this seems to be a universally held belief, viz. women are inferior tc men.

5. I don't know if you have noticed it at all that if not, most then quite a few religious scriptures are written by men : so also interpretations, discussions and leadership positions are occupied by men. Why is this so?

6. In an interesting book by Kevin Harris called *Sex, Ideology and Religion,* some interesting points have been made. Harris points out that in the early chapters of Genesis, there was a lot of begetting. A begets B, B begets C and C begets D. All A, B and C were men : where were the women? Background begetters? An obvious inference is that religion not only determines attitudes towards men but also in undervaluation and denigration of women.

7. Interestingly, if religion is supposed to be so good and is supposed to preach good behaviour amongst all of us, why do we have so much discrimination against women?

I know, I have posed some awkward questions without suggesting any answers : I have done this deliberately so that during your two day seminar, perhaps that participants could examine these issues and come up with practical solutions to religion-related problems faced by women.

And finally, not only as the Chairperson of the National Commission for Women but, as one truly concerned about women's issues, I eagerly await the findings of this seminar—and, any recommendations you may wish to make to the National Commission for Women, you can rest assured, that serious consideration will be given to them.

STATUS OF ASIAN REGION

Two decades ago in Mexico, at the First World Conference on Women, the effort to reduce gender inequality moved from the national to the world arena. This international movement has helped in transforming nearly almost every facet of contemporary life for women as also for men and children. It is a well known fact that even now, notwithstanding the tremendous efforts made by the countries of the region to mitigate the hardship of women—legal, social, economic and political—males and females still live in different worlds, with unequal access, opportunities, rights and privileges and protection. Significantly, however, as they once used to be, literacy among women is increasing, fertility rates are falling and women are entering the labour force in larger numbers.

Empirical evidence supports the view that all over the world, supporting a stronger role for women enhances the quality of their own lives and contributes in a substantial manner to the economic growth, improves child survival and the health of all members of the family.

In the region the critical areas that call for immediate attention would include :

(i) Inadequacy of institutional mechanism for the advancement of women.

(ii) Persistent and institutionalized discrimination against the girl child.

(iii) Feminization of poverty.

(iv) Gender blindness in macro-economic policies.

(v) Invisibility of women's contribution to the economy and environmental sustenance.

(vi) Poor participation by women in decision making structures and processes.

(vii) Gender gaps in literacy, education and health.

(viii) Barriers encountered by women in accessing legal entitlements.

(ix) Gender biased societal norms.

Social issues and challenges of modernity facing the women of the peninsula nations primarily arise on account of the fact that society fails to keep pace with the changes occurring all around and tries and holds on to the antiquated concepts, beliefs and practices. The atrocities committed on women, the inadequacies in decision making, roles for women in economic and political institutions, lethargy and lack of commitment in enforcing social legislations aimed at protecting the honour, dignity and safety of women are other issues, which I am sure along with many other relevant issues will be deliberated upon in this as well as other sessions of the Convention to improve the status of women everywhere.

Pakistan

One of the earliest of the seventy-two country gender assessments carried out by the World Bank was on "Women in Pakistan : An Economic and Social Strategy", in 1989. The report found that the status of women in Pakistan is among the lowest in the world, despite the esteem accorded to women in many social contexts. Pakistan's vigorous GDP growth of almost 6 per cent in recent years and the prominence of its female political leaders have not translated into welfare and productivity gains for its women citizens. Pakistan has the lowest sex ratio in the world : in 1990 there were an estimated 92 women for every 100 men, down from 93 in 1963. The under-five mortality rate for girls in 1991 was 139 per thousand, compared with the average of 96 for all low-income countries. Female literacy at 22 per cent and a primary school enrolment ratio of 32 per cent for girls are among the lowest in the world. In rural areas, fewer than one girl in six completes five years of education.

The report emphasized that Pakistan's under investment in its people—particularly its women—was a serious obstacle to its transformation into a dynamic middle-income economy.

The Government responded with plans for a major multisectoral effort, the Social Action Programme, embodying the government's commitments to substantial budgetary shifts and policy changes to support improvements in the quality of its social services. The programme would, in particular, address the barriers created by the tradition of female seclusion, so that girls and women would have greater access to these services. It pledged significant additional government resources for work in four key areas : primary education, primary health, family planning and rural water supply and sanitation.

Sri Lanka

The island nation of Sri Lanka in South Asia has achieved notable improvements in the major indicators of social development. These achievements are nonetheless marred by lagging economic growth, high unemployment rates, persistent poverty, and decade-long civil disturbances. How cultural definitions of women's roles affect women's access to resources varies by ethnic origin (whether Sinhalese, Muslim or Tamil), religous orientation (Christian, Buddhist, Hindu or Muslim) and social and economic status. The lives of poor, uneducated rural women tend to be more circumscribed than those of the urban, educated elite, while households headed by women are disproportionately poor.

Bangladesh

The lives of Bangladeshi women are being profoundly influenced by socio-economic and demographic changes. Most Bangladeshi women are not only poor but are also caught between vastly different worlds. One determined by culture and tradition confines their activities inside family homesteads; the other, shaped by increasing landlessness and poverty, forces them outside into wage employment for economic survival. However, women have limited access to opportunities for improving their lives and, with little education and access to health care, they are ill-prepared for the outside world.

There are great disparities between the health and nutrition status of men and women in Bangladesh. Mortality rates are among the highest in the world for female infants and children aged one to four and for mothers. Infant and children mortality rates are higher for girls than boys, who receive better health care and food because their parents value them as economic assets and as insurance for old age. Widespread nutritional deficiencies result in poor health and low productivity for women.

Indonesia

Indonesia is a nation of enormous cultural diversity. Its 190 million people from three religious traditions, represent 300 ethnic groups, and speak 300 languages. Amidst such diversity, Indonesia's recent record on socio-economic achievements is noteworthy. Indonesian women compare well with women in other countries in Southeast Asia : primary education is nearly universal, girls' primary school attendance has improved significantly, and female labour force participation rates have risen. The national promotion of family planning and the rising age of marriage for women have contributed to reduced fertility rates. Whereas most health indicators have shown marked improvements over the past few decades, infant and maternal mortality rates remain unusually high.

Kazakhistan

Women in Kazakhistan have long been an important part of the labour force. Girls and women have had good access to education, while a well developed system of childcare and maternity leave made work outside the home compatible with raising a family. At the end of the Soviet era, participation by women in the labour market was higher than in Western industrial countries.

---

*It is trifles that make perfection but perfection is not trifle.

5

WOMEN PORTRAYAL IN THE MEDIA

The National Commission for Women has dedicated this entire week from 1st to 8th March—the International Women's Day—to drawing public attention to some of the serious issues and concerns that women, and in particular, poor women face. This, as all of you know, includes their representation on mass media.

Again this is not a concern that is unique to our country. It is a global issue which was systematically addressed at the Beijing Conference on Women. In fact, in the Platform of Action, there was a series of concrete recommendations for the government, media industry and NGOs.

The government have agreed to collaborate with women in working out guidelines and developing appropriate regulatory mechanisms to promote balanced and non-stereotyped portrayal of women. And towards this end have also committed themselves to promoting research and implementation of a strategy of IEC or Information, Education and Communication. Similarly the NGOs and industry have their share of commitments.

Nothing could have been more timely than this. In an era of liberalization, privatization and globalization, when market forces are supreme and the country is virtually swept off its feet by the satellite information invasion we do hope that the government takes serious note of its responsibilities not only to itself but to civil society as a whole and to vulnerable groups like women and children.

Our concerns are manifold. At one level, we are concerned about the quality of depiction that women are victims and in particular the kind of titillation and sleaze that purveyors of commercial and entertainment media take recourse to.

But at another level we are even more deeply concerned about our abysmal representation in more serious categories of programming such as news and current affairs. Here the odds are still against us and the justification that is often given is that we or our issues are not as news worthy as others, an argument that we are not entirely convinced about.

We realize that media has many facets to it and even at this stage when we are sharing our concerns about it we do not underestimate the media's support to us. I personally recall many instances when media played a very vital role in advocating our concerns.

But notwithstanding their sensitivity and their inclusiveness these issues still lack the necessary institutional support and encouragement. Moreover there is no mechanism barring public interest litigation—of making media accountable not only for its so-called transgression but even more important for it's blatant discrimination against less privileged groups like women.

The government, as we are aware—is planning to introduce in the current session of Parliament a Bill to regulate to broadcast industry. We learn from the Press that although the immediate provocation is the entry of technological inputs such as DTH this effort has also partly emerged from the Supreme Court judgement of 1995 urging government to make airways a public property and to constitute an appropriate authority to oversee this.

What concerns us about this bill is the fact that any effort to make media accountable should be inclusive of civil society and within that sensitive groups like women. In other words what we require is a court of appeal or a public body such as the Broadcasting Council which has been envisaged in the Prasar Bharati Bill. But, such a body should have the public confidence and in particular have a critical representation of people with a proven track record of work on gender issues.

In the absence of such mechanism and effort by the government and the media industry to address the specific needs and concerns of women and in particular less privileged groups of women, all the talk about ensuring rights and constitutional guarantees of non-discrimination and equality to women will come to a naught.

We realise that all these policy changes have to go beyond mere legislative intervention and have to ensure an informed and sustained participation of civil society. This is often easier said than done. Therefore, when institutions like the National Commission for Women recommend policy changes we do so fully realizing the gravity of the issue and are willing to bear equal responsibility for its implementation and realization. So we do hope that the government uses the present opportunity of putting into effect some of the longstanding promises that it has made to groups like women.

I am confident that today's deliberation will throw light on the above issues and policy makers, and planners would help many a parent and citizen to comfortable clean viewing.

Media's role towards women

It gives me immense pleasure in participating in this workshop organized by the Media Advocacy Group. This august gathering of women from all walks of life—women representing different spectra of the society—women activists, women entrepreneurs, professionals and media persons, all converging at one place, is pointer to the concern all of us have for the cause of women.

The subject "Women's Depiction on Television" appeals to all. We live in an informational environment and of all the media, television has the most electrifying influence on our psyche. Even when the television was in its infancy, its impact and influence was tremendous. Television news coverage of Vietnam has been a disaster as far as Washington is concerned. It had alienated people from war. With new electronic gadgets and powerful cameras, television can change the course of events. On small screen, we are exposed to exciting picture stories speaking with extraordinary sensitivity and eloquence.

I am happy to say that television does not make much discrimination between the two sexes at least insofar as depiction is concerned. As you switch on the television set, you find a woman there. She may be an anchorperson, a newsreader, a character of a serial or a woman peddling certain consumer durables. Indeed, this media needs to be congratulated for capturing Indian women in its various moods and shades, costumes and colours, capacities and capabilities. Now women issues do make headlines. We have had serials with middle and lower middle class settings—serials like *Hum Log, Buniyad, Tamas.* Here we find portrayal of Indian women within the family setting—managing domestic chores—to a certain extent content with their environs and at times, register their grievances too. Beyond that she cannot venture. The extended joint family is being rapidly replaced by nuclear family which increases the strains of a single housewife. Even though the role of women is central to our polity, the position is one of sister-daughter-mother syndrome. Indeed because of male bias one half of the population has been subordinated to the other half.

Then we have had and still have serials like *Khaandan, Swabhiman, Udaan, Gumrah, Rajani, Shanti, Banegi Apni Baat*. Here the depiction is quite different. Here the woman is in the lead. Radha of *Gumrah*, Swetlana of *Swabhiman*, Kalyani Singh of *Udaan*, Rajani of *Rajani*, Shanti of *Shanti* are not the faces of individuals—they are the faces of women who have grown, women who have come out in their own right, breaking all social barriers, setting themselves as role models. Doordarshan deserves credit for portraying them as such.

Now, coming to commercials, particularly with the attended system of sponsoring. In this age of image advertising, it is from small screen that the meaning of brand names are learned. Here, also the depiction varies. Some of them exclusively focus on housewives. Commercials on detergents, spices and household goods fall in this category. Then we have depiction of the glamorous woman—woman selling cosmetics, costumes, jewellery and fashion dresses. But to my utter dismay, at times, I have found that in an effort to glamourize women, some of the Ad persons have taken to what we may call obscenity and vulgarity. There is a section in the Advertising world, which, I may be permitted to say, in effort to sell their products depicts women as objects of sex.

Another trend, I may state is the increasing emphasis on consumerism. Very often, the model presented in many of the serials and commercials is of a higher middle class or even upper class which I am afraid, a large majority of our womenfolk will fail to identify with. With the growing haste to sell one's product and to maximize profits, at many places, we find attempt to distort the very face of Indian womanhood. This is one trend against which we should be careful.

Another area which the television might think of emphasizing upon is perhaps, focusing more attention on programmes set in relatively humble settings. The depiction of woman as successful entrepreneurs, lawyers and bureaucrats is appropriate in its own right. But there are several other situations, where television may like to capture. A clerk, a stenographer, a nurse or a receptionist, may be a school teacher—their lives—their dual commitments—commitments at home and in the office—their problem to reach office and return home in crowded buses—all these call for sympathetic depiction. Then, there is a large segment of women in rural India—women, who contribute equally to the family income—women who work in the farms as well as are engaged in different crafts and enterprises—all have their own saga to tell. They may interest television. 36 per cent of agricultural workforce is female. But women's projection on television is mainly as non-products with a very limited role outside home.

Television's depiction of Pulse Polio immunization campaign, AIDS awareness programmes and family welfare campaign is really commendable. But there are other issues, which the television may like to consider. The Human Development Report, 1995 states that India has a Maternal Mortality Rate (MMR) of 460. This is in sharp contrast to 2 in Ireland. Even in neighbouring Sri Lanka it is 80. Television may like to focus such issues to enlighten and educate.

We in the National Commission for Women are in the midst of formulation strategies for ameliorating conditions of women. One thrust area is launching of legal awareness campaign through women's colleges spread all over the country. We also have programmes for organizing, "Mahila Lok Adalats" for delivery of quick and inexpensive justice. We are aware of the problems of prostitutes and are trying to plan out what we can do for them. Anti-liquor campaigns are also on our agenda. Television as a powerful medium can be of immense help in all our endeavours. We have plans to exploit its tremendous potential in propagating our cause and in delivering something worthwhile for the Indian women. I am sure our invitation for cooperation to our friends in television media will have a responsive echo.

*Little things affect little mind.

6

TRAFFICKING IN WOMEN FOR PROSTITUTION

WOMAN AND PROSTITUTION : GREATEST SCOURGE AFFLICTING WOMANKIND DOWN THE AGES

Ladies and gentlemen, friends, I speak on behalf of the victimized, the trapped, the harassed, the branded, the mutilated, the tortured and moulded woman shaped to suit the lust of sexual exploiters. I consider it an honour and a privilege to be with you all, it certainly is an honour to be among such a distinguished gathering, it is my privilege to deliver an address, on a theme which is of great relevance in today's society.

Trafficking in women and children is assuming dangerous proportions threatening the fabric of our society in the region for the purpose of prostitution.

The practice of prostitution is perhaps as old as civilization. Historically, religious beliefs and social customs prevalent in society from time to time provide the earliest accounts of its origin. It is rather difficult to enumerate or identify all factors conducive to prostitution because it has often been argued that prostitution has its roots deep in the fabric of society. Some research studies suggested the factors conducive to prostitution as destitution, desertion, neglect, ill-treatment, strained relations, deception, bad influences, illegitimate pregnancy, illicit sexual relations, ignorance, sex curiousity, sexual urge, desire for easy life, desire for revenge, industrialization, urbanization, tradition, heredity, prohibiting of widow remarriage; and adopting double standards for men and women whereby men are allowed considerable sexual freedom and women ostracized on the score of chastity.

We have a growing population of children and young people exposed not only to the seduction of capitalism, but to the economic pressures of survival. The social condition emerging out of this phenomenon becomes a fertile ground for the easy recruitment of innocent victims into the vicious market of human flesh.

The age-old recourse to trafficking

We are also speaking about a flourishing industry operating worldwide that capitalizes on the sale and trafficking of children through internet and other means. It is an industry that can buy political power.

I am mentioning these because trafficking has direct relationship with commercialization of prostitution and the new trend of introducing young girls in the trade. Three major legal systems are in vogue the world over for the purposes of controlling immoral traffic in women : (i) Regulationist Approach, (ii) Prohibitionist Approach, and (iii) Abolitionist Approach.

International attempts to eradicate trafficking in women were made as early as 1904 when the International Agreement for the Suppression of the White Slave Trade (as trafficking in women was then called) was signed in Paris. The modern standards on the elimination of trafficking in women, are based on the 1949 Convention for the Suppression of the Traffic in Persons and of the Exploitation of the Prostitution of others.

In the nearly fifty years since the adoption of the 1949 International Convention on the Trafficking in Persons, a number of international legal instruments have been developed that deal at least in part, with the trafficking in women. However, despite the growth of instruments in this area, it cannot yet be said that an international legal regime exists that successfully governs this complex problem.

Trafficking in persons has long been recognized as a contemporary form of slavery. Trafficking occurs throughout the world in different forms, including illegal adoptions, theft of body parts, debt bondage of workers and sexual exploitation. Despite a general increase in human rights protection in the past 50 years, women and children in particular have suffered immensely in recent decades as victims of sexual trafficking. For instance, the HIV/AIDS epidemic has made child prostitutes, believed to be free of disease, all the more sought after. The scope today for international travel has made the growth of sex tourism possible. New technology and case of communication by cyberspace have facilitated the spread of pornography and the abuse of 'Marriage' and 'Dating' services, further complicating efforts to protect victims of such abuse.

As the phenomenon of trafficking in women and children becomes increasingly global and modern, new legal approaches are emerging to combat the problem.

International curbs

Unfortunately only 69 countries have ratified the 1949 Convention. There are, however, other instruments, particularly human rights instruments, which address directly or indirectly, the problem of traffic in women. Further, the Convention on the Elimination of All Forms of Discrimination Against Women provides in Article 6 that State parties shall take all appropriate measures including legislation, to suppress all forms of traffic in women and exploitation of prostitution of women.

A lot more work needs to be done at the level of the

international standard to ensure the basic rights of trafficked persons, for example in the areas of summary deportations of trafficked persons and the lack of support services for them. This work is critical to shift the focus from prosecution of traffickers to the needs of victims, and to make it easier for victims to seek help and speak out about their situation.

At times, an argument is put forward that as everybody has a right to earn in one's own way so the prostitutes and trafficking is a part of it. But this theory needs to be rejected with the contempt it deserves for the very obvious reason that an overwhelming majority of girls and women have not joined this trade by their free will, but have been pushed into it by force or through the devices of socio-religious sanctions. It has also been said that it is primarily poverty that drives them into this profession. However, that is also not very true because it is not poverty *per se*, but the exploitation of that poverty by anti-social elements such as traffickers, that drives the innocents into this vice. Some people are in favour of granting licences to prostitutes. But this will amount to accepting prostitution as a profession and permitting commercial exploitation of sex. I do not agree with this argument.

To check trafficking, appointment of trafficking police officers should be made by all countries. We have interfaced with a large number of prostitutes. The responses we got have been very encouraging. We have created awareness. We have earned for ourselves confidence amongst the victims. But the journey is arduous and the goal, if not distant, is definitely difficult. Like Arjuna in the Indian epic *Mahabharata*, we are looking only at the bird's eye—the bird's eye being—to usher in a society, where there is zero level of trafficking. To achieve this, we must formulate a perspective plan of action.

To arrive at the 'priority objective' of zero level, both

positive and negative methodologies must be adopted. Positive methods involve rescue operations and rehabilitation measures for victims already in the profession. Negative measures aim at negating entry to new entrants to the profession. For this, every country should have access to fully developed intelligence network with efficient networking among countries of the region.

Curtailment of trafficking in humans in the context of India

In India, we are planning to have under our agencies an organization based on the pattern of the Narcotics Control Bureau, (proposal for this is under formulation), for an effective information system. This will be a nodal agency which will have representatives from all law enforcement agencies like the C.B.I., Central Police Force, Border Security Force, representatives from the judiciary, the Central Excise Department, NGOs and the National Commission for Women. This body will research, analyse, disseminate information and plan immediate steps for total eradication of trafficking of humans. With this kind of agency we hope to cut across barriers and impediments of protocol and bureaucracy which have slowed down all past measures to stamp out the malaise of child prostitution.

Thinking together we can move forward. Ideas don't need any legs to stride, but, they need institutions to translate all the promises to real life. Likewise, cooperation must emerge. We must all cooperate to free women and children from the deplorable human violations.

I know the path is not at all smooth. I know there is no easy way to solutions. There is no magic wand which can be twirled to remove this blot. I know, too, that no matter how many conferences we have, how many laws we make, the truth is that we cannot wipe off the tears from the face of every girl who has been hurt, abused and traumatized. There are no choices. A bold beginning has to be made. We are far from achieving our goals, but as long as we keep the struggle alive, we can continue to give hope to our children, and vindicate all those who perished as victims.

Let all our voices resound as we commit to restore to the children their dignity, their humanity, their childhood and their bright future.

WOMEN IN PROSTITUTION—HUMAN RIGHTS PERSPECTIVE

Modus Operandi: Forceful Compliance

A highly distressing feature which is a disgrace to any civilized society is the prevalence of crime and violence against women. It manifests itself in many forms such as kidnapping and abduction, molestation, rape, stripping, eve teasing, dowry harassment and death, domestic violence and so on. But forcing women into prostitution is one of the most heinous forms of violence against them which combines in it crimes in a series ranging from seduction, kidnapping, abduction, rape, battering, confinement and compulsion to sell their bodies. All along the line, the women's human rights are trampled with impunity and they are finally reduced from human persons to commodities for sale. Once they are pushed into this trade, their dehumanization is complete and they are compelled to live a life of indignity and brothel bondage. They are in most cases victims, but are unfortunately treated as criminals both by the society and the authority while the offenders involved at various stages of the process of inducting them into this trade manage to go scot-free.

There are brutal ways and subtle ways of forcing girls and women into prostitution. In the brutal method, especially after being lured or kidnapped, they are subjected to intimidation, force, beating, starving, raping or gang raping with the ultimate aim of compelling them into sex work. Those who are bold enough to resist and refuse to submit are either done away with or led to commit suicide. Could one think of a greater human rights violation depriving the human beings of their liberty by such brutal methods? The subtle methods are devices of socio-religious sanctions in the from of Devadasis, Basavis etc. Their entry into the flesh trade is made possible without having to resort to methods of violence and torture, but, ultimately, they are equally deprived of their human rights.

The commonest and most numerical form of prostitution is brothel prostitution followed by the Devadasis/Basavi systems. The two together comprise a vast majority of those in the flesh trade and deserve attention in that order. There are many other forms in which prostitution is practised such as dancing and singing girls, massage parlours, cabarets, clubs, hotels, guest houses, etc. There is also highway prostitution, pavement prostitution, in railway areas and so on. Besides, in certain micro communities in a number of States, prostitution has become a family tradition. Here, the birth of a girl is celebrated since she is a future money spinner for the family.

At times, an argument is put forward that everybody has a right to earn in one's own way and so also the prostitutes. But this theory needs to be rejected with the contempt it deserves for the very obvious reason that an overwhelming majority of girls and women have not joined this trade by their free will, but have been pushed into it by force or through the devices of socio-religious sanctions. It has also been said that it is primarily poverty that drives them into this profession. However, that is also not very true because it is not poverty *per se*, but the exploitation of that poverty by anti-social elements that drives the innocents into this vice. Some people are in favour of granting licence to prostitutes. But this will amount to accepting prostitution as a profession and permitting commercial exploitation of sex.

Prevention, rescue and rehabilitation required

Obviously, therefore, this field of sexual exploitation requires concerted efforts at prevention, and rescue and rehabilitation. There are, without doubt, serious hurdles in the way. Crimes on sexual exploitation are the most under-reported crimes in India. This field is also perhaps the least researched and meagre information and data are available on it. Those daring to take initiative for rescue or even to try access to sex workers for research are exposed to the danger of being assaulted or even killed at the hands of sex-mafia. Besides, there exists little public conscience to combat the vice. The sex workers themselves are afraid that their rescue will not lead to their acceptance by their families or the society. Hence the task is not easy.

The Government have improved upon their past efforts by amending the Immoral Traffic Suppression Act in many ways and renaming the Act as Immoral Traffic Prevention Act. The police can arrest traffickers and customers, rescue girls in prostitution and admit them in protective homes, arrest women in prostitution and send them to lock-up, rescue children of prostitutes and send them to juvenile homes, close the brothels and do many other things. But the amended legislation has not made any significant difference either in preventing the crime or in rescuing and rehabilitating the victims. The police has failed to crack the sex mafia, working both at the inter-state and international levels. In fact, many brothels flourish with the connivance of the police force. The purpose for which protective homes were meant has been defeated because of very deplorable conditions prevailing there. Some of them are even reported to be indulging in sex-trafficking of those rescued.

Social welfare

There are not many voluntary initiatives to be found in this area as in some other areas of social welfare because of the nature of obstacles involved. Their efforts are mostly confined to arranging for education of prostitutes' children, running creches, arranging or supporting marriages for the rescued, creating awareness about AIDS, stimulating awareness through seminars, conferences, media, etc.

As things stand today, major initiatives must lie with the Government machinery. Much more work has to be done by the social organizations also, but for that they should be enabled by the Government through their association and involvement with Government efforts at various levels.

It has been strongly felt in some quarters that the law on prevention of immoral traffic should be restructured and made innovative so that the enforcing agency—the police—and the dispensing agency—the judiciary—do not cling to the letter of the law, but consult the provisions in the interests of the victim. The intention should be made amply clear in the statement of objects and reasons or by way of introducing a preamble to the Act. The Act should also define in detail how the "Protective Homes" and the "Corrective Institutions" would be run with regard to boarding and lodging, education, medical treatment, counselling, freedom to go out and a strong habilitative component. There should be strict monitoring of these homes with the involvement of women's organizations. The suggestion that voluntary agencies be given the powers of search, seizure, investigation, etc., should be seriously considered. As Justice P. N. Bhagwati once suggested, just as there are special training courses for IAS, IFS and other All India or State Services, so should there be for those who are entering the judiciary. Judiciary does require sensitization to acquire a positive attitude towards women. We have had a taste of an insensitive judicial pronouncement recently in the well-known case of Bhanwari Devi of Jaipur who was subjected to gang rape for opposing child marriage; the judgement has let off the culprits.

An important aspect requiring attention is that a substantial proportion of sex workers suffer from related diseases. These diseases generally go untreated and many of the suffering women are left to die unattended. Lately, AIDS is becoming a menace requiring urgent attention. One of the suggestions made for countering the sexually transmitted diseases is that free condoms should be distributed to the sex workers and they should be persuaded to prevail upon their customers to use them.

According to a UN report, India tops in child prostitution in the world with about half a million of child prostitutes in the flesh trade. A more disturbing feature is that their proportion is reported to be increasing.

A good number of prostitutes in the cities of India are from Nepal as they fetch high rates. How menacing the problem can become for the society is exemplified by the fact that in a number of villages in the Himalayan foothills of Nepal, there are no young girls and women, all having being sold off or lured for sex trade in India.

The NGO role

The NGOs face many limitations in expanding their activities in this field. Yet, there are ways of exerting pressure more effectively. They can jointly put relentless pressure on the Government for an effective statutory package. Recently, a team from PRAYAS (a research project of Tata Institute of Social Sciences) followed up a case of some Himachal Pradesh girls escaping from Bombay brothel and reaching their homes. The efforts of the team resulted in the formation of core group consisting of members of the Social Welfare Board, high police officers and bureaucrats and social activists—who are all cooperating to ensure that the Himachal girls are not lured away into prostitution and those rescued are suitably rehabilitated. NGOs can study the case and make a joint effort to set up such core groups in their own States. Himachal Pradesh has also taken another step which NGOs may pressure their States to follow. When a girl or a woman is forced against her will to indulge in sex, it amounts to repeated rape. Hence, H.P. Government has decided to apply the IPC section on rape in combination with the provision of the Immoral Traffic Prevention Act. Government can also be pressurized that the trial of the rescued girls or women should be held in-camera because they get panicky at the sight of brothel owner and his goons in the court and are unable to give independent evidence. The NGOs can identify vulnerable groups in their own states and take measures to prevent them from being seduced away. They can also agitate for providing these women with ration cards and voting rights. Indian Penal Code has a section prohibiting sale of minor girls. There is no reason why women should not be covered under this section. NGOs may make this demand from the Government.

Joint Women's Programme has been active in this field for the last about 15 years. They have done commendable job both in the area of research as well as field work in various parts of the country and have several publications to their credit on this subject. I do admit that prostitution is a sensitive area and access to a person concerned is both difficult and risky and it has therefore become an area in which voluntary initiatives have per force been limited.

AIDS AWARENESS—NEED OF THE HOUR

As Chairperson of the National Commission for Women, I was delighted to receive Shyamala Natarajan's letter informing me about the Regional Meeting which the South India AIDS Action Programme has organized, having as its theme "women in Prostitution". Reading Shyamala's letter I could not help being impressed with the organizational work that has gone into designing and collecting data for this Regional Meeting; and, at the same time, have a feeling that good results could be expected from this very carefully planned, organizational effort.

Preparatory research

At the outset, I must compliment South India AIDS Action Programme on two specific points. Firstly, their idea of sending out a detailed structured questionnaire prior to this Regional Meeting—to no less than 60 NGOs located all over the country to collect data that could give valuable inputs for the Regional Meeting. And, secondly, their getting all those who have come for this meeting to spend one full day before the formal meeting, so as to clarify ideas for discussion.

This brings out the extent of professionalism that has gone into the organizers' pre-meeting work : surely these efforts must have a positive influence on you deliberations during this Regional Meeting.

Research findings

Apart from my heading the NCW, I have a long-standing interest and commitment to issues relating to welfare of women. Consequently, I would be most interested to learn about the pre-meeting research carried out by Shyamala Natarajan and her team. And, I might add, the NCW will certainly give very serious consideration to views and recommendations that may arise out of this Regional Meeting.

AIDS and women in prostitution

The objectives of this Regional Meeting cover a wide field. At this stage, however, I would like to spend some time on two of your objectives, viz. (1) Increasing motivation and ability of women to protect themselves against STDs/HIV/AIDS and (2) Increase understanding of child support issues and needs with women in prostitution.

These two objectives clearly bring out your concern about health of women, children and women in prostitution.

As I see it, the problems faced by women in prostitution really centre around a seemingly unbreakable vicious circle, with health and poverty as its two focal points. Let me try and bring a sort of perspective into these two focal points by giving you some facts and figures from a recent report published by the World Health Organization.

WHO facts and figures

This recently published WHO report brought out alarming and startling facts which could have a bearing on the deliberations of this Regional Meeting. This WHO report, among other things, stated that :

* the rate at which Indians are being affected by HIV virus (which causes AIDS) has trebled since 1992;
* in 1994, around the world, prevalence of adult HIV cases was over 13 million while no less that 6000 people were getting affected daily;
* street children who are at a "high risk" of malnutrition; TB, STDs, parasite and worm infections along with skin diseases form 100 million of the world's population;
* despite a massive Malaria eradication campaign by the Government of India, the number of cases of malaria in 1992 was in the region of 2 lakhs;
* outside Africa, death due to cholera takes place only in 6 countries, one of which is India;
* poverty alone is a major source of all diseases in the world;

* poverty again, is the main reason why babies are not properly vaccinated, clean water and sanitation are not provided, and curative and other treatment are unavailable.

These facts and figures certainly bring out the magnitude of the challenges we face when we try and do something about women in prostitution : they are depressing facts—but facts, nevertheless!

Tradition-bound barriers

Another area where work on women in prostitution is on a bumpy road is linked with tradition. I'm sure you have heard of too often-used phrases like : "Human nature being what it is" and "Prostitution is the world's oldest profession". If one links these two sayings—past centuries of age-old traditions, superstition, and taboos we find they are deeply ingrained in man's thought process : as we approach the 21st century, it is a discouraging thought that superstition and taboos compel man to avoid doing what, rationally, they would do, as preventive. An example would perhaps explain what I am trying to highlight : it is more than well known-especially through various campaigns and efforts by the Government, NGOs and social activists—that the only known prevention against AIDS is the use of condoms. But, despite these campaigns on "Safe Sex" and "Use of Condom", a vast number of mobile persons—such as truck drivers - are reluctant to use condoms citing a host of peculiar reasons. (I don't need to go into all that... you must have heard about them!)

And so, in addition to the depressing facts given by the World Health Organization, social workers—especially women in prostitution come up against these tradition-bound, mental barriers. One can't help saying that it's a tough task but seeing so many of you here today, suggests an encouraging and positive attitude—something which is worthy of emulation by others.

War against AIDS and prostitution

We all know that prostitution has existed throughout the ages. And only in the latter half of the 20th century, has the HIV virus been identified as the main cause of AIDS. The war against AIDS and prostitution is not one which can be fought through one campaign nor won through winning a battle. Many campaigns and fronts need to be opened, using medical, economic and social "weapons" : and this regrettably, will not be a short-lived affair.

Medical science, through research workers, doctors and the scientific community worldwide, is, perhaps, doing its best to fight HIV virus through a sustained campaign involving medical research and experimentation. Unfortunately, no real breakthrough seems to be in sight, so far. But, once in a while, one comes across a stray report that this research effort is slowly unchaining towards that much-wanted breakthrough. Social workers like us can only hope that our friends in the medical and scientific community will soon locate that elusive remedy to this terrible disease. For the moment, then, let's wish them good luck and see what we, as social workers can do on the economic and social fronts of this seemingly never-ending war. Apart from the WHO report to which I had referred a little while ago, it is common knowledge that poverty and the need to earn enough to feed hungry mouths, often leads women especially from the weaker sections of society, to enter prostitution.

Since there is a direct link between poverty and women entering prostitution, I am sure your regional meeting will give some thought to this "link" and consider ways and means as to how all of us—social workers and social scientists—can help in devising methods to overcome the main cause of women entering prostitution, viz. poverty. Here again, philanthropic donations, charities and "poverty doles" are no answers to this problem : we'd only be creating another problem a refined form of another social evil that is begging. We do need to do something which would add to our social problems. But, in our deliberations, I hope you would consider what types of schemes could be evolved so as to wean women away from prostitution by leading economically visible lives.

On the "social front", perhaps this is where NGOs and social activists need to put their heads together. Our goals in this social front are not only clear but linked with action on the "economic front" : the main goal is in the direction of weaning away women from working in or as prostitutes. There are encouraging signs in the existence of a vast number of NGOs and social activists voluntarily working in this field. No doubt, this regional meeting will help you exchange ideas and experiences along with inputs from Shyamala Natarajan's Preparatory Research studies. I would, however, like to leave one thought with you : I hope you will consider how all of you could build on your successes and devise systems and mechanisms of networking so as to reach our common goal of winning this war against AIDS and prostitution.

"Actionable Action Plans"

Since this regional meeting has a very busy work schedule, I don't want to take much time and come in the way of your deliberations. However, in conclusion, I would like to refer to two of your objectives where mention has been made about the National Commission for Women:

1. Increasing direct representation and depositions of women in sex work to the National Commission for Women; and
2. Increase in representation of views of women in sex work in National Commission documentation on prostitution.

Right now, I prefer not to react to these objectives; it'll be like putting the cart before the horse! However, please rest assured that we, at the NCW, are everyready to listen to views and suggestions coming from meetings such as this—but what would be infinitely more meaningful are ideas and proposals letting us know what results are expected if action is initiated on your proposals.

And finally, as we are much too aware, nowadays, there seems to be too much talk and comparatively little action leading to results, and an absence of cost-benefit analyses bringing out hidden and direct costs indicating anticipated benefits of schemes and proposals. I hope your proposals to the NCW will have these cost-benefit analyses.

With these thoughts, may I suggest that when you come to your last session of this regional meeting, you should produce, what I'd like to call, "Actionable Action Plans" : the key word being 'Action'.

THE GIRL CHILD

India with 28,000 kms of spanning dimension and a rich tradition of civilisation, inhabited by diverse people of diverse economic levels and cultural attainments, speaking a variety of languages, is a country which presents a distinct flavour high and low, ugly and beautiful. These contradictions are nowhere more manifest as in the case of prostitution and child prostitution with steady increase in the levels of income, different levels of affluence as a result of international trade, economic liberalization and green and white revolutions. The scene is indeed pathetic when we discuss child prostitution.

We find ourselves today at a particular historical juncture, where progress and development in human society has created two contradictions. On one hand, there is modernity with improved quality of life; while on the other, the same change threatens many aspects of community life, such as the loss of ethics and moral values to the corrupting influence of modernity itself.

In India, despite emphasis and solemn resolves for the safeguard of a child from all sorts of abuse under the Constitution and despite the fact that India is a signatory to the UN Convention which guarantees, rights of a child, the phenomenon of child-prostitution does exist in the country. This has started assuming monstrous proportions as is sometimes depicted in some of the press reports—by foreign media in particular. Empirical studies conducted by us indicate that besides economic factor (poverty being the main motivation) and lack of awareness, two other factors responsible which are: a) growth of international tourism, and b) consumerism.

India has also adopted Universal Declaration of Human Rights which *inter alia* provides that no one shall be held in slavery or servitude; slavery and the slave trade shall be prohibited in all their forms. The victim in the flesh trade is no less than a slave. Article 5 of the UDHR provides that no one shall be subjected to torture, or to cruel, inhuman or degrading treatment or punishment. The trapped victims of flesh trade are subjected to cruel, inhuman and degrading treatment which are obnoxious, abominable and an affront to Article 5 of the Universal Declaration and Article 21 of the Indian Constitution.

The problem, however, does exist. Let us first analyse the situation and circumstances why a girl-child enters the profession. To my mind, it appears, that there are four distinct ways—at times, some of these converge and overlap:

1) Girls are kidnapped, induced, allured and sold (in many cases by parents themselves). Nearly 80-85 per cent of victims come into prostitution through this pathway.

2) About 10 per cent are off-springs of the prostitutes—

unwed or wedded. In such cases even though the mothers do not like their daughters to follow them in their profession, the powerful nexus of *Gharwalis* (brothel keepers), pimps and *pahalwans* (musclemen) decide otherwise.

3) Then there is caste/community specific and area-specific prostitution. Going from generation to generation, this is the type of child-prostitution which is practised in specific areas by some communities under the gaze of the family itself. Some of the known localities of operations are Mandsaur, Guna, Raisen, Bhind, Morena, Shivpuri, Gwalior in Madhya Pradesh, region around Chakrata in Uttar Pradesh, amongst Nats and Sansis of Central India, some tribes in north-eastern states and some of the nomadic tribes following Venkatasani cult in Telangana region of Andhra Pradesh.

4) And finally we have special types—the profession with links in some of the religious customs. Instances are of the Devdasis in Karnataka, Andhra Pradesh, Orissa and Maharashtra, Bhavanis in Goa, Kudikars on West Coast, Jogins in Andhra Pradesh, Thevardiyar in Tamil Nadu, Basavis in Karnataka and Muralis, Jogateens and Aradhinis in Maharashtra.

Why is there an increase in the number of child-prostitutes? (Almost everywhere, in India and elsewhere—in every part of the globe wherever there are human settlements and a semblance of civilization, sex with a child is rape—an offence.) Even though being a blot on the face of humanity, it does persist. The possible factors, which I have analysed are:

a) General degeneration in human values leading to moral degrading; here it is important to point out that brothels are no longer run by pimps only. The operators now could also be a serving police officer, politician or a businessman.

b) Role of media—specially the electronic media leading to indecent exposure of girl's anatomy.

c) Perversion.

d) Increased use of alcohol and other intoxicants.

e) The false belief that sex with young girls may add years to one's lifespan—such beliefs being more predominant in people living in feudalistic environs and moffusil areas.

f) The superstition that sex with a young girl may cure sexually transmitted diseases.

g) The belief that in having sex with young girls there is little danger of HIV infections.

h) The ease with which a young girl can be trapped and initiated into the vice with little fear of her complaining against her tormenters because of elements of fear and social stigma attached.

As I feel, the last factor is the motivator in most of the cases along with the general degeneration in consciousness leading to low morals.

There is, therefore, a growing movement towards a global solution to problems caused by development itself. After all, it does not exist in isolation but in the interdependence of the nation-state system. We have had several regional, state and district consultations to resolve a national dilemma; how to stop the commercial sexual exploitation of children in different forms : prostitution, pornography and sexual trafficking.

We have a growing population of children and young people exposed not only to the seduction of capitalism, but to the economic pressures for survival. The social conditions, emerging out of this phenomenon become fertile ground for the easy recruitment of innocent victims into the vicious market of human flesh.

Every single day, without fail, newspapers carry reports about a child being raped by a neighbour, daughter sexually molested by father, children working as "guest relations officers", a euphemism for sex entertainers in disco houses and beer joints, children servicing the pleasure of the men in ships that dock in our ports, street children who are often at risk and vulnerable to prostitution and pedophilia.

We are also speaking about a flourishing industry operating worldwide that capitalizes on the sale and trafficking of children through internet and other means.

Although admitting that economic poverty breeds exploitation, one cannot assume that in more successful economies, children are safer. They are equally exposed to dangers of commercial sexual exploitation.

The statutory provisions for children particularly girls

Article 19(1) of the Constitution of India provides that the state shall take measures to protect the child from all forms of physical or mental violence, injury or abuse, neglect or negligent treatment, maltreatment or exploitation including sexual abuse while in the care of parents, legal guardians or any other person who has the care of the child.

Human rights for women, which include rights of girl child, are inalienable, integral and indivisible part of Universal Declaration of Human Rights. All forms of discrimination on grounds of gender is violative of fundamental freedoms of human rights. It is, therefore, imperativ- to take all steps to prohibit prostitution. Eradication, of prostitution in all forms, is integral to social weal and glory of womenhood. Development of right of the child hinges upon elimination of prostitution, success lies upon effective measures to eradicate root and branch of prostitution.

One of the principles of the United Nation's "Declaration on the Rights of the Child" was that the child shall be protected against all forms of neglect, cruelty and exploitation. The child shall not be the subject of traffic in any form. The National Policy for Children adopted by government of India contains all elements of the Declaration. Successful implementation is the need of the hour which is unfortunately lacking.

Prostitution in society has not been an unknown phenomenon, it is of ancient origin and has its manifestations in various forms with varied degrees of so-called social sanctions, etc. The victims of the trap are the poor, illiterate and ignorant sections of the society and are the target group in the flesh trade; rich communities exploit them and harvest their interests at their misery and ignominy in an organized gangsterism particularly with police nexus. It is of grave social concern, increasingly realized by enlightened public spirited sections of the society to prevent gender exploitation of girl children.

The prostitute has always been an object and was never seen as complete human being with dignity of person. Their problems are compounded by coercion laid around them and tortuous treatment by managers of brothels and are subjected to discrimination, social isolation and deprived to live normal life for no fault of their own. They should no longer be treated as criminals or as an object of shocking sexual abuse. They are victims of circumstances and hence should be treated as human beings like others so as to bring them into the mainstream of the social order without any attached stigma. In no circumstances, they should continue to be in the trap of flesh trade for commercial exploitation. They need to be treated with humanity and compassion so as to integrate them into the social mainstream.

Statistics on prostitution

86 per cent of the sex workers hail from Karnataka, Tamil Nadu, West Bengal, Bihar, Maharashtra, Uttar Pradesh, Assam, Gujarat, Goa, Madhya Pradesh, Kerala, Meghalaya, Orissa, Punjab, Rajasthan and Delhi. Delhi receives prostitutes from about 70 districts, Bangalore from 70 districts in the country; Mumbai from 40 districts, Calcutta from 11 districts; Hyderabad from 3 districts, etc. There is growing evidence that prostitutes get into flesh trade either voluntarily or by organized gangsters who force women and girls by offering them a rosy picture of the future and trap them often with the connivance of the police.

Several types of prostitutes have been identified, viz street walkers, religious prostitutes, prostitutes in brothel, singing and dancing girls, nude bar massage parlour girls and call girls. So far as age group of the prostitutes is concerned, at the time of entry, 45 per cent of the girls are in the category of neglected juveniles, about 25 per cent are minors between 16 to 18 years. 94.6 per cent prostitutes are Indian while 2.6 per cent are Nepalese and 2.7 per cent are Bangladeshis. 84.36 per cent are Hindus; 18 per cent are Muslims and 3.5 per cent are Christians. In terms of caste classification, Dalits and other tribes constitute 36 per cent, other Backward Classes 24 per cent and others 40 per cent. In terms of marital status, only 10.6 per cent of the prostitutes are married, 34.4 per cent are unmarried and 54.2 per cent are divorcees or widows.

In terms of education level, 70 per cent of them are illiterate, 30 per cent literate, 24 per cent educated up to primary and 1.4 per cent have higher qualifications. Therefore prostitution is primarily, due to ignorance, illiteracy, coercive trapping and fear of social stigma.

In India, the prostitutes lose market by the time they reach 35 years of age. Thereafter such persons either manage brothels or develop contact with high leads. Recent trend is that ladies from higher levels of income are initiated into prostitution to sustain sufficient day-to-day luxurious style of life and to ensure continuous economic support for their well-being.

Indian laws have proved themselves too inadequate to meet the challenges. Sensitization at all levels is needed. The police, the lawyers and even the judiciary needs to be sensitized to the cause of the victims. The girl who has landed in the dungeon after great trauma finds herself incapable of standing lengthy cross-examinations. The Immoral Traffic (Protection) Act requires substantial amendments. We should have a separate Act exclusively for children in prostitution with stringent measures against the clients, brothel keepers and the pimps. The provisions of the Act should not take the victim as an offender. The Indian Penal Code also needs to be suitably amended. All cases of child prostitution should be treated under "Rape Juvenile Justice Act". Indian Evidence Act and Criminal Procedure Code—all require thorough change and amendments with provision for compensation to the victim by the accused just a few months after the institution of the cases. This will prove to be a deterrent and help the victim in rehabilitation.

Nepal appears to be the most significant, identifiable source of child prostitutes for Indian brothels. Thousand of Nepalese females under the age of 20 have been identified in India by various studies. The average age of Nepalese girl entering in Indian brothels is said to be 10-14 years, some 5000 - 7000 of them being trafficked between Nepal and India annually.

There is also the trafficking of children to the Middle East and some South Asian countries through widely publicized advertisements and agents who lure guardians with the promise of big money. The advertisements are usually for domestic help.

It is known that traffickers keep themselves informed about vulnerable communities and areas of the region which are severely impoverished or have suffered from climatic disaster or political upheaval. They may then canvas these regions as sources of children for sale. Calcutta offers a striking example of this phenomenon. Five regions surrounding the city that have locations of depressed silk industry supply almost 60 per cent of the city's prostitutes. Traffickers flooded the area following the downfall of this industry, promising desperate girls and their families employment in the city and paying them a much needed lumpsum in advance.

At the other end of the chain, madams and brothel owners exploit the girl's immaturity by fabricating expenses and presenting "debts" which they may settle through their work. This, of course, translates into perpetual prostitution for the girls since most of their income is taken by their madams as so called "rent". Moreover, because of the added attraction of young girls, especially when they are presented to clients as virgins, fees and profits to purveyors of prostitutes, is on the rise in the cities because of the fear of HIV / AIDS and the prevailing myth that sex with virgins will cure sexually transmitted diseases. In such cases, the cost of having sex with a child prostitute on the first night may range between Rs. 6000 to Rs. 25000 in the higher class establishment. Even the regular charge for young girls appears to be ten times that for an adult prostitute.

The Government of India as also most of the State Governments, are aware of the enormity of the problem of child prostitution. Under orders of the apex court of the country a Central Committee under Department of Women and Child Development has been formed which is looking into different aspects of the problem.

The committee is to submit its report within three months. The committee in its first meeting felt the need for imparting education to students, providing more facilities to migrant labourers, extension of welfare schemes already in operation, to cover child prostitutes and children of sex workers, vocational education to children of prostitutes besides enrolling some of these children in regular schools.

The State and Union Territory Governments have identified the problem as key area of concern. To be assured that we are on right alley, we have formed an "Expert Committee" with eminent and knowledgeable people to give us advice and suggestions. At several places all over the country seminars cum workshops have been organized and at most places prostitutes have interfaced with a large number of prostitutes. In Delhi on July 24, 1996 we organized a seminar on the subject which was attended by good number of prostitutes from every corner of the country.

We have travelled thus far. The responses we got have been very encouraging. We have created awareness. We have earned for ourselves confidence amongst the victims. But the journey is arduous and the goal, if not distant, is definitely difficult.

Positive methods involve rescue operations and rehabilitation measures for victims already in the profession. Negative measures aim at negating entry to new entrants to the profession. For this, we intend to have access to fully developed intelligence network.

Thinking together can move minds and civilization. Ideas don't need any legs to stride but they need institutions to translate all the promises to real life. Likewise, cooperation emerged as an idea.The National Commission for Women held a conference where 50 women working as prostitutes gathered at Delhi and came up with the idea of cooperation. The institutional form of cooperation is cooperative. In a cooperative, each women would have equal share regardless of the value of the share she had, the idea being founded on equality among persons minimizing conflicts and power struggle. Women are known to resist conflict, competition and clash. They are inclined towards harmony and mutual cooperation and have little interests in gaining power by overpowering others. This enables them to form good cooperatives and also confirms equality among persons working. It is thus an appropriate tool for women. The idea that women need to be empowered is true, however, women also have to be empowered from within, although schemes are showered on women mostly from outside which is really weak. The women themselves have power and this power can surface, assert and sustain itself, if women themselves have access and control in matters of decision-making and implementation. The geographical location where such an institution is working should have close, effective participation of women in the day-to-day life. Hence, the cooperative system which was found to be a remarkably flexible system, became the institutional choice to women in prostitution. This emerged as the most eligible way of controlling child prostitution in India. Groups of women were formed to safeguard the interests of little children who would be kidnapped, sold and brought to the brothels and these women family the cooperative would act as rescuers to these children and prevent their entry at the early stage. One of the methods of preventing children from entering prostitution was thus discovered during the day-long meeting of women in prostitution.

Legalisation of prostitution

A section of society is in favour of granting legal status to sex workers. This was echoed at the national convention of sex workers organized by Durbar Mahila Samanwaya Committee at Salt Lake stadium, Calcutta on 14-16 November 1997. Eminent persons like Home Minister Indrajit Gupta, Health Minister Renuka Choudhary have extended their support to the sex workers to form a trade union. The demand has been made on the ground that prostitution is a service industry and the sex workers earn their bread from physical labour and therefore they should be recognized as industrial labourers/workers.

The sex workers are confident that a trade union will enable them to clinch their rights as workers, help them achieve some social acceptability and protect them from regular harassment by police and other forces. Prominent trade unions like AITUC, CITU, BMS, Government Employees Unions and women's groups have promised to extend help to them.

Dr. S. Jana, who has played an important role in conducting AIDS awareness campaigns in the city brothels is in all sympathy with the demand. According to her, such a move would go a long way to usher in the much needed improvements in the red light districts. In countries like New Zealand, Netherlands, Australia and Bangladesh, prostitution has already been recognized, she says.

According to the protagonists of the proposal, such a step will pave the way for sex workers to form societies, improve their economic status and working conditions, prevent entry of minor girls in the profession and a check on girls being sold off as there will be a board run by sex workers themselves to regulate the trade. It will also save women from AIDS and other veneral diseases because the they will be in a position to insist on safe sex. Legislation will also save women from exploitative landlords and other exploiters.

The matter is placed before the committee for its expert opinion and valuable suggestions.

There have been significant advances in meeting the problem head-on over the past three years. Awareness raising and public information campaign on children's issues have been pursued with vigour.

We are lucky to have a strong NGO movement in India. They are in the forefront of the crusade against child abuse and commercial sexual exploitation. We in the National Commission for Women recognize their contribution in resounding the needs of the local children as well as their advocacy efforts both at the local and international fronts.

Thus, it is imperative that all stakeholders—government, NGOs, the media and the communities pay more attention to strengthen response mechanisms; to re-orient cultural attitudes and social values to be more sensitive to the child; to increase advocacy for children's right; and to work towards a more active participation of children in all matters affecting their lives.

I know the path is not at all smooth. I know there is no easy way to solutions, there is no magic wand which can be twirled to remove this blot. I know, too, that no matter how many conferences we have, how many laws we make, the truth is that we cannot wipe off the tears from the face of every girl who has been hurt, abused and traumatized. There are no choices. A bold beginning has to be made. We are far from achieving our goals, but as long as we keep the struggle alive, we can continue to give hope to our children, and vindicate all those who perished as victims.

Dedicated researchers, despite the occupational hazards, have, over the last eight months, collected first hand information on the malaise of child prostitution.

Ten studies, were commissioned by the NCW, and they have candidly brought out the insidious ways in which children are lured, kidnapped and sold to brothels. The enormous network of traffickers is spread far and wide. They are the invisible operators and perpetrators of child prostitution. Through empirical surveys, these studies have uncovered the inter-city and inter-country operations by kingpins of the flesh trade—a practice which has assumed criminal proportions.

Let all our voices resound as we commit to restore to the children their dignity, their humanity, their childhood and their secured and bright future.

THE CHILD AS TARGET

"That children are given opportunities and facilities to develop in a healthy manner and in conditions of freedom and dignity and that childhood and youth are protected against exploitation and against moral and material abandonment"

—Art. 39 (f), Constitution of India

Commercial Sexual Exploitation of Children (CSEC) is a global problem of pernicious nature. In the present contextual framework of the materialistic, multi-ethnic and divisive society, this form of violence on children is flourishing like a major industry/business controlled by well organized international Crime Syndicates. Since it is lucrative, innumerable strong criminal network are very actively involved in the trafficking of children from one state to the other and from one country to another contributing to the rapid growth of this form of violence on both girl/male children/adolescents from a very tender age.

Child sexual exploitation is an abhorrent and intolerable crime that strikes at the heart of humanity. Children inherit the past and they themselves are the future. They own the right to live and grow as children. They must not be treated as sexual playthings, thrown-away entertainment, mere commodities for buying, selling and reselling. Those who investigate the working of this industry are shocked by the volume, spread and nature of the activity. It is an organized crime utilizing the children for profitable business. Tourism has further aggravated the gravity of the situation globally. Asia has been targetted as key destination, sex 'haven' for business and vacation travellers.

We find ourselves today at a historical juncture, where progress and development in human society has created two contradictions. On the one hand, there is modernity with improved quality of life; while on the other, the same change threatens many aspects of community life, such as the loss of ethics and moral values to the corrupting influence of modernity itself.

There is, therefore, a growing movement towards the globalization in the solution of problems caused by development itself.

There is, therefore, a growing movement towards the globalization in the solution of problems caused by development itself. After all, it does not exist in isolation but in the inter-dependence of the nation-state system. Today's consultation is to resolve a national dilemma : how to stop the commercial sexual exploitation of children in different forms : prostitution, pornography and sexual trafficking.

We have a growing population of children and young people exposed not only to the seduction of capitalism, but to the economic pressures of survival. The social condition emerging out of this phenomenon has become a fertile ground for the easy recruitment of innocent victims into the vicious market of human flesh.

Every single day without fail, newspapers carry reports about a child being raped by a neighbour, a daughter or the daughters sexually molested by the father; children working as "guest relations officers", a euphemism for sex entertainers in disco houses and beer joints, children servicing the pleasure of the men in ships that dock in our ports, street children who are often a risk and vulnerable to prostitution and pedophilia.

We are faced with the evil effects of a flourishing industry operating worldwide that capitalizes on the sale and trafficking of children through Internet and other means. It is an industry that can even buy political power.

Although admitting that economic poverty breeds exploitatioin, one cannot assume that in more successful economies, children are safer. They are equally exposed to dangers of commercial sexual exploitation.

Steps for curtailment

There have been significant advances in meeting the problem head-on over the past three years. Awareness-raising and public information campaign on children's issues have been pursued with vigour.

We are lucky to have a strong NGO movement in India. They are in the forefront of the crusade against child abuse and commercial sexual exploitation. We, in the National Commission for Women recognize their contribution in responding to the needs of the children as well as their advocacy efforts both at the local and international fronts.

Thus, it is imperative that all stakeholders—government, NGOs, the media and the communities pay more attention to strengthen response mechanisms; to re-orient cultural attitudes and social values to be more sensitive to the child; to increase advocacy for children's rights; and to work towards a more active participation of children in all matters affecting their lives.

I know that the path is not at all smooth. I also know that there is no easy way to solutions; there is no magic wand which can be twirled to remove this blot. I know, too, that no matter how many conferences we have, how many laws we make, the truth is that we cannot wipe off the tears from the face of every girl who has been hurt, abused and traumatized. There are no choices. A bold beginning has to be made. We are far from achieving our goals, but for as long as we keep the struggle alive, we can continue to give hope to our children, and vindicate all those who perished as victims.

The issues emerging before us are :

1. Can we work out a child-centric and child-friendly judicial system to eliminate CSE and uphold their several rights to which we are committed?
2. Can we sensitize the media to be child friendly and work for the elimination of CSE than promotion?
3. Can we make a realistic implementable plan of action to sensitize the several target groups who are insensitive to the children?
4. Can we have an inbuilt monitoring system to this process of sensitization?

Some of the recommendations that have emerged from our various consultations are as follows :

1. To adopt an appropriate definition of trafficking that will take in all the current trends for use in legislation like trafficking for the purpose of cheap wage labour, organ trading, marriage apart from trafficking for prostitution and sex work.
2. To put the issue of trafficking in women and children in the agenda for discussion at SAARC.
3. Effective measures include on the part of the respective governments and diplomatic missions to give overall support to the victims in terms of voluntary repatriation. Those who do not want to return should be given asylum. And the traffickers should be made to pay compensation to the victims and the legal guardian appointed by judiciary.
4. Sensitization of the law enforcement agencies and the

judiciary to the laws at the national and international levels.

5. Set up a regional mechanism where affected persons can seek unconditional and nondiscriminatory justice like a regional level court for the violence of trafficking.

Dedicated researchers despite the occupational hazards over the last eight months, collected first hand information on the malaise of child prostitution. Ten studies, commissioned by NCW, have candidly revealed the insidious ways in which children are lured, kidnapped, and sold to brothels. They have exposed enormous network of traffickers which is spread far and wide. They are the invisible operators and perpetrators of child prostitution. Through empirical surveys, these studies have uncovered the inter-city and inter-country operations by kingpins of the flesh trade—a practice which has assumed criminal proportions.

It is my fervent hope that deliberations will help those who are committed to working out a pragmatic action plan and developing strategies to combat this evil. These children are being deprived of their childhood. They crave our immediate attention.

NCW in Forefront of Women's Struggle

A very good morning to all of you and greetings to you from the National Commission for Women of India. The National Commission is busy all the time because of men ! Is it not ironical for the National Commission for Women to be busy with men? It is the men who keep us busy with various atrocities committed on women, it is the men who keeps us busy by not changing their attitudes ! It is the men who keeps us busy with formulating the laws adverse to women because they are the decision makers. Today we want to change that. Let us become busy with women and women's issues and together collectively work with women and men. Today shall I address you all as my daughters? Because I really take a sigh of relief to see that this generation has taken a lot of burden that we have been carrying since the last 30 years in our work. It was 30 years ago that I met a group of young women, say 20 or 30 from an institution of typing who were together arrested and the police said that they were soliciting. It was 30 years ago that I thought "Is a woman not safe to walk on the road ?" Is this the condition and since then it has been an unending struggle and I hope this struggle will culminate with your recommendations to SAARC and you would be successful. My congratulations to all of you for having taken on this venture.

Having said that, now what is the reality of the situation of getting this item to the agenda? I have spoken to three Prime Ministers, the Prime Minister of India, the Prime Minister of Bangladesh and the Prime Minister of Nepal and till such time all the seven SAARC countries get together it will be a difficult situation to put it on SAARC Agenda. My appeal to you would be, (the NCW would of course work in my own country to see that this goes on the agenda), to all of you, my appeal would be to start mobilizing support towards that to make it a format in the agenda. Why is the society like that? Men and women both form the same society and let us today at least pledge ourselves while we are talking about SAARC, let us not give up one very important aspect of the whole thing which is the morale in society and what is happening to that. What are we going to do about that?

Rehabilitation by NCW

In India we have found some methods of preventing and rehabilitating : First I will tell you the NCW's efforts towards that : We have gone down to the basic society right at the grass roots level, the Panchayati Raj and we are giving a legal awareness training to Panchayati Raj and we have told them about 29 points of agenda adding one more to see if a girl from her village is kidnapped, if a girl from her vicinity is taken it is her responsibility to see the safeguard and get her back immediately. This would perhaps take care of the larger issue till she is transported to the border and also this would prevent her getting away right from the village border. We have suggested and we have to make a narcotics bureau kind of a bureau at the borders with 5 member NGOs, DIG of Police, and the lawyers, bureaucrats in all the border states and the boarders of India. Where we will prevent children from entry and exit. But this is very important with a shelter home also. So we are now trying to see if we can have a good shelter home in all these borders also. We have made recommendations for vigilance cells in all the local stations and all the local bus stops where these women are taken. In these vigilance cells we have recommended men and women from NGOs to be in the cell and arrest the evil at the entry point. Because in India as in any other countries also it is a big mafia and this mafia is naturally with politicians so we have to stop it there itself.

Now I come to the question regarding what are the country's responsibilities? Each country has got its own responsibilities before we go to SAARC. You will have to make a pressure groups in each country and to see that they mobilize support for women. Now, in India we have in each brothel a force of the women themselves. These women in prostitution are themselves quite responsible for the moment a girl is brought into a brothel she is taken to the NCW network and will report about this to the authorities or to the National Commission or NCW's network like Indrani in each place in each district, in each local village. This is the kind of responsibility we refer. The second responsibility of the Government that we have in India is to see that there is Integrated child development programme in every brothel. The women in the prostitution trade are human beings and her child needs all the amenities that are there for any common child. So these integrated child development programme must be ensured for those children also. We have set 5 per cent reservation for all single women children in all boarding and lodging schools in India throughout the country. These are the country's responsibilities that I am talking about and I will tell you many of these have already been met. Calcutta has just now got 150 ICD programmes through. NGOs because we all know the functioning of bureaucrats and what they can do ?

We have also the process of heavy sensitization of the judiciary because the judiciary has been very biased and from the Bhanwari Devi case of Rajasthan we found that things are not going straight and we have had to file a public interest litigation (Also refer to Appendix V). I have just now commissioned a study for making a country paper of India for prostitutes. We are making it from State to State because we have regional variations, to collect information and get the summary paper prepared so that we have data of what is exactly the situation. Why I am mentioning all these things is in order to have all these preparations before the SAARC agenda. Every country must be prepared with this kind of background information. It will not be possible for the SAARC country to even consider the issue. This homework will have to be done by the various groups over here. I am sorry I have taken more than my 10 minutes. One aspect of the whole thing I would like to emphasize here is the health aspect.

---

*Wisdom lies in the realisation that as we know more about life and nature we know much less than we think we know.

7

EMPOWERMENT : PANACEA FOR WOMEN'S DENIALS

Women all over the world are overwhelmingly concerned with the issue of gender equality through women's empowerment. The countries of the world, and the women's movement everywhere, during the past five decades that the United Nations has been in existence, organized in a systematic and sustained manner the strategies and approaches that would effectively enable women to be equal partners in one's nation's progress and prosperity. The results are periodically assessed in world conferences, of which we have had four since the Mexico Conference, the last one being in Beijing in July, 1995. In the intervening period, national and international conferences deliberated on women's issues including gender equality.

From a perusal of this international conference paper, I find that during the last two days you have been deliberating on various issues crucial to promote women's empowerment.

Since the days of Raja Ram Mohan Roy, we have brought in a great measure of social reform in the country. India's Constitution conferred equality before law, universal adult franchise and equal opportunities for men and women. We are on the eve of completion of our fiftieth year of Independence. It is opportune at this juncture, to briefly take stock of the process of empowerment. As a matter of fact, the last five decades have been momentous for India's women's movement. In terms of constitutional, legal and administrative measures as well as enabling support to improve the working and living conditions of women, many initiatives were taken since 1947. Prominent among them are the constitutional mandates for gender equality and justice, enactment of very many new laws and amendment of existing laws to protect and promote the interests of women, setting up of women-specific administrative and economic structures like separate Women and Child Development Department at the Union and State Government levels, constitution of the National Commission for Women as also Commissions for Women in several States, State Women Development Corporations, orientation in plan strategy to include women specific and women related programmes, launching of special schemes like Rashtriya Mahila Kosh, Indira Mahila Yojana and Mahila Samridhi Yojana and the foremost among them all, the provision to reserve for women, one-third number of seats to be filled by direct election in Panchayats and urban local bodies as also offices in specified rural and urban local self-Government institutions, curbing introduction of 81st Constitution (Amendment) Bill for reservation of seats in Lok Sabha and State Legislatures.

Thus, we have enacted useful legislations to curb indignities on women and provide safety and security and harmony in family and society while some countries are still struggling for the emancipation of women. What we find is that these social legislations, such as those on dowry prohibition, equal remuneration and the like, lag behind implementation because the society has not kept pace with the rapidity of legislations, fast changing societal norms and dynamics of human behaviour and the need of human rights prerogatives. Our culture accord, a high position to women. We venerate women and we accord the highest place for the mother in the family, yet women are denied equality of status, contradictory and strange are the human motives. In this context, I am reminded of what A.C. Pigou said in his Welfare Economics. I quote, "When we elect to watch the play of human motives, that are ordinary, that are dismal and ignoble, our impulse is not the philosopher's impulse—knowledge for the sake of knowledge—but rather the physiologist's knowledge for the healing that knowledge may help to bring" unquote. My purpose here in stating this is to remind all of us that the knowledge that we may gain through conferences and other means must be utilized to heal the ills of society and to bring about sober and sound systems that make the home, the society and the country a place worth living.

Governance is an omnibus phrase. It encompasses social, political and economic empowerment. Achieving through gender equality and the strategies and approaches that a country needs to be adopted to achieve in full measure the objectives is the main theme of this international conference. Gender equality, as in many other areas, is a relative term. While in a female headed household or matriarchal system, the women may have equality to a large degree, but when it comes to the society, the social status varies considerably from community to community. In general, women lag behind in the equality status. The society and the Government have not been able to shed their inhibitions and reservations in according an equal status to women, notwithstanding very many progressive elements found in many of the religions of the world as well as the Constitutions of the various countries. I am deliberately not quoting examples, because it is not necessary to do so for an informed audience gathered here.

When it comes to economic empowerment, while women work along with men equally hard if not harder, their work is neither recognized nor taken into account in computing income. The statistics in our country, so also in very many others, show that the number of women in employment of a regular nature has been increasing and women are now to be found in a variety of jobs once considered to be preserves of men. It is a universal truth that if real empowerment is to be had, women must be economically independent. Many family discords occur mainly because of glaring unequal economic status of couples. It is also essential that the title of property owned should at least be, in the joint names of the couples if not exclusively in the name of female especially if the property was acquired through money brought from parental home. The role of women in taking decisions in the family affecting economic areas must also be a joint effort of husband and wife, father and mother, daughter and son, brother and sister and so on, involving equally the males and females. Then alone can harmony be built. As somebody put it, a happy home is heaven in advance.

In our country, the main obstacle for empowerment is the dismal female educational levels. It is a paradox that even after half a century of independence, according to the 1991 literacy figures, there are social groups among whom female literacy rate is even less than one per cent or negligible. To put it mildly, illiteracy is the greatest casuality among girls and women in many countries like India and is the stumbling clock towards empowerment. It requires no reiteration that the other major challenge towards gender equality and empowerment are the archaic social customs.

The gender disparity that vitiates the development process has its origin at the most vulnerable point in a women's life, viz. girl-child growing up in a family. Education of the girl-child is the best remedy to correct the imbalance and no cost is too high to achieve it. In respect of girls' education, we may not be wanting too much in theoretical formulations and planning strategies, our major weakness seems to lie in the lack of sincerity in execution and vigour in implementation.

Women in decision-making process

In the empowerment route, participation of women in decision making at all levels has special significance, especially in a democratic set-up. It is unfortunate that some countries in the world have yet to confer full voting rights to women. In our country, the process of political empowerment was well begun when we adopted our Constitution and gained momentum when the Constitution was amended reserving for women one-third of seats in local bodies, both rural and urban, as also specified post of office bearers. This process is being taken to the zenith with the introduction of 81st Amendment Bill providing for one-third reservation of seats for women in Lok Sabha (lower house) and State legislatures. Many State Governments have reserved specified quota, generally 30 per cent of posts in public services for women. The Government of India has also under its consideration a proposal to reserve 30 per cent posts in the Union Government services. It is to be expected that these measures should hasten the empowerment process in adequate measure.

The empowerment of women and the achievement of equality should not be considered in isolation. The realization of these goals is the only way to build a harmonious, just and balanced society. Let us pledge ourselves to actively pursue these essential requisites for the good of humanity.

Empowerment of Women Through Various International and National Agencies

It is indeed appropriate that in this International Year for the Eradication of Poverty, UNDP has decided to release the book "Sites of Change—The Structural Context Empowering Women in India" which is the outcome of a seminar organized jointly by the Friedrich Ebert Stiftung (FES) and UNDP in December, 1995.

In India, one can see three stages in the process of attaining sustainable development. The first, the paternalistic conservative stage, where curing the worst ill was enough; the second, the liberal stage, where safeguarding against inequalities was enough; the third, the actual democratic stage where helping people to help themselves is the prime concern. In our country, sustainable development had its origin in efforts to deal with poverty. Unfortunately, this is still the priority concern, although our efforts must also be for freedom from exploitation and oppression, environmental protection, gender equality with social justice.

Social development presupposes the evolution both of the individual and the society in a manner that happiness for both is ensured. Even as society recognizes the individual's rights to live in a manner she or he wants, the individual also should recognize the rights of other members of the society and of the society itself.

In spite of the diversity of opinion among experts on the methodology of measuring poverty, the importance of quantifying it has been well recognized, especially since poverty alleviation has become an important plan objective and successive plans have been specifying poverty alleviation targets.

Confronting poverty

Defining a poverty line is the first step in estimating poverty. A poverty line dividing the poor from the non-poor is used by putting a price on the minimum required consumption levels of food, clothing, shelter, fuel and health care, etc. The definition of poverty line in the Indian context was attempted for the first time in 1962 by a working group of eminent economists and social thinkers.

While being aware that the poverty line is only approximate and stylized indicator of a complex, multifaceted and changing reality, it is also necessary to recognize the continued necessity and utility of poverty estimation. A practical approach will, accordingly, have to consist of:

(i) improving the set of poverty estimates as may be feasible from time to time with reference to (a) concepts (b) data (c) methodology;

(ii) supplementing the poverty line approach with indicators and information on various aspects of the conditions of the poor; and

(iii) promoting research on the understanding and estimation of poverty on a sustained and cumulative basis, under different recognizable groups.

Where there is a commitment to social development, the deployment of resources for it will depend on priorities and whose interests the state wishes to servc. Social development alone may not bring gender equality. Power hierarchies, legal structures and political conditions that offer space for dissent are other parameters. Gender is linked to poverty through unequal relations within the household. In gender equality, two indicators can be seen, one is the availability of basic resources on an equitable basis and and the other is that intra-household distribution of resources and their control are important. For empowerment, economic aspects have to be tackled effectively.

Poverty eradication assumes great significance in this context. Poverty eradication and empowerment of women are now at the centrestage of development. The release of the book is timely and a welcome measure. Friedrich Ebert Stiftung and UNDP have been in the forefront in matters of women development. Their contribution deserves grateful acknowledgment.

NCW as vehicle for empowerment

A nation can ill afford to leave behind half of its population in its march towards progress and prosperity. Advancement and empowerment of women, therefore, has to be accorded high priority in the country's development efforts. Under section 10(1) (h) of the National Commission for Women Act, 1990, the Commission is required to suggest ways and means of ensuring due representation of women in all spheres of development and identify the various constraints in their advancement.

Regular elections form the backbone of democratic functioning of the State. Participation in elections, candidature and representation, are fundamental rights of citizens and are perceived by all citizens as a moment of greatest participation in democracy.

India goes to the polls regularly every 5 years. Voter turnout is uniformly high at around 64 per cent. An electorate returns 545 representatives to the Lok Sabha from 25 States and 7 Union territories. 51 per cent of women voters turn out for elections. However, of 6160 candidates standing for elections in 1989, only 198 or 3.2 per cent were women. Of these 14.1 per cent were elected. Women in the Lok Sabha account for about 5 per cent of the total representation. At ministerial level this decreases to 3 per cent. Despite this, analysis of women's voting and candidature trends indicate that even as women are more and more eager to participate in politics their share in representation is seriously undermined. All political parties, whether national or regional, continue to undervalue women as voters and as representatives. In the absence of quotas, the lesson of women's successful participation in Panchayati Raj are yet to be reflected in State and national levels.

Equality between women and men is a condition for social justice and is also a necessary and fundamental prerequisite for equality, development and peace. Yet the under-representation of women as people's representatives and decision makers at State and national levels forecloses adequate representation of almost half the country's population. Analysis of past manifestoes brings out the fact that inevitably women's issues and interests cannot be sufficiently addressed. Inequality in the public area is symptomatic of the existing unequal power relations, economic disparity, and social discrimination. These conditions continue to prevent women from enjoying her human and citizenship rights to the full, as also equality as guaranteed in the Constitution of India.

Equal opportunities to take part in elections and to take part in decision-making at all levels is a necessary condition for achieving equality. It ensures women's perspectives and realities are taken into account in agenda setting, policy formulation and resource allocation. Balanced representation mirrors the makeup of the society and is required to strengthen democracy and promote proper functioning.

Furthering equal participation of women in the political process

The under-representation of women in the electoral process is a serious impediment to the achievement of her real equality. The National Commission for Women proposes to suggest ways and means which would encourage the participation of women in elections, ensure the freedom of ballot, increase their ability to stand as candidates and eventually bear office in all sphere of public life.

The National Commission for Women will initiate a dialogue with leadership, manifesto committee members, women parliamentarians and candidates, workers, organizers and youth leaders of political parties to address the issue of women's equal representation in political decision making.

In order to investigate and examine the constitutional safeguards of equality for women, the Commission will undertake promotional and educational research on the ability of women to participate in the electoral process in certain constituencies across the country.

In order to examine matters related to ensuring constitutional safeguards provided to women and promote their socioeconomic development the Commission will also undertake the examination of party political manifestoes.

In this regard the National Commission for Women urges all political parties to ensure that national manifestoes reflect the obligations of the State to ensure the enhancement of women's political, economic and social rights as undertaken in the various national plan documents, and in the light of India's international obligations undertaken through its ratification of international treaties and in particular, the obligation to ensure nondiscrimination in all areas of public life and development undertaken by India under the Covenant for the Elimination of All Forms of Discrimination Against Women.

The due representation of women in all spheres requires the effective participation of women voters in the elections in secure and non-threatening circumstances in which women can operate as voters and candidates. The National Commission for Women will seek the cooperation of National Election Commission in voter education for women, special training for electoral staff, and in particular care and attention to ensuring the safety of women in the electoral process. In particular, the National Commission for Women recommends the review of existing model codes of conduct and election guidelines to reflect the realities of women's lives and experiences so as to meet their special needs.

In order to promote women's informed choice and equality in the political process, the National Commission for Women urges the mass communication fraternity of radio, television, and print media particularly those using national and regional languages to vigorously disseminate relevant information concerning women's issues and her right and duty to exercise her choice through casting the ballot.

RIGHTS AND CURRENT STATUS OF WOMEN

It has always been the contention that equality in all spheres is inseparable from active political participation and is integral to the progress of women. Without active and continuous participation of women at all levels of Government including local party structures, equality in true sense will continue to remain deceptive. It has now been accepted that equal rights to vote and to be elected to national offices are fundamental to women's status.

In 1945, when the UN was founded, only about half of the 51 members had extended franchise to women. The Commission at first concentrated on political rights which were regarded as fundamental. The Convention on the Political Rights to Women adopted by the General Assembly in 1952 stated that "Women shall be entitled to hold public offices and to exercise all public functions, established by national law, on equal terms with men, without and discrimination". This was the first instrument of international law aimed at granting and protecting of women's rights on a worldwide basis.

The United Nations declared 1975 as the 'International Women Year' and 1980 as the 'Year for Development of Women'. The decade 1975-85 was hailed by the member nations of the world who were expected to focus their attention and resources on the problem of women with the objective of integrating women with the social, economic and political activity. However, after half a century of women's suffrage, the number of women in high positions of political power and influence is still small. Although there have been women Prime Ministers, women ministers, some of cabinet rank, in many countries, very few have held office outside the spheres that are usefully considered women's interests such as social welfare, public health and family affairs.

The Government of India Act published in 1919 did not enfranchise women, but it did empower provincial legislatures to remove the sex barriers at their discretion. In the first election in 1926 the Act enfranchised less than one per cent of the total female population.

Bapu's concern for women

Mahatma Gandhi who was instrumental in bringing hundreds of thousands of women out of their homes to fight in the freedom struggle, did not equate legal equality of sexes with equality of occupations. He believed that there was a basic difference in the roles and functions of men and women but they were complementary. He further asserted that they were not inferior to men and that men and women were equal in law. The amelioration in the condition of women was a necessary precondition to the regeneration of Indian society. So he mobilized women into the national movement, apart from working for their emancipation.

Political status of women implies the degree of equality and freedom enjoyed by women in the shaping and sharing of power and the value given by the society to the role of women. The equality is inseparable from active political participation. Participation of women in political life is integral to the advancement of women. Their political participation means not only using the right to vote but also power sharing, co-decision making and co-policy making at all levels of Government and within party structures.

The institution of local Government in India has a hoary past. Many types of local Government institutions flourished in ancient India. The Government of India Act of 1919 is considered as a turning point in the field of local Government. Eminent persons like Pandit Jawaharlal Nehru, Sardar Vallabh Bhai Patel, Purshotamdas Tandon, Sathya Murthy and a host of others entered into municipal councils. Thereafter, the evolution has been continuous.

The first Municipal Corporation was established at Madras in 1687 followed by that of Calcutta and then Bombay. But it was only in 1793 that these bodies were placed on a statutory basis.

In recent decades, the pace of urbanization has been on the increase. This has resulted not only in the increase of population in the existing cities and towns but also in the creation of new towns. There has thus been more than a tenfold increase in the number of municipal corporations. This has been due to the elevation in status of a number of towns from municipalities to municipal corporations.

Representation of women in governance

In the annals of evolution of local self-government in the country, June 1, 1993 occupies a prime place. It was on that day a constitutional status to municipal administration in India was accorded by bringing into force the Constitution (Seventy-Fourth Amendment) Act. 1992. It is well known that earlier the Constitution did not make local self-government in urban areas a specific constitutional mandate. While the Directive Principles of State Policy refers to village panchayats, there was no specific reference to municipalities except implicitly in Entry 5 of the State List which places the subject of local self-government as a responsibility of the States.

It was the weakened status of urban local bodies which mobilized public opinion in favour of a constitutional guarantee to ensure :

- regular and fair conduct of elections of these bodies;
- holding of elections within a specified time limit in case of supersession;
- adequate representation of women and SC/ST in the elected bodies;
- placing on a sound footing the relationship between the State Governments and the urban local bodies with respect thereto;
- functions and taxation powers of the urban local bodies;
- arrangement for revenue sharing between the State Governments and the urban local bodies;
- involvement of elected representative at the grass roots level in planning and implementation.

It is also significant that in many ways the leadership of our freedom movement was nurtured in the civic bodies.

the State Legislature may, by law, endow :

(a) The Article 243 enjoins that the municipalities with such powers and authority as may be necessary to enable them to function as institutions of self-government and such law may contain provision for the devolution of powers and responsibilities upon municipalities, subject to such conditions as may be specified therein, with respect thereto :

(i) the preparation of plans for economic development and social justice;

(ii) the performance of functions and the implementation of schemes as may be entrusted to them including those in relation to the matter listed in the Twelfth Schedule;

(b) the committees with such powers and authority as may be necessary to enable them to carry out the responsibilities conferred upon them including those in relation to the matters listed in the Twelfth Schedule.

It is here that the challenges lay for our women representatives in urban local bodies. The problems of women in urban areas are many, varied and complex. To cite a few examples, let us take the case of urban poverty, slum dwellers, migrant women workers, street children, mothers at work or even housewives and urban violence against women.

Each metropolitan city is a miniature India representing aspirations and hopes of millions and deprivation and callousness to millions. On this count, women figure prominently.

Urbanization is a natural consequence of the economic changes that takes place in a country. The positive role of urbanization is often overshadowed by the evident deterioration in the physical environment and quality of life in the urban areas caused by the widening gap between demand and supply of essential services and infrastructure. Maharashtra has the distinction of occupying the first rank in terms of level of urbanization with 38.73 per cent of its population living in urban areas, which is about 13 per cent more than the All India figure (25.72 per cent).

Apart from providing regular and routine civic amenities like drinking water, public health, sanitation, street lighting, slum improvement, etc, some of the important programmes now being implemented in urban areas include :

1. The Integrated Development of Small and Medium Towns (IDSMT) Scheme
2. the Scheme of Environmental Improvement of Urban Slums, an integral part of the Minimum Needs

Programme;

3. the Urban Basic Services Scheme (UBBS);

4. the Urban Basic Services for the Poor (UBSP);

5. by far, the most important programme for poverty alleviation is the Nehru Rozgar Yojana targeted towards persons living below the poverty line in urban areas.

My intention in briefly mentioning the particulars of some important schemes was only to impress upon the need to sensitize the elected women members to assess the impact of such schemes on the family and consequently on the women members who are always deprived of the real benefits. Take any item, migration for example. It is the women migrants to urban areas who suffer most and also are sometimes subjected to various forms of atrocities. Take poverty as another example. The deprivation that women and girl children undergo are definitely more severe than other members of the poor family. In all these and many other matters our women representatives in the local bodies could bring about solace and comfort by appropriate interventions. In this connection, the Resolution adopted at the 25th meeting of the Central Council of Local Government and Urban Development held in May, 1994, is extremely relevant. It read "The Council is deeply concerned about the rising incidence of urban poverty as revealed by the Lakdawala Committee report." Considering the magnitude of urban poverty and the fact that the present outlay would enable coverage of hardly 10 per cent of the urban poor the Council recommends that :

(i) the Central and State Governments should substantially step up funding of programmes related to the urban poor, particularly those benefiting women and children;

(ii) the Commercial Banks and other financial institutions increase their lending to the urban poor and evolve simplified application and appraisal procedures and recovery mechanisms suited for such portions of society.

I am not sure whether any corporation has acted upon it. In any case, the thrust of the resolution is very clear.

A word about finance. A study by the National Institute of Urban Affairs. New Delhi in October, 1994 brought out that analysis of available information on municipal finance in India suggests that local finances are unable to cope with rising demand on municipal services. The pattern of municipal revenue indicates that the self sources continue to be the dominant mode of resource mobilization at the local level. However, dependence of municipal governments on inter-governmental transfer has increased. Municipal finances, based on available data, suggest a very poor financial base of municipalities. State Finance Commissions are confronted with the task of bridging the fiscal gap of municipalities. Given the fact that the demand for urban services will continue to increase, it will be necessary to examine various policy options available for SFCs to augment municipal revenues.

I would like to stress the importance of training, especially for the women members. Again, in May 1994 meeting of the Central Council, it endorsed a resolution, which read as quoted "Recognizing the complexity of urban planning and management tasks, in particular financial management, in the context of the growing responsibilities of municipalities, the council recommends that :

(i) the Central and State Governments should make an assessment of the training needs in the urban sector immediately;

(ii) training and research institutions should be identified at the regional and State levels which could take up these training programmes;

(iii) steps should be taken to strengthen such identified institutions by way of both financial and technical assistance;

(iv) suitable research programmes should be evolved which would provide necessary inputs into the planning process and feedback on programmes under implementation; and

(v) networking among such institutions should be evolved with a view to exchange experiences and information between local bodies and State Governments in the areas of urban planning and management.

Rajiv Gandhi's concern for women

Proposing to extend reservations for women to Nagarpalikas on the same pattern as in the Panchayats, our then Prime Minister Rajiv Gandhi had said that "there is no section of our society more oppressed, more exploited and more neglected than women. In every segment, class or community, women suffer all the disabilities inflicted on that group and, in addition, suffer also the consequences of gender discrimination. Yet, their contribution to economic life, social well-being, cultural continuity and ethical standards is far greater than their share of the population. We must make a determined beginning to bring women into the mainstream of local self-government".

The municipal corporation is entrusted with the task of laying down of the policy in the assigned area, organization, execution and management of the vital affairs of the city. It is, therefore, duty-bound to evolve a suitable framework within which there should be adequate scope for satisfying the legitimate requirements of the urban women and to find practical solutions to their problems. Only by getting into positions of power can women bring about changes quickly and effectively in the society.

Here is an opportunity for women to contribute their mite in improving the status of women and thereby the

Empowerment through grass roots democracy

Everything must start from the beginning. So also is the case with progress and development for these to be meaningful. Moreover, it must involve both men and women, from the lowest possible levels—grass roots level, as we often refer to them, to enable their total involvement and participation. Unless we the people help ourselves and thereby strengthen the hands of the nation towards peace, plenty and prosperity, there can be no future at all for this nation nor for the suffering millions. While eradication and total abolition of poverty, illiteracy and disease must be the main plank for us to commence our programmes and policies, what needs to be worked out is the *modus operandi* for successful implementation of these schemes and programmes. Be they any of the multi-pronged phases involving integrated rural development with its composite package of potable water, housing, fuel and electricity, health, education and introduction of innovative appropriate technologies, all of them perforce have to deeply involve committed villagers of both sexes.

Then and then alone can we see the beginning of a great future for this great nation with its grand manpower of skilled, trained competent band of administrators and scientists. We do not have a dearth of either technologies or people to transmit these technologies to the relevant strata of society, making them the beneficiancies of the fruits of a grand endeavour. The lacunae must be identified and the gaps filled without any further delay in order to enable both the village and urban level populations subsisting at villages on the fringes of big metropolitan cities.

To this end we must set up task forces involving as many people at various levels, as possible including recently retired officers of the Government to enrich the programmes with their excellent experience. While men at all levels must be drafted into these schemes, since women form often more than 50 per cent of any population be it rural or urban or even semi-urban, success will be assured to most programmes by their active involvement and achievement. But many of the women are either hesitant or even reluctant to enter these programmes although several of them have already been drafted into them by various processes of mediation, awareness of their own potential, and actual gains for themselves individuals as well as for the whole family and village at large. Despite lack of formal education, many of these women have a native intelligence quotient rather of a high order and are able to master the three Rs. (i.e., reading, writing and arithmetic) rather rapidly particularly the arithmetic part of it including computing, etc., of accounts. Better roads and commuting facilities, lighting, availability of fuel for cooking, will free them from unnecessary drudgery of long and arduous chores, and make them available for work for society, village and the nation.

Benefits of modern science and technology must reach the masses in various appropriate levels and phases. This is an ongoing process and many women have adopted and adapted to these facilities. The stress and emphasis on Panchayati Raj and the 33 per cent reservation for women is a great and laudable step in this direction. There is a general feeling that village menfolk not only discourage their women to participate in the great national adventure, they also prevent and condemn their involvement. While it is so in some cases I have seen that by motivating the men and impressing on them the benefits for the whole family that whole family that would accrue because of such scheme many men are willing and what more, are even glad to have their womenfolk enter all arenas. This is nothing new. The men have been working shoulder-to-shoulder in the fields and have taken it as a matter of fact and necessity. By persuasion and coaxing of men it is easier to ensure the smooth transition into other fields also, mainly political which would then usher in an era of politics and socio-economic progress.

Political empowerment of women

This brings us to the question of political empowerment, a very crucial issue in many of the ongoing debates and concerns throughout the length and breadth of the country. Where do we begin to enable active participation of women in the decision making levels? Understandably it must be at the grass roots level of the Gram Panchayat and to repeat, the 33 per cent reservation for women at all tiers of Panchayat has made a significant beginning and a major contribution. In order to get the elected women to function effectively and safeguard the interests of the village and in particular of women and children adequate training and authority have to be provided to them, by continuous motivation and awareness procedures of the rich dividends inherent in such empowerment. The constant and beneficial interaction of women with bureaucracy will usher in an era of new perception and comprehension for the women, who thenceforth will need no further guidance. Most of them are quick learners and the spirit of enthusiasm and optimism will affect the entire village population especially the women, most of whom are already in a socially cohesive group, due to the great vision and mission of the Father of the Nation Mahatma Gandhi, who spread the concept and message of cooperative farming, cottage industry benefits, etc., which have grown into small industries.

It is here the NCW has a vital and significant role to play. By constant interaction with the rural women, by providing them with necessary awareness, advice and guidance from the urban sisters, who could be both from private NGOs and from Government circles, who may be honorary or paid workers, this movement must gain greater force, pace and momentum. We at the NCW are engaged in various exercises to ensure that the benefits of the various schemes actually reach the beneficiaries as rapidly and as effectively and as much as possible. This will be a constant endeavour on our part and we have a dedicated band of women, who are determined to ensure the success of implementation of these schemes by the turn of the century. We are already poised for a great victory. But in this scenario we would like to involve and motivate our urban women population, factory workers, construction site labour, so that they, a very hard working group are not left behind in the race.

In this context the 73rd and 74th Constitution amendments which apart from providing a statutory framework for a decentralized democratic polity are intended to ensure the smooth functioning of the three-tier structure. It is now for the Gram Panchayat bodies to take full advantage of this opportunity and through elected men and women start regulating and governing themselves. The women must take full advantage of the 33 per cent representation and without hesitation or fetters of *Ghoonghat* (veil) forge ahead, in this great effort to enable these women to come forward and acquire and sustain their rights and contribute to the development of the nation. Political empowerment is both a weapon and device in the struggle of women for emancipation from poverty, disease and illiteracy, for by active involvement in the decision-making machinery of the country at all levels will ensure and carve a place for themselves and their girls, daughters, the future citizens of this nation.

Greeting from the National Commission for Women. May I extend to you all, on my own behalf, on behalf of the National Commission for Women, the State Comissions for

Women and millions of Indian women, our good wishes in this 50th year of our Independence and 40th successful anniversary of ECA. I hope that during this year South-south Cooperation would attain further empowerment for women.

I feel proud to be a part of the process of transformation which is taking place not only in India but all over the world. The widespread and vibrant womens movement in my country has been responsible for catalyzing changes in attitudes, policies and laws. Realizing that knowledge is power and awareness, sensitization and enlightenment are the prerequisities for changes in the social system, the National Commission for Women in India, of which I have the privilege to be the Chairperson, has taken up measures in this direction.

The South is part of a world whose interdependence is constantly widening and deepening, and our vision is of a cooperative world made more secure for all its people. Our vision is for the South to achieve a people-centred development : a form of development that is self-reliant, equitable, participartory and sustainable. We envisage a process of development achieved through the active participation of the people, in their own interests as they see them, rely primarily on their own resources, and carried out under their own control.

The objective should be not only to secure economic growth but also to ensure that it benefits the mass of the people. Development must be conceived of as a process which enables human beings to realize their potential, build self-confidence and lead lives of dignity and fulfilment. Development does, of course, require sustained economic growth, for only in an expanding economy can poverty be eradicated. But, development cannot be measured solely by the growth of the gross national product. What is produced, how and at what social and environmental cost, by whom and for whom—all this is just as important as a higher GNP. Hence, in conditions of mass poverty, priority must be given to policies aimed at ending poverty, increasing productive employment, and ensuring that the basic needs of all the people are met, with any surplus being shared fairly. Such goods and services as food, shelter, basic education and health facilities, and clean water should be accessible to all and without discrimination on grounds of gender, race, colour or religion. In addition, our vision includes a democratic form of government, together with its supporting individual freedoms of speech, organization and information, as well as an effective system of justice which protects all the people from actions in breach of just laws which are known and publicly accepted.

The need for developing countries to rely on their own resources and efforts to revitalize development in the 1990s applies not only at the national but also at the South-South level. Increased reliance on the collective resources of the South, through diversified and reinforced process of political, economic and social cooperation, will be of vital importance in the response of developing countries to the many challenges they face. By expanding the flows of finance, trade, technology and skills within the South, through stronger links which take advantage of complementary assets, South-South cooperation can fortify the development of all countries of the South.

The strength the South can gain by making more use of its collective energies will give it greater importance in the world economy and a more favourable position to exert influence on global economic management. Pursued with determination, South-South cooperation can, in the long run, change the world economic map; criss-crossing links within the South can mitigate the dependence that imperial rule built into North-South links.

The search for a more rational and equitable world order, which the South has pursued for so long, requires a more effectively organized South to present its case and negotiate its demands in world forums. On the issues that concern humanity in common no less than on those of special relevance to the South, it is necessary that the South should speak with one voice. It is equally necessary that its voice should not go unheard—or unheeded—because of its organizational failings.

Another vital task to be accomplished before one could assess the prospects and map out the strategy for future South-South cooperation is to re-evaluate the strategy of cooperation pursued up to the present.

South-South cooperation really needs that there should be a good strategy for cooperation based on economic and political structures of the countries. So far the objectives of cooperation have been pursued in a haphazard manner. Hence, there have not been viable and effective strategies. We definitely need a global strategy for South-South cooperation that would serve as a basis for elaborating more specific regional, sub-regional and national programmes for cooperation.

A development strategy committed to equity and participation must also give priority to the raising of the social and economic status of women. Throughout the South, women play a vital role as producers and agents of social progress. Yet they carry the double burden of discrimination and greater than average poverty. No nation can truly develop so long as half of its population suffers discrimination. It is, therefore, essential that development programmes should purposefully seek to advance women's status in society, ensuring that womens concerns are treated in a comprehensive manner, adequate resources are made available to meet their needs and the obstacles they face in important economic areas are eliminated.

Macro-economic policies, especially those bearing on the allocation of resources and technological choices, need to take account of their likely impact on womens productive activities. Policies ought to be pursued that enhance womens income-earning capacity and give them a fair share of social services. Womens right to social justice and equity should be legally protected. Deliberate endeavours to foster a gender-sensitive culture should support these reforms.

Whenever we talk of partnership, we would first see partnership in changing the mindset of man. Only then would "Gender Revolution" be possible. That is the only way of ending the subjugation of women. In India we have achieved grass roots solidarity like the Sathins of Rajasthan, women in chipko movement, women in prostitution, Self Employed Womens Association or SEWA, women in agriculture, women entrepreneurs, women in the anti alcohol movement. Because of this solidarity, women have got *bargaining power*, e.g. recently, during elections in India, a group of trib women exercised their right of rejection to cast their votes unless the road leading to their small huts was built and water made available to them. Then again, in the Indian States of Andhra Pradesh and Haryana, the Chief Ministers won their Assembly Elections because they promised prohibition in their States.

On another front if today India can boast of a White Revolution in milk production, it is due to a network of several thousand village women organized into cooperative societies as in Gujarat and other States. On one side in milk collection and on other on value added products produced in modern plants and marketed even internationally under the brand name "AMUL". Amul has become a household word in India. These women in reality are employing top management experts and are also reaping the benefits that accrue.

For a good framework of partnership it is neccessary that this sort of grouping together is undertaken which achieves remarkably successful results.

The 73rd and 74th amendments to the Indian

Constituiton brought about a sea change in the statutory shield for women. However, the womens movement in India has not remained just a bargaining force but a vibrant development forum/agency which is self-sustaining and powerful because of its large numbers.

Our vision goes beyond the South to embrace the whole world. We look to a world in which there is no "South" and no "North", in which there is no one part rich, developed and dominating while the other remains poor, underdeveloped and dominated. During the framework of partnership, we need to identify middle level functionaries to interact for South-South Cooperation.

Our societies are varied but our problems are more or less the same. Cooperation between the South-South would therefore prove highly beneficial because of similarities of issues being discussed. What we need is a viable strategy to guide sustained cooperation in various fields. I look upon with great optimism that even though the task is not easy we can imbibe a new confidence for gains in South-South cooperations. Despite the challenges, many problems can be overcome particularly if we target women and children. We in India have achieved major successes with little means especially when communities have been motivated to effect profound and lasting change.

We in India look to our African sisters who are always full of energy and enthusiasm to take up challenges against all odds and we learn lessons of courage from them. I would like to add that a group of 27 African women entrepreneurs are due to visit India shortly. It would not be out of place ot mention that India and South Africa are among the strongest supporters of a separate agenda item on human rights in the Commission on Human Rights.

In conclusion, I would like to say that women unqestionably, cannot be treated any longer just as a special interest group, as we represent half of humanity. Therefore, it is necessary to maintain a gender perspective in all policies.

Enlightenment : Key to progress

It is hardly ten days since the world celebrated "International Women's Day" : that important day in the Calendar of the Women's Movement was on the 8th of this month.

To commemorate International Women's Day, we — in the National Commission for Women — held a one-day workshop on that day. And, exactly at 11.00 a.m., all participants of the workshop — including Mrs. Vimala Sharma, our First Lady, Mrs. Margaret Alva and quite a few dignitaries — remained in pin-drop silence for 5 minutes, signifying the women of India "*Akhri Maun*" : our "Last Silence". From that moment onwards, the women of India have ceased to remain silent spectators and watch our sisters suffer indignities heaped upon them by society. With centuries-old traditions and varying attitudinal behaviour by sections of our society, I know the task ahead of us a is huge one; and we need to mobilize our resources, join hands in a common endeavour and wipe away as much tears as we can from the eyes of the women of India.

Our Constitution and our laws give Indian women a number of "Rights" and "Guarantees" : protecting women's liberty, equality and freedom. Unfortunately the gap between legal "Guarantees" and "Ground Realities" is, vast. Certain sections of our society — especially the urban ones — do find women in almost every walk of life successfully contributing to social welfare, industrial development and participating in legal profession and even legislative services. But, if you consider the very low percentage of women legislators in the 10th Lok Sabha, it would be obvious as to where women stand in Indian society today. Hopefully, the coming elections will change this situation.

The gap, therefore, between "Guarantees and

Ground Realities" threatens to increase or widen, not decrease or reduce. I believe that this potential threat to Indian women is the strong motivating force behind our "*Akhri Maun*", which gave a clarion call to all of us — women (as also men) of India — bringing out that we need to do so much, in so short a time, to better the lives of Indian women and as, the theme of your seminar suggests, to empower women.

When Prof. Zakia Siddiqui first wrote to me about this seminar, I was informed that several subjects/themes were being considered for discussion during this seminar. Among the topics mentioned were :

(1) Education of disadvantaged women with special reference to Backward minorities.

(2) Enrolment and dropout of the girl child.

(3) Vocationalization of education for women.

(4) Legal literacy and human rights education.

(5) Leadership education for elected representatives at Panchayats and local bodies; and

(6) Role of NGOs and non-formal education.

NCW's contributions

As Chairperson of the National Commission for Women, I would be very interested to receive feedback and ideas generated as a result of discussions centering round themes such as the ones I've just mentioned. I am sure feedback of this type could lead to greater cooperation between the Women's College of Aligarh Muslim University and the N.C.W. bearing in mind that the latter has launched action-based programmes to help women in India.

Legal awareness and human rights, I am sure, will be discussed at length at this seminar. At the field level, the N.C.W. is in the process of launching a nation-wide programme to create legal awareness among women. This programme will be in collaboration with the National Law School University in Bangalore : the basic principle involved is through a structured "Training of Trainers" programme for university lecturers, there will be a multiplier effect leading to young women students being updated in legal awareness of their rights.

Another major programme launched by the N.C.W. is a series of nationwide Mahila Adalats. Our objective here is to assist women disputants receive justice by reducing our judiciary's very large backlog of pending cases. Thanks to the active cooperation of State Legal Aid Boards and judiciary interested NGOs over 3000 pending cases involving women, hopefully, will be settled in Gujarat by the end of this month. Apart from Gujarat, Mahila Adalats are being conducted in States like Maharashtra, Kerala, Madras, Andhra Pradesh and Delhi as elsewhere too.

I thought I'd mention just these two programmes of the N.C.W. mainly with a view to suggest that with a little foresight cost-effective schemes could be implemented — by accepting and using scarce resources and friendly assistance — and, in turn, these actions could benefit many women.

This is a two-day seminar and I should not delay it from getting started, in a brisk manner. I would however, like to make an observation with regard to education. As an educational institution, the Women's College of Aligarh Muslim University surely would be concerned about the state of literacy in our country, as revealed in the 1991 Census. Having an all-India women's illiteracy of 60 per cent is not something to be proud of. However, certain States like U.P., M.P., Rajasthan and Bihar, makes us unhappy. The 1991 Census shows literacy levels (for women) in these States as being less than 30 per cent! There are, of course, several factors that have led to this situation but, instead of worrying too much about the "causes", perhaps greater discussion should centre on how to come out with action plans which would answer the question "Where do we go from here?" And I can assure you that any idea, suggestion, action plan which you may like to share with the N.C.W. will receive our serious consideration.

Fifty Years of Independence and Status of Women

Greetings from the National Commission for Women. May I extend to you all, on my own behalf, on behalf of the National Commission for Women, the State Commissions for Women and millions of Indian women, our good wishes in this fiftieth year of our Independence and fifty years of 50 per cent successful democratic rule. We hope that during this year, the Indian women would attain further empowerment in continuation of the process initiated three years back at the grass roots level by adequate representation in the apex legislatures.

I feel proud to be a part of the process of transformation which is taking place not only in India but all over the world. During the past 2-1/2 years I visited about 350 districts in the country and on asking "What do women want?", the answer always was "full and equal partnership with men in all aspects of development, governance and in society". Needless to say that it is for all of us in our various capacities to decide how we will keep the doors of transformation open, to walk through them and to avail the opportunity with open mind, to work together to make appropriate changes. It is a continuing commitment to the difficult but crucial task of improving the lives of people everywhere and of course with special emphasis on women and children.

On the threshold of the 21st century, the eyes of the world are turned towards India which is witnessing positive transformation in economic field as a result of the reforms initiated a few years back, with an unattached diversity of political and social systems. Our efforts towards redressing gender inequality are more pronounced than in many other countries.

We are now recognizing that if women are healthy and educated their families do better. If they are free from violence their families do better. If they have the opportunity to earn and work as equal partners in societies those families do better. Needless to say when those families do better then the communities and nations of which they are part also do better.

Institutionalized mechanisms for gender equality

Institutionalized mechanisms in a democracy for gender equality would naturally include micro and macro level strategies and initiatives. At the micro level, India's record of initiating social legislations and positive discrimination through quota system in local self-government institutions are unparalleled. At the macro level, policy prescriptions for compulsory education, State policies on women, health policy, special dispensation for weaker social groups are too, well known. It may be added that our national policy on women is yet to be officially adopted. Indeed, in a democracy, impediments en route to realizing the goals of gender equality and gender justice could stem from the nature of Government, whether it is secular, whether it is truly representative, whether it is one party or coalition and so on. In this matter, we are fortunate in that we have a national Government with wide representation of different shades of public opinion and a common, minimum programme, committed both by the constituent parties election manifestoes and through public pronouncements of leaders. Their adherence to empowerment of women is a significant aspect which cannot escape notice. It is a different matter that for some unclear internal differences of some constituents of the

United Front Government, some of the measures, such as the 81st Constitution Amendment Bill aimed at providing $33_{1/3}$ per cent seats for women in State Legislatures and Lower House of Parliament (Lok Sabha) have not been acted upon. We are all sure that this will be done through the support of women's commission, women's council, women's board, etc., constituted by the Government, apart from those of the independent NGOs working in various fields. It should, however, be admitted that balanced and sustainable development is not a simple matter of Government alone. It is in this context that the relevance of various specialized institutionalized arrangements rendering requisite inputs are recognized and appreciated.

Governance is a very broad based concept while democracy has very many shades. As somebody put it, democracy is like a hat which has almost entirely lost its original shape in the process of it having been worn by many. It has to be acknowledged as a participatory system which provides adequate, unhindered, universal opportunity for all in the promotion of an equitable and sustainable social and economic order. For achieving optimum results in a democracy, there has to be a partnership accord between women and governance ensuring as also safeguarding individual liberty and dignity and common interests. In almost all cases, the failure of democracy happens because of the failure of Government. In one of the works of Subhash C. Kashyap, it was mentioned that "governance has become a casualty of Government" with Government themselves more concerned with survival rather than attending to the needs of the people. Democracy thrives through democratic institutions. It is not an isolated and insulated phenomena. The effectiveness or usefulness of democracy would depend upon the structures supporting it. It will be agreed that what really matters is the quality of democracy by which it is meant that everyone, and especially the poor and the marginalized like backward social groups and women, have access to decision making levels through inbuilt appropriate strategies so that their voices are heard and heeded. Further, as is the present case in our national government, democracy based on the principle of "consent" is more beneficial. The success of democracy, in so far as it concerns women would definitely be tested on the question of sensibility, sensitivity and suitability to answer to the needs of feminist concerns, though not divorced from society, nation, regional and international interests.

I would submit that we are witnessing an enormous transformation in human history; that the changes in women's lives and voices are both cause and effect of larger processes at work. The world is becoming smaller and more interdependent.

From the experience the world over, poverty has been considered to be an important women's issue, for poverty has a feminine face. In addition, everywhere women are the poorest of the poor with very limited livelihood resources or access to them. The Human Development Report, 1997 has this much to say on the issue of poverty and women:

"Poverty affects women more severely. Already suffering from societal bias, they are more vulnerable than men and bear a heavier burden when poverty strikes. Poverty and gender are inextricably linked—gender inequality is strongly linked to human poverty. Generally, the face of poverty is changing, but female poverty continues to remain a constant factor."

Tackling of poverty issue in a democracy is a ticklish problem not because of "a Government of the people, by the people, for the people." Here, in India as in most countries, women are severely under—represented in decision—making levels. The efficacy of democracy for the good of the people, including women, in such a situation is doubtful. Look at our own planning process. In the early stages of our Plan era, women as a target group did not receive any specific cogent treatment. It took four Five Year Plans to mount specific plan strategies to meet the minimum needs of rural population in which female members of the family have high stakes. Rural poverty alleviation programmes by all counts constitute one of the largest segments of our development plan. A succinct account of the erosion of standards in administering development programmes and declining status of implementing structure in a vibrant democracy where fifty per cent of voters are women, is to be found in the report of the Task Force on Self-Managed Institutions for Integrated Development (Planning Commission, 1991). The Report states: "The entire pool of resources for development available in the country has been so allocated that they support proliferation of officialdom and bureaucracy. Little expenditure on priority areas of education, health, agriculture and energy is planned."

Women sustain the community

Women's place in every community is vital to the well-being of that society; without them both in the formal sector and in the family, most communities would not survive. It is now well recognized that enhancing women's status and enforcing their rights on an equal basis with men will do much to achieve the objectives of Equality, Development and Peace adopted at the Fourth World Conference on Women held in Beijing in September, 1995. These are the guideposts for nations and movements to take note of and act upon.

In conclusion, it may be said that for women, democracy is the best suited political system for the system provides for women representation at all decision-making levels. However, equality and gender justice cannot be had through fragmented and routine approach. In the structure that supports democracy and governance women must be represented not merely by the fact that they are females but by women of dedication understanding and goodwill. It should not degenerate into a statistical phenomenon of filling up "male"/"female" columns in a proforma.

Vande Mataram!

Socio-economic development of women

May I, at the outset acclaim the aptness of the theme of the workshop. The role the women politicians and parliamentarians could assume may largely influence development options affecting half the population of every nation directly and much more indirectly through promotion of regional cooperation. The women functionaries in political parties and parliamentary institutions have opportunities and capabilities not only to understand and convey the needs and aspirations of the common people to the decision making and implementing authorities but also the authority to ensure that the intended benefits reach the target group of women in full measure.

The topic of this working session is so wide and all embracing that every aspect of women's concerns and development will ultimately have a bearing on the socio-economic sphere. India's emphasis in all programme has been on improving the socioeconomic conditions of the disadvantaged and deserving population groups like women, particularly in rural areas. They deserved higher priority not only because of egalitarian and humanitarian ideals but also because it had been proved that the long term social rate of return on investments on these groups could be the highest.

The ultimate goal of development planning is improvement in the quality of life. This not only includes the efforts for accelerating economic growth but also those bearing on the distribution of economic prosperity, removal of disparities and the creation of a healthy vibrant, homogenous polity.

The last five decades have been extremely important for Indian women. This period witnessed far-reaching developments in almost all spheres—political, economic and social. In terms of constitutional, legal and administrative measures, many initiatives were taken. Prominent among them are the constitutional provisions for gender equity and justice, enactment of new laws and amendment of existing laws to protect and promote the interests of women, setting up of women-specific administrative and economic structures like separate Women and Child Development Department at the Union and State Governments levels, constitution of the National Commission for Women in several States, State Women Development Corporations, orientation in plan strategy to include women specific and women-related programmes, launching of special schemes like Rashtriya Mahila Kosh and Mahila Samridhi Yojana, Indira Mahila Yojana and the foremost among them all, the provision to reserve for women one-third number of seats by direct election in Panchayats and Urban local bodies as also offices in specified rural and urban local self-government institutions.

The UN perspective for women's development

The United Nation's document entitled Platform for Action (PFA) tabled and adopted at the World Conference on Women at Beijing listed out a dozen dimensions in respect of women development. These twelve areas are required to be redressed through concrete government and NGO actions. Here the women political workers and women legislators can contribute immensely in realizing the desired goals. The areas identified are :

(1) the persistent and increasing burden of poverty on women,

(2) unequal access to and inadequate educational opportunities,

(3) inequalities in access to health and related services,

(4) violence against women,

(5) peace and conflict resolution and their impact on women,

(6) gender equality in economic structures and employment,

(7) participation in decision-making at all levels,

(8) mechanisms to promote advancement of women,

(9) women rights as human rights,

(10) access to communication,

(11) women and environment, and, lastly

(12) survival of the girl child.

This is a timely and commendable effort. In general, all these areas are relevant to our country as well as those of the neighbourhood. India has welcomed these action points.

Education of the girl-child is the best remedy to correct the imbalance in development process vitiated by gender disparity. Indeed, no cost is too high to achieve it. "Destiny of India is now being shaped in her classrooms", declared the Education Commission (1964-66) in their report. It is unfortunate that females constituting almost half the population of the country have missed their "tryst" with destiny. Even after a quarter of a century , since the stirring assertion of the Education Commission, the female literacy rate, according to the 1991 Census is only 39.19 per cent as against 64.20 per cent for males. In respect of female education in our country, we may not be wanting two much in theoretical formulations and planning strategies. Our major weakness seems to be lack of sincerity in execution and vigour in implementation.

"The web of poverty is too frail to bear the weight of

gender." Someone had remarked that "women are like rails, they carry the burden but if they are moved then it means society will be derailed and there will be chaos." Women are important economic agents. Women's income in the poverty groups is critical for household survival. The subject is so vast that time does not permit to go into the details, suffice it to say that there is an urgent need to ensure timely and effective economic resources like credit, skill upgradation and skill formation, organizational support, marketing facilities, working atmosphere and generally an appreciative outlook towards women in economic activities both in rural and urban areas.

Noted economist Amartya Sen had recently opined that "India's population problem has only one remedy; social development in a gender-sensitive way what is required to check the growth in fertility rate is education, social awareness and emancipation of women."

Although women provide health care to the whole household, their own access to health care is generally limited. The factors responsible for women's lower reach to health facilities are lack of sufficient protection, lack of capacity to meet the cost of the facility and lack of a felt need to avail the services. However, the expectancy of life for women at birth as per latest projections is marginally higher than men, this being 61.2 years as against 60.6 years for men.

An added dimension to the general proposition as contained in the twelve items listed, insofar as it relates to India would be, the wide rural-urban differences as well as some socially and economically backward communities, e.g. the Scheduled Castes and the Scheduled Tribes women. In addition to this, a specific strategy would need to be worked out to direct interventions in respect of different income groups.

In tackling the socio-economic problems of women in

India different strategies have been adopted. These include area approach, target group approach and individual beneficiary approach. What has been found in many cases is an absence of coordinated, cohesive and complementary approach. Sometimes, there is even competitiveness in achieving "targets" by different governmental agencies. These need to be corrected.

We have done much, but much more remains to be done. Sometimes critics in our country harp on what has not been done but the truth is that they shy away from saying what has indeed been done by us so far, not only in the realm of women's development but in other spheres as well. We have achieved tremendous progress in notable areas though we could have done still better. The journey towards progress is long and arduous. In a world of challenges and competition, we have to constantly attune ourselves to demanding needs, which we are now accustomed to adjust to. Lasting progress could be achieved when we are able to tackle issues at household and family levels, both in urban and rural areas. Socio-economic development will have content and meaning when the family members enjoy the fruits of development in an atmosphere of contentment.

In the context of prevalent phase of India's development, having intense bearing on economic, social and political spheres, it is perhaps not necessary that one should spell out the nuances through which the system works in bringing about gender equality and gender justice. May I hope that these remarks, though inadequate, will generate adequate responses for a meaningful discussion.

We will regret we lived in the age of decline and decadence. History spares none and posterity will never pardon us.

I shall not begin, as I probably should by offering to define terms. Transformative politics is a loaded word in that it reflects a dynamic situation with critical variables. It also encompasses different regions, social groups and economic status of widely varying nature. In a country like ours, which has often been described as a nation exhibiting "unity in diversity"; transformative politics also reflects varying shades and shapes. The status of women in such a hetrogenous setting undergoes dominant changes under the influence of politics.

The last two decades have been marked by the growth and development of women's movement. During preindependence period it was a part of the freedom struggle. Events over the last few years have demonstrated that in Indian politics, there is a lot of difference between political theory and practice, concepts or preachings and acts. It is significant that despite proclaiming in unambiguous terms the intention of the political parties to accord $33_{1/3}$ per cent reservation in State Legislative Assemblies and Lok Sabha for women as manifested in their election manifestoes it was not converted into practice when the occasion arose to demonstrate their unhindered support during the tabling of Joint Select Committee Report on 81st Constitutional Amendment.

Rights and equality : how to attain

Women's rights and women's equality cannot be achieved unless women in large numbers are visible and active. With this end in view, the National Commission for Women has been advocating distribution of tickets for more women candidates and further have been lobbying for this with the various political parties on the eve of the Lok Sabha elections.

Despite our efforts only a limited number of women got the tickets from the various political parties—491 out of a total of 14,724 candidates were women. There were large number of spurious arguments on the part of the political parties to prefer men over women. This is despite the fact that under the Panchayati Raj and Municipality Act (73rd and 74th Amendments to the Constitution) one-third of the total members have been women. They have also been functioning more or less effectively and enthusiastically in the length and breadth of the country.

NCW, hence, undertook a study to examine the various factors which contribute to the success/failure of the women (and men candidates) in the elections. How valid and correct are the various arguments laid against women candidates? The study was undertaken in six Lok Sabha constituencies across the nation from where women candidates contested—South Calcutta (West Bengal), Gaya (Bihar), Hapur-Ghaziabad (UP), Ludhiana (Punjab), South Madras (Tamil Nadu) and South Delhi (NCT of Delhi). The studies were undertaken by Women's Studies Centres and Women's Research Organizations on behalf of the NCW.

The study revealed that women's political empowerment and equal participation in all decision-making institutions are critical elements in the struggle against their subordinate status within the family and society.

The two major obstacles for more women not emerging in political sphere are lack of support from family and friends, women's fear of the world of politics which has become aggressive and competitive and lack of infrastructural facilities and strong family background. Thankfully, the trend is slightly changing because of political awareness. Let not gender equality suffer in transformative politics.

Female respondents reported that if more women came into power, politics would become cleaner. Given the chance, women can run the country more effectively since they have the experience of running the family. Further, the shift in the election campaign has to be in positive direction to enable the electorate to cast its positive vote instead of the negative vote by rejecting those with greater demerits.

The irony of the situation is that women are not even treated as a political constituency to be wooed and won, much less as political actors on their own right.

Political will needed

The criterion for political parties selection of the women contestants were work in the constituency, but is not based on party affiliatious or on other considerations, which had not at all political. There were exceptions, however. The parties reflect the established values of a male dominated society, which would be difficult to alter without certain structural changes in the socio-political set-up and herein lies the need for a directed approach in clean politics.

Women's political pressure groups should encourage and build confidence among women with the necessary political will and commitment to contest for political offices in the forthcoming elections. Sincere and committed persons should enter politics and change the state of affairs.

Women parliamentarians should be aware of their rights and strength and train themselves in parliamentary procedures and in the art of influencing parliamentary decisions.

Networking of women's groups in support of women contestants cutting across parties and regions, is required. Women should come together to take up issues, directly relevant to them. Women's groups need to look into the possibility of setting up a trust/fund to support them in the initial stages of the move to ensure gender equality in politics.

Independence brought with it the opportunity for equality in the social and political spheres through the instrumentality of the Constitution. Nevertheless, women remained under-represented in the decision-making bodies, although they were in the forefront of national movement as well as various social reform movements. Their presence in representative institutions was never commensurate with their strength in national life. In the fiftieth year of India's Independence, this lopsided and imbalanced state needs to be reversed and the women in India must attain their rightful place.

It is worthwhile recalling what the Committee on Status of Women which submitted its report on the eve of the International Women's Year, December, 1974 observed:

> The reason for this lack of concern among the political elite to the problems of women is the absence of an active women's movement. While the number of political organizations seeking to mobilize women is now higher than in the earlier period, their identification with different political parties prevents most of them from arousing women's consciousness for the solution of the problems which are specific to women.

Thus, alongwith this passivity the emergence of autonomous organizations and revitalization of some of the mainstream organizations, has been one of the major achievements of the two decades of Indian women's movement.

Today, it is no more the absence of strong, vibrant, dynamic and purposive women's movement that prevents empowerment of women, but to my mind it appears that the transformative politics is afraid of women's power. Men fear losing 1/3rd seats but they should be emboldened by the fact that they are strengthening the nation by agreeing to share power with women in a spirit of cooperation and partnership. Women in transformative politics of representative coalition governments, common minimum programmes and united fronts would achieve much more for the people and for the country in pursuit of strengthening democracy and democratic institutions and achieving gender equality. Let us hope that fifty year's experience would surely pave the way for heralding a new era of gender equality and gender justice.

Women in Decision making

It gives me great pleasure to address you at this Commonwealth Heads of Government NGOs forum. It is an excellent opportunity to meet hundreds of field functionaries from all over the Commonwealth. The British Council deserves congratulations for facilitating this meet and helps achieve common goals towards progress of women. I bring with me the greetings of 450 million women of India when we are celebrating the 50th year of our Independence.

It would be appropriate at this moment to recall what the Universal Declaration of Human Rights states on the subject: "Everyone has the right to take part in the government of his/her country". The United Nations Economic and Social Council endorsed a target of 30 per cent women in all levels of decision-making by 1995. In spite of this, globallys women constitute ten per cent of legislative bodies and less in parliamentary positions. The countrywise position in respect of selected few is as follows :

Per cent of Parliamentary Seats in the Lower House Occupied by Women in Selected Countries, 1994

Australia	9	Mexico	8
Austria	21	Netherlands	31
Bangladesh	10*	New Zealand	21
Belgium	9	Norway	39
Chile	8	Poland	13
Czech Republic	10	Russian Federation	10
Denmark	33	Sweden	34

Finland	39	Thailand	4
France	6	Turkey	2
Germany	21	UK	9
India	7#	U S A :	
Japan	3	Senate	9
		House of Representatives	11

* 30 seats are reserved for women, chosen by the elected MPs.

The 1996 figure has dropped to 6.4 per cent.

In some of the State Legislatures of India, we had as high as 18 per cent women members.

Representation of Women in State Legislatures

States/UTs	*Year*	*Total*	*Women*	*Year*	*Total*	*Women*
Andhra Pradesh	1957	252	11	1994	294	9
Karnataka	1957	179	18	1994	224	7
Kerala	1957	127	6	1991	140	8
Madhya Pradesh	1957	218	26	1993	320	12
Punjab	1957	101	5	1992	117	6
Rajasthan	1957	136	9	1994	200	9
Tripura	1957	30	0	1992	60	2
Uttar Pradesh	1957	341	24	1993	425	12
West Bengal	1957	195	11	1991	294	18
Delhi	1972	56	3	1993	70	3

While dealing with gender issues, it is important to mention that the Constitution of India has guaranteed equality before law and equal protection of laws (Article 14) and prohibits discrimination on the grounds of sex and it has empowered the state to make special provision for women and children (Article 15). It has made provisions to prohibit traffic in human beings and for just and human conditions of work and maternity relief (Articles 23 and

42). It is a constitutional duty of every citizen to renounce practices derogatory to the dignity of women (Article 51A). One-third of seats in local bodies are reserved for women (Article 243D). There is a plethora of legislations in the form of affirmative action to protect, ameliorate and empower women which could be brought into the 'result equality' approach of legal feminism.

We are fortunate that in our country, there is a well established tradition whereby political parties, opinion makers, public leaders and social activists do not generally oppose moves for women empowerment or very strongly object or disapprove measures aimed at bringing about gender equality and gender justice. The evidence is not far to seek as demonstrated in the case of 81st Constitution (Amendment) Bill proposing for $33_{1/3}$ per cent reservation for women in State Assemblies and Lower House of Parliament, or as it happened in the case of 73rd and 74th Constitution Amendment Acts providing reservation of 1/3rd seats in rural (Panchayati Raj) and urban (Municipalitics and Corporation, local bodies) local bodies, or in enacting social legislations to curb harassment and oppression of women or to improve the status of women.

The widespread and vibrant women's movement in my country has been responsible for catalyzing changes in attitudes, policies and laws. Realizing that knowledge is power and awareness, sensitization and enlightenment are the prerequisites for changes in social system. The National Commission for Women in India, of which I have the privilege to be the Chairperson, have taken up measures in this direction.

In our country, the basic issue has been as to how can the goals of empowerment of women and enlightenment of men be achieved so that gender equity and gender justice prevails. At the outset, we need to acknowledge our immeasurable indebtedness to the thousands of women who have sensitized us, as we have tried to sensitize them, through our programmes and frequent exchange of views in meetings, seminars, conferences, etc. In particular, in the NCW, we focussed attention on certain thrust areas, namely, speedy justice for women (through Parivarik Mahila Lok Adalats); Legal Awareness Programme, custodial justice, steps towards rehabilitation of women and children in prostitution, widows, women in mental asylum, released women prisoners, destitute; and also anti-arrack movement. The Members of the Commission and as also myself have visited 345 districts of the country to gain first-hand knowledge of the problems facing women belonging to different social groups. When I used to ask," What do women want?" the answer has always been "full and equal partnership with men in all aspects of development, governance and in society."

An extensive programme of legal literacy awareness was sponsored by NCW through women's colleges. So far 160 colleges in the country have conducted training covering about 13,000 teachers and girl students. Apart from this, six regional legal literacy sources were held in different regions in which thousands of women participated.

Realizing that the women members in Panchayat Raj bodies require awareness and training, NCW sponsored 40 such training camps in rural areas wherein hundreds of women attended. These are all promotional steps towards empowerment of women.

All our efforts have been to prepare our sisters to make them aware of their responsibilities in shouldering power and being at decision-making levels.

Government commitment to empowerment of women

As observed earlier, we as a nation are committed to the empowerment of women. In clear terms, country's approach paper to the Ninth Five Year Plan (1997-2002) commits:

> An integrated approach will be adopted towards empowering women. This underscores harmonization of various efforts on different fronts, viz., social, economic, legal and political. Further, a special strategy of earmarking of funds as 'women's component' will also be adopted with a close vigil to ensure a flow of adequate share of resources and benefits for women from all development sectors both in the Center and States. To this effect, the Ninth Plan recommends expeditious adoption of the 'National Policy for Empowering Women' along with a well defined Gender Development Index to monitor the impact of its implementation in raising the status of women from time to time.
>
> In the political and administrative spheres, the proposed strategy of quota system for women both in Parliament and State Legislatures and also in Services will be adopted so as to strike a gender balance in decision making.
>
> For capacity building of women, it is essential that attention is paid to their health, especially the reproductive health and their access to health care services. A life cycle approach to women's health with a special focus on reproductive health and choices will be adopted.
>
> Economic empowerment of women is based on their participation in decision making process with regard to raising and distribution of resources, i.e. incomes, investments and expenditure at all levels. The entire effort of empowering women is to help them to exercise their rights in decision-making at all levels and in every sphere both within and outside the household as equal partners in the society.
>
> A media policy will be framed in such a way that it

becomes an instrument in projecting a positive image of the girl child and women. Strict ban on the depiction of demeaning, degrading, negative and conventional stereotypical images of women and violence against women will be enforced through legislation, regulatory mechanisms and media policies.

In civil services, many provincial governments have legislations providing for 30 per cent reservation for women.

India had made five commitments at the Beijing Conference.

These were:

(i) Formulation of a National Policy on Women.

(ii) Increased investment of 6 per cent GDP on education by 2000 A.D.

(iii) Universalization of mother and child care programme through the Integrated Child Development Services (ICDS) Schemes; and

(iv) Setting up of Commissioner for Women's Rights.

As a follow-up to this commitment, a National Policy for the Empowerment of Women has been drafted after wide ranging consultations throughout the country. The proposed National Policy will continuously guide and inform action and policy in every sector, by incorporating a gender perspective into all plans, policies, programmes, budgetary allocations, appraisals, monitoring and evaluatory exercises.

As a part of support services we have committed to universalizing child care services. We have since done that by sanctioning ICDS projects in the whole country which include 5291 Community Development Blocks and 310 major urban slums in the country. The scheme had been operationalized in nearly 4000 blocks and preparatory work has been started in the remaining areas. We are in the process of finalizing Gender Development Indices and situational profiles of states and districts. This is expected to channelize Social Development programmes with greater intensity in the areas where low levels of development are indicated.

Setting up of Commission for Women's Rights is also likely to materialize soon for which necessary ground-work has been initiated.

In brief, the process of increasing women's representation at decision making levels is proceeding with commitment and dedication. We are confident that as in many other matters like democracy, peace, international cooperation—India will lead the way in protecting and promoting gender justice.

Vande Mataram!

IMPARTING OF SKILLS TO WOMEN

"Our glory lies not in ever falling, but rising everytime we fall"

KARUNA needs no introduction. It's President, Smt. Margaret Alva is not merely a Member of Parliament but a vibrant and dynamic activist promoting the cause of Indian women everywhere. Earlier, a national workshop on training of women elected to Panchayats was organized in Delhi. As a follow-up, four regional workshops are to be held and this is first of the regional workshop. Undoubtedly, these small efforts go a long way in strengthening the local self-government machinery and empowerment of women.

Our democracy is 50 years young. We are preparing to celebrate the Golden Jubilee year of our Independence. It is opportune that at this moment in our polity we take stock of the need to create increased awareness among women to involve them more and more at decision making levels. Needless to say that parliamentary democracy is the rule of the majority. 50 per cent of the women population cannot be left behind in the country's march towards attaining the goals of justice, liberty, equality and fraternity under a well established regime of social, sovereign, socialist, secular, democratic republic.

To bring about a meaningful training programme at the rural and urban levels for women elected to local bodies, and to make them aware of their powers and duties constant efforts are required. A large measure of funds would be in their hands now. The accountability rests with those elected to the local self-government institutions, i.e. the Panchayats, the Municipalities and the Corporations. The financial provision during 8th Plan for rural development alone was Rs. 30, 000/- crores. It will be manifold during the 9th Plan. In order to bring about sustainable development by removing glaring inequities and poverty conditions prevailing in most parts of our country, the women representatives at these grass roots level institutions may have to share and discharge heavy responsibilities. This training programme, as well as many more that would follow are aimed at empowering women representatives to enhance their capabilities to administer policies and programmes in Panchayat and urban areas to bring about perceptible, balanced and sustainable development.

I would like to conclude by emphasizing the fact that learning and becoming aware, is a continuous process. Training workshops help in maintaining this continuity. T.S. Eliot once lamented that "humanity had lost its wisdom in the acquisition of knowledge. "The process of learning, always leads to a progressive acquisition of ignorance." The only thing I know" said Socrates, the most learned man of his time, "is the fact of my ignorance". Let these small efforts of ours help reduce such ignorance.

EMPOWERMENT OF WOMEN

I consider it a privilege and an honour that I have been selected for the Bhavna Jain National Award for Social Awareness and National Harmony. Many qualities have been attributed to me. I am not very sure whether I really possess them. I shall certainly try to do so.

I will be attempting an impossible task if I start explaining who Swami Vivekananda was. The only answer one can give in brief is, "Who was he not? And what was he not?". Humility, courage, renunciation, service—these are all the ideals which Swami Vivekananda put before us. Let us remember the lessons he taught us, and not merely utter them but assimilate them into our very being.

> Woman is the companion of man, gifted with equal mental capacities. She has the right to participate in every minute detail in the activities of man and she has an equal right of freedom and liberty with him... By sheer force of a vicious custom, even the most ignorant and worthless men have been enjoying a superiority over women which they do not deserve and ought not to have. Many of our movements stop halfway because of the conditions of our women. Much of our work done does not yield appropriate results; our lot is like that of the pennywise and poundfoolish trader who does not employ enough capital in his business.

During the past $2_{1/2}$ years, I visited 345 districts in the country and when I used to ask "what do women want?" the answer has always been "full and equal partnership with men in all respects of development—governance and in society."

Empowerment of women, meaning thereby adequate access to resources, power and decision-making is a prerequisite towards gender justice. Such a situation can come about when there is equal participation in decision making at family, society and other institutions of government. It needs to be recognized that any strategy which aims to empower women must be based on an understanding of, and to overcome the causes of the lack of power which lie behind it. While there is much debate at the theoretical level as to what empowerment comprises and how best it can be achieved, there has not been enough study at the grass roots level covering, different strata of society as also urban-rural-tribal regions to contribute to our understanding of what empowerment means in everyday terms. Before one can find a satisfactory answer, the questions that would emerge would be : (1) what are the causes of the subordination or oppression of women; (2) is it that women's powerlessness is because of patriarchy as an over-arching gender system which determines women's role and relationships; (3) is it that women experience subordination or powerlessness in all domains.

The usual strategy adopted to empower women could be broadly classified into three categories :

(1) integrated development approach; (2) economic approach; and (3) consciousness raising-cum-organizing approach. In the first category, that of advocating integrated development approach, the assumption is that women's disempowerment is due to their lack of education, low economic status, lack of access to resources and low decision-making power. The second category, i.e. economic intervention is considered necessary because of their low economic status and consequent dependence as also due to their lack of decision making power. In the third strategy, i.e. through awareness building, the premise is that disempowerment is a result of complex interplay of historical, cultural, social, economic and political factors.

While dealing with a complex issue like empowerment of women, it has to be conceded that the life of a human being is many - sided. There is an economic aspect, a legal aspect, a political aspect, an aesthetic aspect, a personal aspect, a religious aspect and so forth, but blending into them all is the social aspect. Society is the marvelously intricate and ever-changing pattern of the totality of these relationships. Empowerment of women is influenced and determined to a very great degree by societal attitudes towards gender issues.

When we are to deal with empowerment which has close social relationships, we must discriminate their specific forms, varieties and patterns. We must observe how they criss-cross and how they combine. We must note their responsiveness to changing conditions, changing demands and changing needs. These will enable us to adopt acceptable strategies.

Women's issues cannot be considered in isolation. It is the society which liberates and limits the activities of human beings, sets up standards for men to follow and maintain whatever the imperfections and tyrannies it has exhibited in human history, as it is a necessary condition of every fulfillment of life. Society is a system of usages and procedures, of authority and mutual aid, of many groupings and divisions, of controls of human behaviour and of liberties. It is the web of social relationships. And it is always changing.

The Commission felt that many of the laws that were framed prior to Independence were not women-friendly and also not relevant to the present-day needs. Many legislations concerning women have been taken up for review. Recommendations in respect of 14 bills have been sent to the Government of India for revision.

It is my conviction that empowerment of women can take place only in an atmosphere of "give and take" attitude and partnership accord. It is also my firm belief that for any improvement to take place in the status of women, the society has to render unhindered cooperation.

We are aware that many social legislations aimed at improving the status of women are not really implemented for want of social acceptance, e.g. Dowry Prohibition Act, Child Marriage Restraint Act, etc. Our endeavour should be to inform and influence the society about the need to enlist men and women in partnership towards progress of every section of people—men, women and children. There is too much of violence against women but the society remains a silent spectator. Men opress women not because of their biology, nor because they are innately more aggressive, they do so because they benefit from doing so. This is the origin of 'class' legislation creating and upholding an insurmountable difference between the sexes.

I would appeal to every citizen of this country not to neglect one's duty to our fellow human being, be it man or woman and treat everyone with honour and dignity.

Participation of women in public affairs

The National Commissicn for Women considers it a privilege and an honour to be associated in this 50th year of our Independence, with a function in the Institute dedicated to the memory of Madabhushi Ananthasayanam Ayyanagar, an illustrious son of India. I am happy that the Institute has chosen an extremely important national issue for its symposium in that "Participation of Women in Public Affairs" is both a subject of topical interest and potential instrument for social change.

Public affairs, as such, is a very vast topic. In our present times when the State as an agent of society, is taking upon itself more and more areas of common interest to the citizens, the realm of public affairs goes beyond an easy definition. Public affairs certainly denotes those activities involved in carrying out the policies and programmes of Government which includes planning, organizing, directing, coordinating and controlling of Government operations. In India, this will indicate broadly the functions of the executive. To my mind, we must also include such of those functions under the legislative and judiciary as well in the definition of public affairs. Thus, the topic covers a very wide field. I note from the structure of the symposium that many of these items would be covered during the deliberations today.

In order to appreciate in its proper perspective the relevance of the topic of the symposium, it would be appropriate that we have an understanding of the current status of women in our country.

Women's deprivation has many facets. These encompass not only denial of social and economic rights, but civil and political rights as well. In every society, women are denied opportunities which can be economic, political and social in every field, be it access to health and basic education, employment, information and technology, access to productive assets, access to shelter and so on.

One of the main reasons impeding the march of our Indian women to progress and equality is the essential structure itself. Unless the archaic patriarchal attitude towards women is altered, no positive changes can happen in the affairs of any nation. I am reminded of the characteristic words of the scientist Erasmus Darwin, who summed up such an attitude :

> The female character should possess the mild and retiring virtues rather than the bold and dazzling ones, great eminence in almost everything is sometimes injurious to a young lady; whose temper and disposition should appear to be pliant rather than robust; to be ready to take impressions rather than to be decidedly marked, great apparent strength of character, however, excellent is liable to alarm both her own and the other sex, and to create admiration

rather than affection."

(Quoted by R.M. Maciver and C.I. Page, Society, An Introductory Analysis, 1950).

To manage public affairs, the crucial prerequisite that a person must possess is education. Let us have a look at the female literacy scenario in country.

Despite intensive efforts to improve literacy levels, it has been low. Literacy rose from 18.3 per cent in 1951 to 52.2 per cent in 1991. The sex differentials in literacy are very pronounced. While the male literacy rate in 1991 was 64.1 per cent, female literacy rate was 25 percentage point has persisted from 1961. There are Scheduled Tribe Communities with less than one per cent literates. This is a dismal situation. It is recognized that knowledge is an important element of human development for it constitutes the basis for expanding opportunities and making informed choices. Being educated is not only a valuable achievement in itself but also enables one to achieve other goals they value. Knowledge is empowerment.

Employment of women is an index of their economic status in the society, especially with reference to equality. According to the census data, the work participation rate (i.e. proportion of employed or total workers to population) of females rose from 14.22 per cent in 1971 to 19.67 in 1981 and to 22.27 in 1991. The rise in work participation of rural females is even steeper from 15.92 in 1971 to 26.79 in 1991. The rise in work participation of urban females is much less impressive between 1971 and 1991 starting from a low level of 7.18 per cent to 9.19 per cent. During the 1991 census, conscious efforts were made to count women workers more completely and remove their invisibility. This could have also contributed to the increase in the work participation ratio between 1981 to 1991.

A matter of great concern is the unemployment rates

for female workers. The rate of unemployment is more significant for urban females at 4.7 per cent compared to 0.3 per cent for rural females.

The founding fathers of our Constitution, realizing the handicaps of socially disadvantaged groups, incorporated in our Constitution positive discrimination provisions, for example, for the Scheduled Castes and the Scheduled Tribes, Women and Children. The provision for "reservation" is a unifying instrument and not a divisive mechanism. It was believed that by providing seats in the legislature, the executive and the educational institutions for some specified groups, the socially depressed and the deprived would be enabled to join the main body of the nation in ushering in an egalitarian society. Our earlier statesmen, constitutional experts and leadership did not anticipate that this socially relevant mechanism will in times to come be employed by self-seeking politicians to create bitterness, caste-based vote banks and perpetuate the male-female divide.

We are all aware that the representation of women in State legislatures, Parliament, public services of the State and the Central Government are very low. Facts need no evidence. One can prove with statistics the grossly inadequate representation of women in all these fields, which may be termed as public affairs. I quote the conversation between Tagore and Gandhi. "Once Gurudev Rabindranath Tagore asked Gandhiji :

> Gandhiji are you so unromantic? When in the early dawn, the morning sun rises, does it not fill your heart with joy to see its reddish glow? When the birds sing does not your heart thrill with its divine music? When the rose opens its petals and blooms in the garden does its sight not bring cheer to your heart?" The Mahatma replied "Gurudev, I am not so dumb or insensitive, as not to be moved by the beauty of the rose or the morning rays of the sun or the divine

music of the birds. But what can I do? My one desire, my one anxiety, my one ambition is when shall I see the red tint of the rose on the cheeks of hungry naked women? When shall I hear the sweet and melodious song of the birds in place of the agonizing sigh of the women? When will such music come out of their sound and when will that day come when the light of the morning sun will illumine the heart of the common women in India? When will I see its lustre and brightness on her face?

I have briefly touched upon some of the important areas, leaving many others. There cannot be any disagreement that women's participation in public affairs should be much more than what is obtaining today in order to ensure efficient, equitable and harmonious structure that would benefit all our people. I do hope that the symposium will discuss all the concerned issues. I am confident that the suggestions and recommendations of the symposium would be helpful in building a more healthy and prosperous nation.

Status of Women in Developing Nations

We are passing through a critical stage in human development. There are perceptible disturbances and disharmony in societies of many countries, not merely because of economic deprivation and disparities but also due to ethnic conflicts, gender discrimination and exploitation of one human being by another. One wonders, whether even after some 20 million years of life upon this planet, the lot of major part of humanity is still, as Hobbes once described it as "solitary, poor, nasty, brutish and short". To clarify this statement one has to turn the pages of history. What a sordid and miserable plight it would have been with people toiling to meet their needs without the aid and support of modern tools, sophisticated gadgets and skills available with the advancement of science and technology. Today, we have leaped forward manifold, particularly in terms of superior technology and communication advancement. The distance between places have been vastly reduced and one is able to comprehend the happenings in any remote part of the world instantly and intimately. There has thus been a lot of bridging in terms of sharing ideas and material benefits primarily due to this space reduction.

Notwithstanding this advancement, the primitive and primordial instincts of man are still clothed in a very thin veil of civilization. Man is still the exploiter of mankind. The strong exploit the weak : the process goes on, warranting human rights safeguards to protect the exploited. Greed, lust, authority, superstition, regionalism, parochialism religious intolerance and the like divide human beings. The challenges before women all over the world, nay, the entire humanity is, therefore, to work towards curbing tendencies of human beings capable of intimidating, interrupting and intervening the process of furthering growth in a most humane way guaranteeing peace, progress and prosperity to every individual man and women like in a civlized manner.

In my understanding, the two prominent obstacles to rapid balanced and sustainable development would be poverty and illiteracy. The poverty levels of many developing countries in Asia, Africa and Latin America, pose unprecedented challenges to the authorities in its form and intensity. World over, children die due to malnutrition and inadequate food. In many countries, children, especially the girl child are abused beyond comprehension. In such poverty conditions, it is the womenfolk who suffer the most on account of deprivation and family responsibilities. Statisticians and economists tell us that work partcipation of women in almost all societies are more or less equal to men, if not more. The world order tolerates existence of islands of affluence with pockets of penury. The world leadership must acknowledge that deprivation anywhere is a serious obstacle to sustainable development everywhere. Human rights, development, international cooperation and gender justice are all related to one another. The world community has a responsibility to respond to human rights needs everywhere. The trade agreements, tariff treaties and regional alliances must accelerate growth and not hinder development. The challenge, therefore, is to mount a worldwide campaign to educate, propagate and sensitize on the essentials needed to achieve and sustain development guaranteeing human dignity.

In some of the countries, the literacy levels are so low that it becomes difficult to introduce measures that would lead to decent living for all the people. In this illiterate category, women and specific social groups dominate. There have been international conferences on combatting illiteracy among females and also on empowerment strategies. Excellent decisions are taken, millions of rupees are spent; but the results are not commensurate. It appears that lack of community involvement and sincerity in implementation of people-friendly strategies are responsible for negligible gains as a result of which the target groups are left high and dry.

Status of women in India

Let me now add a few words about the conditions in my country. Abode for over four hundred million women, a country acknowledged for its plurality of traditions, customs and institutions and proud of its heritage of eclecticism, India's contribution to womens development has been rich and diverse. India's culture accords a high position to the mother as also family linkages. Because of diverse customs, it would be inaccurate to try and posit a generalized picture of the Indian woman across social, economic and cultural space. The formidable task is to try and capture these contributions, experiences and struggles of the Indian women, their achievements, their concerns, their despairs, their perspectives and their visions in its diversified pattern. The truth of the oft quoted saying "unity in diversity" is to be felt and experienced nowhere else but in India. Areas and intensity of diversity among Indian women are innumerable and generally well known that it is not perhaps necessary for me to recount them here.

A deep concern with the status of women and the recognition that the progress of the nation is integrally linked with the advancement of women, have underpinned Indian approach to planned development since Independence. Mahatma Gandhi was a champion of womens rights. He emphasized that, "subjugation and exploitation of woman was a product of mens interested teachings and womans acceptance of them". The leaders of the nation recognized that freedom gained without the active involvement of women would be a hollow and fragile freedom. The Constitution guarantees equality to women, it also empowers the State to adopt special measures of affirmative discrimination in favour of women. The Constitution further imposes a fundamental duty on every citizen to uphold the dignity of women.

It is ironical that in matters of deprivation and gender discrimination there is a certain amount of uniformity. Lack of education and training and absence of awareness intensify deprivation. In such a situation, women of all groups are excluded not only from political, social and economic power but also from the power of knowledge as well. While comprising half of humanity, contributing two-thirds of the worlds workforce, they earn only one-third of the total income and own less than one-tenth of the worlds resources. The objectives of development are to enlarge peoples choices for a reasonable living and increase peoples capabilities to exercise such choices. When fruits of development reach the intended groups, human rights violations are also curbed, as a consequence. Nowhere are these challenges more stark and daunting than in case of poor women. The situation is aggravated due to a general societal inability and apathy to be able to discern these inadequacies of the development response. Many women are often conditioned into insensitivity and unquestioned submission to biases and discrimination, which they view as socially ordained and irrevocable. It is this ideology of patriarchy and the accompanying culture of silence which needs to be challenged and broken if development is to touch the lives of women, no matter to which diversified groups they may belong to.

It is the empowerment strategy which is today emerging as a unique Indian response to the challenges of gender justice, sustainable development and human rights guarantees. If women are to be empowered, it is necessary to provide support services. If women are to be economically empowered, they are to be provided with additional channels of credit, training, employment, mangement skills and social security. And if women are to be politically empowered, the imperative is to resort to different forms of affirmative discrimination, such as quotas of reservation in various political apparatus, to enable them to participate in decision making process. Women have to be given access to knowledge, power and resources. If women are to be persons in their own right, they must be in control of their own bodies. In India we have moved a long way in all these fronts and the results are not disappointing. A strong womens movement supported by NGOs and national machinery keeps a vigil to ensure gender equality and justice.

It is noteworthy that the last decade of the 20th century has seen the emergence of gender as one of the basic issues of human progress. Concern over the status of women has permeated both thinking and rhetoric. The immediate need to capture womens insight for solving basic problems of poverty, illiteracy, environmental degradation and violence is being felt increasingly and at different levels. The challenges before us is to use this concern and this increased awareness to break the stereotypes and move towards a new generation of men and women working in partnership to build a better world for all of us and posterity.

Let us meet the challenge unitedly and with determination. It cannot be denied that "empowered women constitute nations strength". Let us all work together to make 21st century, the womens century.

---

*Today's opportunities erase yesterday's failures.

8

GENDER JUSTICE

GENDER JUSTICE AND SOCIAL GROUPS

Women all over the country face many handicaps—social, economic and political—preventing their march towards equality, equity, justice, progress, security and safety. In particular, these handicaps are more severe and telling in the case of rural women and among them especially those belonging to the Scheduled Caste and Scheduled Tribe communities. You are all familiar with the extreme cases of deprivation and indignities SC/ST women in some parts of our country have had to suffer. You are all aware that Congress, as a national party is committed to the cause of women and especially the disadvantaged groups like SC/ST women. Our Prime Minister, Hon. P.V. Narasimha Rao has taken many initiatives to consolidate and expand activities and programmes designed to accelerate the development of women. You are all in an advantageous position to assist the deserving SC/ST women because your area of work is closer to their habitation. Before I mention some of the important programmes now under implementation for the benefit of SC/ST women, I wish to emphasize that as field level, grass root workers of an organization committed to social justice and secularism, you have to act as an effective link, a catalytic agent, a philosopher and guide to the hapless SC/ST women. For the discharge of this function meaningfully you have to necessarily acquire knowledge about governmental as also non-governmental programmes. This knowledge is an asset for ever and gainful for access to programmes. This knowledge is the key to prepare SC/ST women to obtain optimum advantage of intended programmes as well as to avoid negligence, nepotism, favouristism and misuse in the implementation of scheme. In essence you are the eyes and ears for the authorities bestowed with implementation duties. You perform a watch dog function so essential in a democratic framework. Well, to put it bluntly, Block and Panchayat level SC/ST women cell workers are the true grass roots level functionaries available to large majority of SC/ST women.

Indeed, the last fifty years have been momentous for Indian women including SC/ST women. This short period in the march of a nation, saw epoch-making initiatives enabling enhanced employment of women in almost all spheres of reckoning. The more important of them and more relevant to SC/ST women include the constitutional provisions enabling positive discrimination in favour of SCs and STs and women, enactment of new laws and amendment of existing laws, such as the Protection of Civil Rights Act, 1995 and the Scheduled Castes and the Scheduled Tribes (Prevention of Atrocities) Act, 1989 to protect and promote the interests of SCs and STs, setting up of SC/ST and women-specific economic, administrative and protective structures like Special Component Plan for Scheduled Castes, Tribal Sub-Plan, National Commission for SC/ST, National Commission for Women, separate state departments for harijan and tribal development as also women child development, separate specific development scheme like pre-matric and post-matric scholarships, other educational incentives, hostels, ashrams, assistance to NGOs, SC/ST and Women Development Corporations, Indira Mahila Yojana, Rashtriya Mahila Kosh, Mahila Samridhi Yojana, National Scheme of Liberation and Rehabilitation of Scavengers, and above all provision for reservation for women and SC/ST against seats to be filled by direct election in Panchayats and urban local bodies as well as offices in specified rural and urban local government institutions. You are all aware of these measures. What is needed is full realization of benefits by SC/ST women from these measures. In the attainment of results, you could lend a helping hand through advice, guidance and counselling.

Our nation is passing through a critical phase in its evolution as a strong democratic country. Challenges are many and rumours far greater in number. As dedicated party workers, you have to conduct yourself in a dignified manner without causing any embarrassment to anyone. I commend your work. Our good wishes are always there in your efforts to bring about perceptible improvement in the working and living conditions of SC/ST women.

I welcome you all to this meeting on my own behalf and on behalf of the National Commission for Women. Although, we in the NCW have done considerable amount of work in regard to strenghtening legal protection for the women by examining laws, constitutional provisions, etc., and recommending amendments, our attention towards specific social groups in regard to their economic needs *vis-a-vis* plans and programmes have not been to the extent we would have liked. We thought it appropriate to designate this 50th year of our Independence as year of gender equality with social justice with the conviction that we have not been able to do as much as we should have, in accordance with the vision of our Father of the Nation, Mahatma Gandhi. Women among the weaker social groups are deprived of the benefits of development not so much because of lack of policy framework and financial provisions. Our experience and study of specific problems particularly those relating to the women of the Scheduled Caste and Scheduled Tribe Communities has been that we have erred in implementation of plans and programmes and have not been able to lay emphasis on reaching actual benefits to the identified specific groups. Otherwise, as we find in some states the literacy percentage of ST communities would not have been as low as of 4 per cent.

We have here senior officers with experience both in the states and the centre. They are fully familiar with the problems of women and the weaker social groups. We have also here the member secretaries from the national level commissions who have specialized knowledge of specific social groups. We in the NCW believe that the present meeting will be useful in channelizing benefits to the women of specific social groups. In particular the issues of prominence insofar as the women of the weaker groups are concerned are those of economic independence, educational problems and working and living conditions. In most of the programmes that are now being implemented under various components we do not have the focus that would enable women of these sections to benefit from. Further, what is lacking is an integrated approach whereby the people could derive maximum benefits in a concrete and sustained manner. One or two other issues which I would like to mention about are :

(1) the need to provide drinking water facilities. These must be available within easy reach; (2) the women headed household should receive priority attention in matters of development inputs; (3) the Member and Secretary, Planning Commission in his letter on formulation of Ninth Five Year Plan has stressed that for the Ninth Plan it may also be desirable to identify a woman component in the various schemes and programmes of the States and Central Ministries.

In a few months from now we will be finalizing the Ninth Five Year Plan. This is an opportune moment to concretize our approach to women of weaker sections and in this effort your contribution would be most vital. I would request each of the ministry and department to provide the needed impetus to the so-far neglected groups and ensure that from the fifty-first year of our independence, our less fortunate sisters would get a better deal.

SEXUAL HARASSMENT AT WORKPLACE

I am thankful to the People's Council for Social Justice to have given me an opportunity to share views on an important topic affecting women, that is harassment of working women. I note that the Council which has just entered its second decade of useful functioning is engaged in propagating legal literacy, especially among women and the Scheduled Tribes.

Legal literacy is vital to usher in social justice in a democracy. This is especially true when the authority of law has to be established not only to protect and promote the interests of women, but also to give full opportunity for their development in an atmosphere where fear and favouritism are absent. Our millions of working women, in the fields, the forests, the factories, the offices, the schools and the colleges are under constant threat of being deprived of their honour, dignity, safety and security. Appropriate counselling when needed by the harassed women provides remedial routes. If one is ignorant about legal remedies, one cannot go to the court to seek redressal of grievances and justice. The People's Council for Social Justice, I am told has an impressive track record of conducting 500 and odd legal literacy classes, about 20 para legal training courses and about 170 Neethi *melas* (Lok Adalat). I wish the Council may continue its good work.

It is not even a month since I took over as Chairperson of the National Commission for Women. The Commission is greatly concerned with problems of harassment of women in general and working women in particular. Hon. Justice Krishna Iyer heading the panel of judges at the public enquiry on crimes against women early this year will recall how deeply concerned, the National Commission for Women was over such issues affecting our young, energetic, hardworking and competent women all over the country.

The Commission had also sponsored a few research studies on employment related issues.

Traditionally, Indian women's occupational profile has been associated with the family and the attitude of particular communities towards working women. After attaining independence, definite and positive changes have been occurring because of what may be termed as 'modernization'. This has occurred, particularly because there have arisen tremendous opportunities for women; there has been substantial rise in educational levels and to some extent attitudinal changes at family and community levels. The working women, in that real sense, is not an addition to the Indian scene. In the real economic sense, women of lower strata have always been in the category of working women. Others work at home and its related fields but these were not recognized. It will be agreed that the level of economic equality and independence are the true indicators to determine the status of women. Employment of women, therefore, is a necessary corollary to achieve gender equity, gender equality and gender justice. No doubt, there are many occupational hazards in case of working women, the prominent among them being 'harassment' because of personal greed, lust, indecent and inhuman behaviour on the part of male colleagues, superiors and others. In the context of recently introduced economic reforms and structural adjustment programmes, there has been a demand from women's movement in the country that in addition to providing safety nets and reducing hardships caused by the new economic policy, it would be essential to explore approaches, in which women are at the centre of the policy changes. It will be agreed that research studies and documentation on various facets of employment of women and the nature, extent and consequences of their exploitation and harassment in different settings are not quite adequate. In this connection, I would like to emphasize that the knowledge of concrete local experience lends credence in formulating specific gender related policy formulations whether it be poverty, employment or harassment. In one recent publication the gender-specific causes and consequences of seasonal rural migration in Orissa, Kerala, Gujarat and Maharashtra have been ably presented. In the book *Women and Seasonal Labour Migration*, graphic details of exploitation and harassment are given. A reading of the book arouses at once a feeling of dissatisfaction with the systems. Then there are the woes of the contract women labourers. Their condition in work sites is deplorable and their exploitation knows no bounds. I feel that there is a need to enquire and study in depth the rural scene in all its manifestations where women toil for their livelihood amidst harassment and exploitation.

I would like to recall four important positive developments which have recently taken place in the context of working women. Firstly, the Supreme Court judgement upholding the constitutional validity of Andhra Pradesh Government orders on reservation of quota for women in public services in the context of the Constitutional provision under Article 15(3).

Secondly, the judgement of the Supreme Court in *Ms. Radha Bai vs Union Territory of Pondicherry and others*, which is about harassment of working women. The judgement delivered by Hon. Justice K.S. Paripoornan indicting the union territory administration observed which I quote, "It cannot be gainsaid that the modesty of a woman is very precious to her from all points of view and when attempts were made to molest her and also to thwart the genuine attempts made by her to set right the undesirable happenings in the shelter home for women, any person placed in the position of appellant will certainly feel annoyed and ashamed. There is every reason for the appellant to feel greatly humiliated. There is bound to be moral indignation or resentment"—unquote. We are all happy that at last justice was done to her, though belatedly. After all the good prevailed over the evil.

Thirdly, the directions of the Supreme Court to the Government of India to formulate guidelines to check sexual harassment at the workplace on a public interest litigation filed by a non-governmental organization called "Vishakha" against the State of Rajasthan. (Refer to Appendix V). The National Commission for Women is closely involved in the task in association with concerned Central Ministries and Departments. I am sure something purposeful would come about in due course.

Fourthly, the concern and sensitiveness displayed by women parliamentarians in the matter. A Bill was moved by Ms. Kamla Sinha in the Parliament in May 1994 to provide for the prevention of sexual harassment of women employees at their workplaces. In the statement of objects and reasons, it was explained by Ms. Sinha that in almost every field of economic activity women form a large part of the workforce. The number of working women is increasing everyday. At the workplace women are compelled to work in the worst service conditions. They are harassed sexually at the workplace by their male colleagues, bosses, employers and others. Cases of sexual harassment of women at the workplaces occur but more often these are not reported for fear of social ostracism, family pressure or reprisal in the form of threats and discriminatory treatment. Though offences like physical assault and molestation have been made punishable under the Indian Penal Code, yet working women feel insecure since all aspects of sexual harassment are not covered by that Code. Accordingly, an urgent need is felt to deal with the situation more stringently. The Bill therefore takes care of the offences related to sexual harassment of women at the workplace.

As the seminar is extremely relevant to formulate possible remedies to the menace of harassment of working women, I dwelt on more areas than I intended to, yet am leaving a large part uncovered. I have great pleasure in inaugurating the seminar. I trust the conclusions will be available to the National Commission for Women on whose behalf I assure that we will do everything possible to mitigate the hardship of our fellow working women to the best of our ability.

*Much is said about what is wrong with India. Not enough about what is right with India.

9

SOCIAL REFORMS AND WOMEN

RELIGION AND WOMEN

Namo Buddhaya

Greetings to you all on this auspicious occasion of 2540th Buddha Jayanti celebrations.

I consider it an honour and a privilege to address you during this special function to commemorate the birth anniversary of a great son of India. The organizers have desired that I should speak on the 'Contributions of Religions to Women's Rights' on this occasion. Well, as Chairperson of the National Commission for Women, the choice has fallen upon me, though I believe that there are competent persons in this august audience to speak on such a vast yet contemporary topic affecting almost half the world's population.

Let me preface my presentation with the observation that in general I propose to deal (i)—more in the Indian context; (ii) as the situation obtains as of now; and (iii) religions' role in the area of social reforms for the benefit of society and in recognition of women's rights.

During the last fifty years since India attained Independence vast changes have taken place affecting the life and work of millions of our people, including women. Under the impact of growth of population, industrialization and urbanization, the weakening of traditional values and institutions including the joint family system and the care and protection they offered to the old and the young, men and women, the weak and the indigent, new social problems have come to the fore and many old social problems have become more intense and complex. Women in all walks of life suffer a great deal. Altogether, strains and stresses on individuals and families have tended to increase without commensurate growth in the capacity of local communities and groups belonging to different religious faiths to find answers to women's problems. Challenges loom larger than before. They are multidimensional in nature and the texture is complex and every aspect takes on a multi-disciplinary dimension as to how far religions have helped in facilitating the womenfolk in resolving crucial issues.

It is the cardinal principle of every religion—be it Buddhism, Hinduism, Jainism, Islam, Christianity, Sikhism, Zoroastrianism,—the religious practices or rituals, the social customs or the position accorded to women, these had to stand the acid test of human welfare or else they would be irrelevant and unacceptable. Indeed, the true aim of every true religion is, reason against superstition and welfare of humanity against discrimination.

Some 5-6 years back an NGO, the Joint Women's Programme, New Delhi had held a National Consultation on the "Authority of the Religions and the Status of Women". The consultation came to the unanimous conclusion that while all religions in their scriptures accorded some status to women, discrimination emerged in practice due to improper interpretation of the scriptures by those who preached the religion. The consultation, inter-alia, stressed the need to view the positive aspects of the religion to establish right relationship in the society. It is here that the social reformers play their role.

Reformist practices prevalent earlier

It may be recalled that during the late eighteenth and

early nineteenth centuries, Protestant missionaries with the support of allies in India and England took the initiative in advocating a number of social reforms in Hindu society. They drew attention to practices such as infanticide, child marriage, the deplorable conditions of widows, the exposure of the sick and dying on the banks of holy rivers, Hook-swinging at the Hindu festivals, the practice of Sati, the prevalence of caste system that dehumanized a great part of the society, bonded labour, exploitation of the poor, etc.

From the beginning, it must be conceded that, the Churches had been the greatest single source of education, till the government stepped in a big way after 1947.

In 1820, Raja Ram Mohan Roy emerged as the first modern Hindu exponent of social reform.

The personal laws of a community in many ways, are a part of the culture of the individuals, like marriage laws, guardianship and wards laws, divorce, adoption and succession. It is now increasingly recognized that Christianity need not find expression through the Western medium of culture; it would be more appropriate for it to find expression though the native medium and indigenous ways.

After independence, the Hindu community has taken advantage of Article 44 of our Constitution (The State shall endeavour to secure for the citizens a uniform civil code throughout the territory of India) and brought forth the Hindu Code Bill that was first framed under a special committee in 1941, and which found its way into the Statute Book in several forms, such as the Hindu Marriage Act of 1955, the Hindu Succession Act of 1956, the Hindu Minority and Guardianship Act of 1956. All these new Acts brought far-reaching changes in the status of Hindu women in society, though the adequacy or otherwise of the quantum of relief could be a matter for further action.

The current position of women governed by personal laws

But the Christian women still live under the Indian Christian Divorce Act, 1869, the Indian Christian Marriage Act, 1872 and the Indian Succession Act, 1865 which are inadequate to meet the requirements of changed social conditions and concepts.

The personal law applicable to a community is a part of their culture, and law should promote justice and equity in the relationship among the members of the community according to the Indian value system, such as protection to a widow, to a dependent mother, and to the woman who suffers under the obsolete Divorce Act of 1869.

It was in 1871 that the Privy Council, in *Skinner Vs Ford (14 Movies Indian Cases 309)* said, "while Brahmin, Buddhist, Christian, Mohammedan, Parsee and Sikhs are one nation, enjoying equal political rights and having perfect equality before the tribunals, they co-exist as separate and very distinct communities having distinct laws affecting every relation of life. The law of husband and wife, parent and child, the descent, devolution and disposition of property, are all different depending in each case on the body to which the individual is deemed to belong and the difference of religion pervades and governs all domestic usages and social relations."

In the present Indian context, notwithstanding the position accorded to women's rights in different religions, the Indian constitutional provisions and the judicial pronouncements thereof have an important bearing in according the rightful place for women in society. The preamble to our Constitution spells out the ideals almost like the surest guarantees to Indian women towards attaining justice, equity, equality and dignity in all matters of public life. This preamble reads:

'We, the people of India, having solemnly resolved to

constitute India into a Sovereign Socialist Secular Democratic Republic and to secure to all its citizens:

Justice, social, economic and political;

Liberty of thought, expression, belief, faith and worship;

Equality of status and of opportunity;

and to promote among them all

Fraternity assuring the dignity of the individual and the unity and integrity of the Nation'.

I am sure, in days to come, the women's movement in the country would gear itself to realize in full measure the equality status enshrined in the Constitution for all India's women.

Hinduism is very catholic. It has no creed, no single prophet and no single sacred book. This enabled Hindu society to adapt to changing conditions and introduce social reforms. One of the earliest social reformers was indeed Buddha. He revolted against the caste system and ritual ridden society. Buddha was followed by Mahavir and Basava Saints like Kabir, Dnyaneshwar and Tukaram also carried on the tradition of social reforms. The effect of their teaching was to humanize society and to emphasize the doctrine of tolerance.

The legal status of Hindu women in ancient India was not as pitiable as it was at the beginning of the 19th century. The reformers turned their attention to women's education and established various institutions. Kardondas Mulji, during 1852 to 1861 through his paper *Satya Prakash* campaigned against the Maharajas, the spiritual heads of the Vaishnava-Vallabha community, who at that time were known for their debauchery and licentiousness. He carried on his fight against the degenerate religious heads, with crusading zeal, with a view to freeing religion from their clutches and restoring to Hindu women their dignity.

Dhondo Keshav Karves' Hindu Widows' Home established in 1896, played a significant role in the social reform movement. In fact, it became a model for similar other homes. Karve's Home was also an educational institution for girls. This was in a sense the humble beginning of the movement of women's education which culminated in the establishment of Dr. Karve's Women University in 1916.

Among Muslim, Christian, Buddhist, Sikh and other religious communities of India, the Jain community occupies an important place.

The Jain community is one of the most ancient communities of India. Their mythological and historical personages, their language and their sacred places have their roots in the traditions and culture of our country. Jainism has special ethical rules of conduct based on the fundamental principle of *Ahimsa*. In view of the close social affinities between the Jains and the Hindus, we find the occurrence and prevalence of similar social conditions and problems among Jains.

There is little or no difference in the teachings of Islam between legal and religious matters. The Islamic way of life, i.e. the Shariat, is comprehensive enough to include beliefs, rituals, practices, public and personal laws, dress, personal appearance and rules of behaviour in social dealings. The formulation of the Islamic code of conduct containing these teachings and incorporating women's rights was accomplished by Muslim scholars two hundred years after the death of the Prophet. The absolute validity of the Quran—the revealed book—was accepted by everyone. In such cases where the Quran was not explicit, reference was made to the sayings and doings of the Prophet, known as traditions or *Hadith.* If no act and opinion of the Prophet could serve as a relevant precedent, the decision was to be made by the consensus of the Muslims (*Ijma*). The consensus or an agreement of the

Muslim scholars or of the community as a whole on a particular issue was to be based on a text of the Quran, the traditions of the Prophet, analogical deductions (*Qias*), or general practice (*Url*).

Reform movements among Muslims of various countries originated in different periods. The first significant movement in India for social reform among Muslims appeared in the first quarter of the nineteenth century under the leadership of Sayyid Ahmed of Rai Bareli (1786-1831). The ultimate aim of the movement initiated by him was the revival of fundamentals of pristine Islam. Later, the Indian modernist movement led by Sir Sayyid Ahmed Khan (1877-1898) had a great influence in spreading educational activities. Moulvi Karamat Hussain and his disciple Sheikh Mohammad Abdullah popularized modern education among female section of Muslim society. The central theme of later efforts led by Dr. Mohammad Iqbal was that Islamic society must create a balance between the elements of performance and the elements of change.

Islamic laws governing personal relations such as marriage, divorce and inheritance had been for long sources of conflict and controversy between the modernists and the conservatives. The three major social institutions affecting women's rights under any religion are marriage, divorce and maintenance, apart from succession to property. These issues are now posing serious challenges almost everywhere, including Muslim personal laws.

I have during this talk covered a large portion of the issue leaving uncovered some portion. The thrust of the issues are, however, very clear.

Conclusion

Let me conclude this talk with the observation that at the level of ultimate divinity, all distinctions vanish, even that between the divine power and the humans; the distinctions of sex also become irrelevant. At the wordly level, different persons perform different duties, but these do not create denial of rights or status differences, even though there could be functional distinctions of superiority, etc. There have been academic and technological advances as well as marked improvements in standard of living of vast majority of the urban and rural people. The prevailing situation is in a state of transition and there are perceptible evidences of a certain sense of crisis among the women of all shades and beliefs, as indeed also among vast majority of men. To me, to our Indian citizens, it appears that apart from religion, the role of the legislature and judiciary will be crucial in coming years in providing equal rights to women of different religions to lead a life worth living and guaranteeing to women, honour, dignity, safety, security and freedom.

*It is prudent to be heard less but is wise to hear more.

10

IMPACT OF DEVELOPMENT EFFORTS

WOMEN'S DEVELOPMENT

I do not know whether those who are getting their lamps lighted on this solemn occasion are going through a new experience, because I am myself undergoing a unique experience.

I can surely say that your experience will in no case be less important than my own.

It is certainly an excellent idea that a lamp should be lit on this day and all those who have attained a certain level of education in this university should light their own lamps and go out into the vast world to use the knowledge and experience that they have gathered here. I have presided over many functions and addressed students at very many places, but I must say that almost all of them were very conventional. I never had the same feeling of a new vision or of opening eyes on new things as I am feeling today.

The symbolism used here is indeed very significant, deep and impressive as it is sure to sink into hearts of those who are to participate in it. On this occasion, I am reminded of the words of Buddha, when he was approached during his last days by one of the nearest of his disciples for a message. He said, *Atma deepo bhava* (Be a light unto thyself). This 'Mother Lamp' which I lit here is the divine light from which you partake of the divine wisdom. You will cherish it all your life as your own. Whenever there is any moment in your life when depression, confusion or darkness set in your mind look into yourself and remember this day when you lit your lamp from there. Ultimately, it must be admitted that one has to depend upon oneself and the light within. This simple symbol of Lighting Ceremony today takes us back to the basic truth of our existence.

Coming to the important part of the ceremony today - to the 'Mother Lamp' itself—I am one of those who have received inspiration from the teachings of Sri Ramakrishna Paramahamsa and Swami Vivekananda. Incidentally, I also learnt Bengali in order that I may understand the teachings of Sri Ramakrishna better. The purpose of mentioning this here is only because I feel that but for Swami Vivekananda, Sri Saradamani Devi and Sri Ramakrishna, the modern India would not have had the same insight into spirituality. Many of our countrymen had come under the influence of these great leaders. The interpretation of life given by them to the world is one of the most cherished contributions of India and a great tribute to them.

As women, many challenges will be there before you in your life. The knowledge and the awareness you have acquired would be of immense value and it must be put into best use for the benefit of not only of self but also of the family, the community and the whole mankind. Please remember that knowledge is power and awareness is the driving force. Let this lighting of lamp light your soul with spirit of conviction and courage to face the realities and challenges of life with competence. My good wishes are there with you always.

It is my request that we must look at this lighting ceremony with these sublime thoughts. It would be realized that there is something deep, brave and powerful in it because many "Shaktis" are having their lamps lit here. I pray to the Almighty to give each one of us light, inspiration, power and provide peace, plenty and prosperity.

Thank you.

EDUCATION FOR WOMEN FOR DEVELOPMENT

'. . . Women hold up half the sky'

— Confucious (commenting upon on the Mandarin ideograph for households).

It is a matter of great satisfaction that FICCI has been in the forefront in contributing towards promotion of education among women. I note that the federation has already organized a few seminars and conferences to deliberate upon the issues that contribute towards evolving a strong educational base to give impetus to economic programmes.

Today, human development is at the centre-stage of debate everywhere. It is a process of enlarging peoples choices. In fact, balanced human development is a synonym of gender justice, gender equality and gender equity. Empowerment can be brought about in a sustainable manner through human development of which education would be a prominent component. The correlation between human development and empowerment needs to be appreciated in order to plan and promote education among women.

The relevance of empowerment and human development does not have to be explained to its "object", "beneficiaries" "target groups", for whom, schooling, health care, access to basic necessities like drinking water have a direct immediacy and relevance. In this sense, we can say that the poor and the marginalized live and breathe the reality of human development. They may not articulate the concept, but as a day-to-day problem of sustenance and of work, it is a direct experience for them.

It is now a decade since the National Policy on Education (1986) was formulated and a series of implementation strategies were outlined. A national system of education was envisaged which would lay the greatest stress on elimination of disparities and promote the equality of women, with special attention to the needs of minorities and other disadvantaged sections, so that the system could "move towards the ideals enshrined in the Constitution." Subsequently, a 'dual track' approach was posited to simultaneously focus on adult literacy and primary education, which after the Jomtien World Conference in 1990, came to be reaffirmed by the collective emphasis on 'Education for All' (EFA).

The world declaration lays stress on universalization access and promoting equity, the two issues which are vital to empowerment of women. Notwithstanding the revised National Policy on Education and subsequent Programme of Action, and recent initiatives for girls' education, implementation of certain aspects has lagged behind. Education for the females has not received the impetus it was expected to receive. Certainly, the thrust that the national policy on education and subsequent female education programmes were expected to impart is nowhere visible. Such small momentum as it has picked up is attributable to normal incremental growth from the concerned sectors. Female education did not make the promised progress. During the decade 1981-91, the female literacy rate improved from 29.8 to 39.2 per cent. The percentage of illiterate females declined by mere 10 per cent during the decade. However, there are wide regional variations ranging from literacy levels of 86 per cent in Kerala to 20 per cent in Rajasthan.

Even after 50 years of Independence, we have in our country backward pockets and backward social groups where the female literacy is negligible, for example, 4 per cent in Rajasthan and amongst certain Scheduled Castes and Scheduled Tribes communities, nil.

Educational priorities for women in India

No doubt, many initiatives for women's education have been taken in recent times at national, regional and even global levels. For example, Mahila Samakhya is one where literacy is taken up as a response to need felt and articulated by women themselves, rather than as a predetermined programmes input. In 1991 Lok Jumbish (movement of people) was launched in Rajasthan where 80 per cent women are illiterate. Also, the Shiksham Karmi Project started in Rajasthan in 1987 on the potential of ordinary people to teach. The programmes such as the World Bank assisted DPEP (District Primary Education Project) and UNICEF supported Bihar Education Project are some other examples. The Condensed Courses Education and vocational training for adult women started in 1958 and recast in 1975 by the Central Social Welfare Board (CSWB) also provide new vistas of employment through continuing and vocational training for women and girls who are drop-outs. The SAARC and G.15 level meetings were also, devoted to promotion of education in the region.

Never in the past has the topic of female education been given so much prominence as of now. Unfortunately, the educational requirements in terms of resources, orientation, etc., of disadvantaged groups have not been given the priority and prominence they deserve. It needs reiteration that education of women is linked to their social and economic well-being and empowerment. Down the ages, the female population, have by and large, remained marginalized, unaware of and indifferent to developmental benefits, and more particularly deprived of education. A female weighted education policy is an imperative and spread of education from grass roots level is the need of the hour. In many of the societies, woman is the pivot around which the family moves.

An increase in female literacy and educational level will have wide, positive effects in combating exploitative practices manifest in many spheres, as also enhancing professional capabilities in day-to-day economic chores as also population control, morbidity, health care, nutrition hygiene and sanitation, thus making empowerment a meaningful proposition. The gender disparity that vitiates our development process has its origin at the most vulnerable point in a woman's life, as a girl child growing up in a family. This has to be realized and tackled effectively both as a means to empower women and effecting a social process that would enhance the prospects of ushering in an equitable society.

The draft National Policy for the Empowerment of Women (1996) observes that "A synergy of development measures will be effected and affirmative action designed for the holistic empowerment of women. Women will be given complete and equal access to and control over, factors contributing to such empowerment, particularly health, education, information, life-long learning for self-development, vocational skills, income earning opportunities, technical services, land and other forms of property, including through inheritance, common property resources, credit, technology and market, etc." The draft policy further mentions that :

"Equal access to education for women and girls will be ensured. Measures will be taken to eliminate discrimination, universalize education, eradicate illiteracy, create a gender-sensitive educational system, increase enrolment and retention rates of girls and improve the quality of education to facilitate life-long learning as well as development of skills by women. Sectoral time targets in existing policies will be achieved with a special focus on girls and women." So much the better after fifty years of Independence.

Corporate initiative

The corporate sector and specific commerce and industry institutions like FICCI, CII, ASSOCHEM have lately envinced keen interest in social issues. They have also been taking up projects on social problems for the benefit specified groups. It is reported that comparatively, the success rate of these projects are better than Government—run projects. When an issue is taken up with a certain amount of conviction and commitment, the success rate will definitely be of a higher order. Examples of such instances are many and perhaps I need not quote them. My plea to FICCI and similar other organizations would be to take up on a larger scale educational projects for the benefit of girl children and women in various parts of the country, as a part of our celebrations of 50th year of Independence.

I believe that we do not suffer from the lack of theoretical formulations and planning strategies. It seems that our weakness lies in the lack of sincerity in execution and vigour in implementation. Dissemination of education cannot be achieved by mere desk-work. One has to get down to the field to work among people through measures of confidence-building. It is in this spirit that we suggest here the strategy of sustained application of extension work particularly in geographic pockets identified as low literacy pockets. It is in this context that my suggestion to the corporate sector to launch education projects for women has to be seen. For related statistics on women refer to Appendix VI.

I do hope that my suggestion would be given serious consideration.

Means of attainment

One other point which I would like to emphasize is that the main objectives of women's education should be on mainstream gender issues and strengthening the capabilities of women to face the challenges of modern day. In other words, it is not the intention to make them mere literate in the three R'S. A series of measures will be needed to achieve this objective. These would *inter alia* include training, sensitization, advocacy and lobbying. The methodology to be adopted has to suit each individual situation. The conventional type of formal schooling system may not take us to 100 per cent success. An informal setting which could have many options like peripatetic camps, flexible timing, voluntary responses, women friendly atmosphere, etc., may have to be evolved.

We should seriously look at the problem in which many more women will be enabled to become a part of the political process starting from the lowest level. We have now reservation for women in Panchayati Raj institutions and urban local bodies. Unless adequate steps are taken to educate women on the essentials of local administration, the revolutionary steps we have taken towards political empowerment of women may not yield the desired results, particularly when we are in the process of presenting reservation for women in State Legislatures and Lok Sabha. During the first fifty years of this century, women's literacy rose from 0.69 to 8.86 per cent and later during the fifty years of independence from 8.86 to 39.29 per cent. These figures are revealing. The pace of progress is too slow which calls for policy level changes and operational techniques. We may have to adopt result yielding techniques in the field of education for women so that we have in the next decade more literate women than the illiterate women.

---

*He who does not prevent a crime when he can encourages it.

11

PROHIBITION ESSENTIAL FOR WOMEN'S EMANCIPATION

IMPROVING HEALTH STANDARDS VIA PROHIBITION

Duty of the State to raise the level of nutrition and the standard of living and to improve public health—The State shall regard the raising of the level of nutrition and the standard of living of its people and the improvement of public health as among its primary duties and, in particular, the State shall endeavour to bring about prohibition of the consumption except for medicinal purposes of intoxicating drinks and of drugs which are injurious of health.

—Article 47 of the Constitution

Prohibition is one of the few social security measures which are firmly founded on moral and spiritual values and economic considerations. At the philosophical level, it seeks fulfilment of an ideal—the ideal of creation of a society which is free from all kinds of vices and exploitation. At the most mundane level, it is an instrument for maintaining law and order, a means of saving the poor from squandering their meagre income and protecting them from social deprivation and health hazards. In spite of these laudable objectives, prohibition has suffered serious setbacks in execution.

The attitude of Indian society towards the consumption of alcohol has all long been a mixture of approval and disapproval.

From time immemorial, society has given approbation to the use of fermented beverage. On ceremonial occasions or rituals, alcohol had even acquired a social value. Among the tribal societies, it has been customary to use alcohol at important events like marriage, child birth, death, etc.

This ambivalence arising out of the approbation-reprobation syndrome has become a part of the body politik leading to far-reaching consequences like fast rise in production and consumption of liquor and dilution of the force and spirit of the philosophy behind prohibition.

Over the years, consumption of liquor in India has been showing an upward trend. No wonder, the liquor industry has become a highly lucrative enterprise. Alcohol is easy to make and simple to sell. In the words of a study team on prohibition, the industry thrives by trying to make "every non-drinker, into a drinker; every casual drinker into a regular drinker and every regular drinker into a heavy drinker."

At one time, or the other many States introduced prohibition. Today, barring Gujarat and Haryana all other States have stepped back from prohibition. The main reason attributed for lifting prohibition is loss of revenue through excise duty. But this is not true.

In a study conducted by the All India Institute of Medical Sciences, New Delhi in a few villages in Punjab, alcohol abuse was found to be more common among those who were better educated and having a higher per capita income. Another finding was that alcohol abuse started in many users around the age of 10 and in the age groups of 15-19 years, 35 per cent were found taking alcohol. It immediately increased in the next age-group that is 20-29 years and remained fairly high for the rest of the age groups.

Evil effects of alcohol

It has been universally accepted that alcohol causes

considerable deleterious effects on health. It creates, for example, inebriety, stupefaction, deterioration of intelligence, perversion and unhappiness. It creates social problems like disruption of family and neglect of children and industrial problems as a result of accidents and absenteeism. Alcohol also causes corruption and law and order problems.

The medical opinion on it is that far from having any health giving and disease-curing properties, alcohol causes many diseases and contributes to many more in an indirect manner by adversely affecting the normal resistance of the human body to diseases. According to the expert group on alcohol, human health and nutrition,consumption of alcohol among the poorer sections of the people tends to divert the meagre financial resources and adversely affects optional intake of essential nutrients such as proteins and vitamins by the family as a whole, producing damaging effects particularly among pregnant and lactating women and preschool children. Also, there is "evidence to suggest that pre-existing nutritional deficiency, by interfering with the production or activity of ethanol exidizing enzymes may not only intensify the toxic effects of alcohol, but may also impair the regenerative and reparative activities of the damaged cells of the liver."

Gandhiji was so decisive in his views against drinking that he said : if he were to be a dictator for a single day, his first act would be to close all liquor shops. He wrote in 1921:

> "you will not be deceived by specious argument that Indians must not be made sober by compulsion and that those who wish to drink must have facilities provided for them. The State does not cater to the vices of the people. We do not regulate or license houses of ill-fame. The State does not provide facilities for thieves to indulge in thieving. I hold drinking to be more damnable than thieving and perhaps even prostitution. Is it not often the parent of both? I ask you to join the

State in abolishing the liquor shops.

" Prohibition was not a programme in isolation; it was part of a general programme of reconstrucion arising out of the social, moral and spiritual uplift of the country's freedom struggle.

Under Schedule VII of the Constitution, the production, manufacture, transport, purchase and sale of intoxicating liquors and duties of excise on them have been brought under the State list. Therefore, prohibition is a State subject. The Central Government helps the State Governments in taking appropriate steps in fullfilling the constitutional obligations.

Prohibition Policy 1975 : To reduce the consumption of alcoholic beverages and prepare the ground for the introduction of total prohibition, the Government of India announced in 1975 a 12-point programme for implementation. The major thrust of the programme was to build up social pressure at the national level against drinking.

"Prohibition means a type of adult education of the nation and merely a closing down of grog shops," said Mahatma Gandhi. Social education and rousing the public consciousness about alcohol and its deleterious effects on health is not only imperative, but should also be a constant endeavour. This should be supplemented by systematic and sustained audio-visual publicity campaigns against the evils of drinking.

The role of the press in instructing and educating the masses is indeed very important. Equally important is the role of voluntary organizations in creating public opinion in favour of prohibition. Another effective source through which excellent work for prohibition can be done is women's organizations. Women can spearhed the crusade against drinking as they have the first-hand experience of the ruin that liquor brings to their domestic happiness and to that of their children. To make the campaign more effective, workers of voluntary organizations, including those of women's organizations should be given adequate training in the field.

---

*Like a candle in a holy place, so is the beauty of an aged face.

12

WOMEN AND THE MODERN WORLD

We have almost completed 50 years of our Independence. The founding fathers of our Constitution had envisaged the concept of full equality of women in competition with men which has not fully become a reality till date and women who theoretically enjoy an equal status with men in the Constitution of India have not been able to exercise that equality in letter and spirit.

In spite of several laws, women have not been able to get justice. There has been constant increase in the number of crimes against women. Harassment of women at workplaces is also on the increase which is because women do not come forward and raise their voices. Increasing participation of women in political processes and trade union activities is one of the major ways in which the traditional male dominated value system can be challenged.

In the modern world, the role of the women goes much beyond the home and the bringing up of children. She is now adopting a career of her own and sharing equally with man the responsibility for the development of society in all its aspects. This is the direction in which we shall have to move and to move fast.

Women took active part in the struggle for freedom. They fought shoulder to shoulder with men. Their contribution to the country's development process has by no means been less. It has been a source of unique strength for reaching national goals. As housewives, women have kept the home fire burning so that their menfolk can go out to work and their children attend schools and colleges. It is a different matter that unpaid job of bringing up the family has never been evaluated in terms of money. A wholly dedicated lot, working silently, most of them have been too busy to think of their own rights.

The sex ratio between the males and females in the population: 1000 males to 927 females is a matter of concern since child deaths among girls are higher than among boys. Also the dropout rate of girls from schools is higher and their admission to schools is lower compared to boys. However, there are hopeful signs for improvement in women's situation. The number of women job seekers through employment exchanges has also gone up sharply, the average age of women at marriage has gone up and their expectation of life at birth has improved.

Dear sisters, my plea would be that you must take part in organized activities. In this, the trade unions can be of great assistance and you must take more and more interest to promote your career-related prospects. You are perhaps not aware that it is your fundamental right to form associations or unions. It is high time that at least now you awaken and take active part in decision making bodies. It is in our own interest that we unite and fight for our rights. Only then we will be able to enjoy equality with men. I can assure you that NCW will always support your cause. Dear sisters, you must remember that participation of women not only makes the women visible but also strengthens the movement and gives it publicity. Further, their participation helps to steer the movement in certain directions often away from sexism and violence. In fact, women's participation in wider social movements and agitations like anti-arrack have been more common.

It would, however be worthy of women's participation if they could have, in the cause of the agitations and struggles at least paid attention to the women issues and the rights of women both as women and taken specific steps to facilitate increasing participation of women both as members as well as at the decision making levels. It is only recently that women have awakened and realized their strength. Anyway it is never too late.

You should feel proud that the All India Bank Employees Association is a leading trade union organization of bank employees. It has done yeoman service to the bank employees. The credit for improving working conditions in the banking sector should also go to this association.

It is a time of rejoicing for the women employees of the banks that a women cell is being formed in Delhi. It is also a matter of pride for me that I have been invited to inaugurate the convention. It is hoped the women bank employees will take keen interest and effectively participate in the trade union activities like their counterparts in other regions of the country.

Organization of women required

There is no denying the fact that for betterment of their service conditions the women will have to organize themselves. They will have to play their due and desired role in the routine and the running of trade unions, sharing power, position and responsibilities with their male colleagues.

It is hoped that the association will create a climate and conditions congenial to women employees increasing role in the unions at all levels, consistent with their self-respect and dignity.

The women employees should have positions and responsibilities right from grass roots to above levels. I call upon the women employees to fight for their due rights in the unions and be not only passive members of the union but active and vocal for their own rights, redressal of their own grievances and overall growth and strengthening of the trade unions.

In a male dominated society, the women suffer from varieties of gender bias and repressive laws in all fields of life. Right from the moment of birth up to that of death, they suffer from severe handicaps in the field of education, health care, child bearing and rearing, laws relating to marriage, inheritance and also personal laws. Women must muster enough courage and fight against all these inequalities and repressions in whatever form and resolutely.

Atrocities against women are showing sharp rise. It is the task of the trade unions to raise their powerful voice against all these exploitations and atrocities on women so that an exploitation-free home, work place, society and country is established in the true sense of the term. The NCW will extend all help in this task.

Let us not forget that the perpetrators of gender fallacies are to a certain extent unenlightened women too. We should try to remove the age old superstitions and mental cobwebs. Women's liberation and emancipation is possible only if men and women together talk about the issues. What is essential is the need for evaluating and respecting the competence of each other and sharing the responsibility. With women realizing the need to progress, to fight for the due rights, the future will ensure a society where women gets her social dignity.

Last but not the least, although our country has

made rapid strides in various fields, still a lot needs to be done to improve the women's lot. I am of the view that political empowerment of women is the only decisive catalyst which will bring about a crucial change in the lot of women. Induction of women in Panchayati Raj institutions has already proved that given responsibility, women discharge it more conscientiously than men. This is the reason why NCW is stridently championing the Bill for reservation of 33 per cent seats for women in Lok Sabha and State Assemblies. The nationwide solidarity of women activists, women MPs cutting across party lines, on this issue, speaks of women's determination not to accept the status quo but to strive for political empowerment.

With these words, I inaugurate the convention and once again thank the organizers. Let me conclude this speech by saying that 21st century will be women's century and let us all work unitedly to shape it.

---

*If you don't defend your honour, people will assume you have none.

13

HABITAT FOR THE 21st CENTURY

HABITAT IS A MUST : IT AFFECTS WOMEN

Among several cross-sectional issues on habitat, namely shelter provision, environment, management, tenure, governance, transport, communication, drinking water, sanitation and others, undoubtedly gender issues provide the common denominator in as much as it has the potential to underwrite the success of the best of the initiatives related to all others.

Habitat, as is well known, is a wider term than mere shelter or housing. The dimensions and problems of housing need to be viewed in the overall environment of human settlement. The physical dwelling unit is not the sole element of housing: equally important is the provision of basic services like potable water, sanitation, drainage and electricity. Further, the type and location of housing is inextricably linked to the employment and affordability of the occupants. A durable shelter is one of the basic requirements for people to be able to organize their thoughts, discipline their actions and undertake plans and programmes for creative pursuits. People without a home tend to be uncertain, worried and unstable which affects their every action (p.174 Huq and Sultan, 1991). Environmental sanitation and personal and community hygiene play a significant role in promoting and preserving the physical, mental and social well-being of the people.

Any estimate of housing shortage depends essentially on a minimum acceptable standard of housing which a country might adopt for itself. Shortage of housing resulting in overcrowded conditions of living in urban areas existed even before Independence. The shortage in housing in 1948 was roughly estimated to be of the order of 1.8 million. According to the National Buildings Organization the total backlog on housing was estimated at 31 million in 1991 of which 10.4 million was in urban areas. According to the Eighth Plan document of the planning Commission the housing shortage in the year 2001 is estimated to be of the order of 40.8 million (26.5 million rural and 14.3 million urban). Thus, the magnitude of the problem is indeed massive. It is revealing that a comparison of housing condition in rural and urban areas over the last 10 years , as revealed from the different NSS rounds data, suggests that while proportion of pucca houses has increased over time, the service level has not improved. For example, between 38th and 44th round (1998-89) percentage of pucca house in rural areas has increased from 16.7 per cent to 27.1 per cent and in urban areas from 57.6 per cent to 71.0 per cent. In rural areas 'no latrine' households have marginally decreased from 91.4 per cent to 89.2 per cent. These aspects are brought in specifically to highlight the gender issue involved in not having sanitary latrine in a household.

Despite the planning process, housing standards have not much improved *vis-a-vis* the requirements. On the contrary, there have been some deterioration, qualitatively and quantitatively, both in urban areas and rural areas. Under the Constitution, though housing is included in the State list, assistance for housing is provided both by the Central and State Governments. In line with the National Housing Policy which is a settlement of the long term objective, the core strategy of the Eighth Plan consisted of creating an enabling environment for housing activity, viewed as an important component of the national economy, by eliminating various constraints and providing direct assistance to the specially disadvantaged groups including rural and urban poor households, SC/ST, physically handicapped, widows and single women. It is to be noted that the problem of housing in rural areas is more qualitative than quantitative. Congestion is widely prevalent. The results, however, are not encouraging.

In today's context when considering habitat for the 21st century, gender issues will need to be taken into account in the interest of good governance and people centred environmentalism. The notion of equity goes beyond the arithmetic of political elections or quota systems. In the popular sense 'equity' signifies 'natural justice' or 'fair-play'. In the wider sense, equity may be described as the ethical notion of 'fair treatment'. 'Fair-play' and 'fair treatment' is at the core of all women's demands. For women as agents of change, the need is for 'equitable development' and not 'unequal development'.

Inclusion of women in joint ownership of property

In practical terms in acquisition, allotment, etc, of house sites and houses, the ownership should always be on a joint basis. In respect of female headed household it should naturally be in the name of women. In the context of the 73rd and 74th Amendments to the Constitution, good governance depends on spreading democracy at the grass roots level and associating women in planning, designing and constructing houses and developing habitat. In the development of housing colonies, resettlement projects, etc, the views of womenfolk are generally not taken account, of which we have examples where resettlement colonies and housing complexes have been abandoned especially those under government sector. Another important point, where drinking water facilities are not available, the women have to spend extra time and energy in fetching water at the cost of day-to-day employment or in the case of girls, their education time lost.

Sanitation needs improvement in rural and poor areas

In the case of slums, the deprivations that women face are much more. It is felt that a particular area becomes a slum, more because of poor environment conditions, poor sewerage and sanitation rather than the poor state of structure.

Using a Gender related Development Index (GDI), the 1995 Human Development Report of UNDP places India in the 99th position among 130 countries in relation to the status of women. In dealing with habitat related issues, especially drinking water, sanitation and environment, attention has necessarily to be given to removal of hurdles that impede full participation of and derival of benefit by women. A research study had recently revealed certain shortcomings in implementation of low-cost sanitation programmes that adversely affect women beneficiaries. The women appreciated the harmful effects of open defecation or for that matter about the use of dry latrines on health and environment grounds. Though they knew about the use and maintenance of P.F. latrines, many of them were not using them in the absence of superstructure. They were thus compelled to go for defecation in the open. Until and unless the privacy for women is ensured by constructing the superstructure on P.F. latrine, women would have to go for open defecation.

For maximizing the use of common facility in general and women and children in particular, issues of location, accessibility, user charges, availability of water and electricity, sanitary latrines, etc, will need to be attended to

An important point is that human settlements far away from the scene of employment for women affect them immensely.

Employment participation of women

In another instance, in the Indo-Dutch Environment and Sanitary Engineering Project (IDP) in Jajmau area, Kanpur, a need was felt for creating opportunities for the development of women in the given social context. It was realized that the restrictions on women entering into the fields such as plumbers, fitters or masons are not so much, because these vocations are hard enough or too tiring but as they are historically and culturally being done by men only. So it was resolved to train women so as not only to question the very basis of gender discrimination but also to prove a point for women that they can do the same as men. Three different types of skill training programmes were carried out in the field of water and sanitation. These were as masons, as plumbers and in fabrication.

The assessment of these ventures indicated that not only women got successfully involved in construction, plumbing and fabrication, but they also acted as motivators and promoters for proper use of sanitation and other facilities. The female masons during construction of pour flush latrines also communicated messages relating to health, hygiene and sanitation to the occupants of each house.

In another habitat related community based sanitation and environment improvement programme in Indore, Baroda and Ahmedabad, it was found that the urban poor are trapped in a vicious cycle of poverty, ill health, miserable living conditions and illiteracy in which the causes cannot be clearly distinguished from the effects. In slum networking many of the community development interventions are focused on women and girls, who will in turn be tomorrow's mothers. The reason for doing so is to stem the carry over of the disadvantages from one generation to another. On the physical front, women in slums face the worst hardships of environmental and sanitation degradations. The Baroda project came to fruition in spite of a long incubation period of three years simply because of the persistence of the women there to have individual water taps and toilets.

Imagination and innovation are required to give a fair treatment to women in habitat planning and management for the ultimate benefit of all the inhabitants of Twenty-first Century which is to be Women's Century.

Habitat and its concomitants

Shelter without minimum facilities like sanitation, drinking water and electricity is meaningless. Man has reached the moon, landed remote controlled instruments on Mars and on planets farther away, compressed knowledge spanning several centuries into a tiny chip, cracked genetic codes and cloned life. Yet for all that impressive achievement, half the world's people have no access to a toilet or a decent latrine and must therefore remain susceptible to epidemics like cholera and other water-borne diseases. What is worse, the number of those denied sanitation facilities have increased from 2.6 billion in 1990 to 2.9 billion in 1996.

Highlighting the absence of rudimentary sanitation facilities in half the world, a UNICEF report has pointed out that about 2.2 million children die annually of disease caused by unhygienic conditions. At issue is waste matter contaminating water supplies, polluting open areas and breeding vermin, the report has said and underlined that the problem is most acute in rural areas where only 18 per cent of the people worldwide have access to a toilet or a latrine. In urban areas of developing countries, over 37 per cent lack such facilities. And even there, according to the report, the definition of "adequate" sanitation varies widely from country to country. Uganda, for example, claims adequate sanitation in about 80 per cent of households, but the figure shrinks to just three per cent if pit latrines are excluded. Considering that the cost of providing adequate toilet or latrines ranges from 5 to 60 dollars, the UN agency estimates that the problem can be solved in ten years if an amount equal to ten per cent of a year's global military spending is set aside for toilet construction programmes.

When considering issues on habitat for the 21st century, gender issues well need to be taken into account in the interest of good governance and people centred environmentalism. The Trivandrum Declaration on Habitat Education emphasized:

(a) encourage children and youth to form clubs and societies to undertake voluntary concerted activities of habitat planning and maintenance;

(b) generate fora for discussions and debates on land use, water management, sanitation, wastage disposal, pollution control, socio-psychological dimensions of living in habitats, etc.

(c) link habitat education to such socio-economic issues as employment, migration, health, forestry, energy and similar areas of concern but ignored gender related issues.

I would emphasize that for a "habitat" without female concerns built into the system, the place would be uninhabitable.

The Nirmithi concept has a special significance for inducting the 'habitat-making' competencies into education which would then pave the way for 'education for the habitat' and help us to transcend verbalism in habitat education.

The Approach Paper to the Ninth Five Year Plan

1997-2002 states that the housing shortage in 1997 has been estimated to be 7.57 million and is projected at 6.64 million in 2001. These estimates, however, throw light only on one aspect of the scenario. Access to basic services is equally important.

The National Housing Policy (NHP) has been adopted by the Government and the long term goal of the policy is to reduce houselessness, to improve the housing conditions of the inadequately housed and to provide a minimum level of basic services and amenities to all.

The Ninth Plan strategy will be to provide housing for all by the terminal year of the Plan by taking into account the upgradation of kutcha units to semi-pucca and pucca units.

EDUCATION AND EMPOWERMENT

Education is the vaccine for violence
—Edward James Olmos

It is opportune that the S.N.D.T. University, in celebrating our 50th Year of Independence, has aptly chosen a subject of importance to women for the seminar.

Education, conceived as organized instruction is part of the development process. Theoretically, education must enable persons to acquire knowledge and necessary skills. This knowledge and skills should further enable them to compete for and acquire better occupational status or higher social status in life. Thus, education should lead to social and economic productivity of the individual and, as a corollary, of the society. These are some basic assumptions about education in an open and competitive society. Fair competition requires equality in the initial social status or situation affecting the person or one's community. Hence there is a need for protection or support by the State to those lacking such initial advantage or those who suffer from social and economic disabilities.

It is universally recognized that "mother is the first school of the child", yet the formal educational system keeps her out of the school because of socio-economic reasons, foremost among them being the bias towards girls' education, primarily because of patriarchal attitudes. Thus, the society is deprived of 50 per cent of human power for human development. No doubt, in the course of history, the status of women in our country has changed for better in some spheres and for worse in some others. In particular, education has come to be considered more important for women than men at least in theory.

The University Education Commission (1949) remarked:

"There cannot be an educated people without educated women. If general education had to be limited to men or to women, that opportunity should be given to women, for then it would more surely be passed on to the next generations."

As elsewhere, there is a good deal of discrepancy between the idealistic notion of the Indian women and the actual life situation in which she finds herself.

As Linsay Mackie and Polly Pattalo pointed out:

> The education of women has ever been a matter of great debate. Opinions expressed about it have often been reactionary i.e., sometimes absurd and occasionally extraordinary insulting. It comes as no surprise that Dr. Johnson said that a man is better pleased when he has a good dinner upon his table than when his wife talks Greek.

In India, as in the developed countries, women are less likely than men to continue their education to higher levels and are more likely to be found concentrated in stereotyped occupational roles.

Various commissions and committees, as also policy

documents have stressed the importance of women's education and recommended very many measures. These include University Education Commission (1948-49), Secondary Education Commission (1952-53), National Committee on Women Education (1958-59), Kothari Education Commission (1964-66), National Policy on Education (1986), NPE Review Committee Report (1990), Report of the CABE Committee on Policy (1992), National Commission on Self Employed Women and Women in the Informal Sector (1987-88) and National Perspective Plan perspectives, prescriptions and guidelines and reports of specific study groups on different social groups like the Scheduled Castes and the Scheduled Tribes. In particular, the working group on higher education of Planning Commission for the Ninth Five Year Plan has specifically examined the issue relating to higher education of women. Dealing with access and equity, the working group observed:

> The major issue concerning higher education is expansion versus consolidation, access and equity versus means to maintain quality of education. While the issue has been highlighted in plan after plan, it has not been addressed squarely. Hence, even the increased plan outlays have not made visible impact on expansion of programmes and the development of infrastructure with the large percentage increase in student enrolment. Unless, in the Ninth Plan this is redressed, the system will continue to be paralyzed by the sheer numbers entering it. Both conventional and non-conventional solutions will have to be addressed in the Ninth Plan. These would include a leap forward for open education, not only as separate institutions, but also within conventional universities offering the dual mode to both separate student populations as also to the same student.

There is also a need to be concerned about access

and equity for groups in the system which remain marginalized. These are women who form almost half the country's population, the reserved categories, the minorities, and the differently disabled. It also recommended to develop special schemes for women and other social groups.

A look at women's education scenario

If one analyses the women's education scenario, one would find that women's education is an area cluttered with contradictory complexes, opposing theories and tremendous emotions. In brief:

1. On the one hand, India has a large mass of people either disinterested in or ignorant of the problem of higher education for women; on the other hand, a few enlightened women alone express deep concern about the problem.
2. The area of higher education for women is at cross-roads between intellectual rationality and social conservatism. It is often emotional and ends in negativism.
3. Some people believe that education cannot be different for males and females. Hence, men and women should have the same curriculum content. But, there is another school of thought which believes that there are inherent differences between girls and boys. Therefore, the content of education should also be different. However, there is consensus of the common general objectives of higher education, namely, character formation, personality development increasing employbility competence and inculcation of civic sense.
4. Since higher education needs to be geared to the needs of individuals, one of its objectives for boys is employment, while the twin objectives of employment and home-making hold good for girls.

The women aspiring for higher education could broadly be classified into four categories:

1. Employment oriented
2. Marriage oriented
3. Employment-cum-marriage oriented
4. Unspecified others.

In taking up higher education and choosing a subject of specialization then, I need not emphasize, there is both waste of human resources and lack of national objectives. I have had occasions to discuss with experts about the non-availability of services of women agriculture graduates. After spending much time, energy and funds they do not utilize the knowledge they have acquired for the development of the society. Realizing the importance of women's higher education vis-a-vis utilization of their professional knowledge and skill we have sponsored at the National Academy of Agriculture Research Management, Hyderabad, a workshop on "Issues of Professional Women in Agriculture" from today which will last for another two days. The NCW is eager to evolve a system by which higher education resources are so channelized as would meet the demands of women, both in rural and urban settings. Women have generally been engaged in such traditional areas like teachers, nurses, etc. A shift in a substantial manner, not in token is needed.

Current status of women in higher education

The growth in the number of women students in higher education since independence has been phenomenal. While women constituted only 9.3 per cent of all students in institutions of higher education on the eve of independence, the percentage of women students enrolled in all colleges and universities was 34.1 in 1995-96.

The pace of growth has been particularly faster in

the last two decades, or so. The number of women enrolled, per hundred men, registered a four-fold increase during the period from 1950-51 to 1995-96.

Noteworthy factor of the general increase in the number of girl students in higher education is the uniformity in their enrolment at all levels of education. Faculty wise, Arts stream accounts for the highest, followed by Commerce, Science, Education, Law, Engineering and Technology.

The number of women colleges in the country has recorded a substantial increase. It increased from 780 in 1986-87 to 1146 in 1995-96. It is significant that the University Grants Commission has a programme for promoting women's studies wherein it gives assistance to universities for setting up Centres/Cells for women studies. As on 31st March, 1996 the UGC had provided assistance to 33 universities and colleges for setting up such Centres/Cells (22 Centres and 11 Cells).

At the time of Independence in 1947 we had only 20 universities and 500 colleges. The number of students and teachers in higher education system was very small. At the beginning of 1996-97 we have 209 universities and there is a tremendous increase in the number of colleges, i.e. from 500 to 9278 in which the number of women colleges is 1146.

The latest annual report of the Ministry of Human Resources Development (1996-97) proclaims that : Women's education has always been a priority area and NEE envisages the entire educational system to work for women's education and empowerment. It has been emphasized that gender concerns must be built into all educational process. Emphasis has been laid on enrolment and retention of the girl child in formal and non-formal schooling, recruitment of rural women as teachers and removal of gender bias in the curriculum.

One aspect of unequal relations of society, the world over and in our country, is the disadvantaged and marginalized position of women and girls in education, and specifically in higher education. While women form fifty per cent of the population, in higher education they form only about 34 per cent in graduate and postgraduate studies and 26.6 per cent in diploma and certificate courses.

The issue is even more of social justice and gender equality. One of the main reasons for the majority of the girls not being able to take up higher education is the weak base, i.e. at the school stage, particularly in the rural areas. Added to this are economic deprivation, lack of motivation and strong partriarchal attitudes against girls education.

The number of Women's Universities in the country is five, though a very small number, still they could take a lead in this matter in association with the UGC and the women study centres. They could specifically examine the issues and recommend to the government and the corporate sector the needs of girl students, desiring and deserving, and to at least render financial and motivational assistance to those who go in for higher education.

The NCW would eagerly look forward to the recommendations of this seminar so that we could also take up the issues in appropriate manner with concerned authorities to augment the enrolment of girls students, retain them in the stream for the full term and help them to opt for a career of their choice and beneficial to the society.

---

*It doesn't matter how hard you fall, what matters is how fast you get up.

14

GENDER EQUALITY WITH SOCIAL JUSTICF

EXTENSION OF CIVIL RIGHTS TO PEOPLE FOR IMPROVING SOCIAL ORDER

At the outset, I would like to mention that rights have always had a close link with man's civilization wherever that concept has flourished, and even today their existence or otherwise is symbolic of the standard of civilization attained. In fact, the Buddhist doctrine of non-violence in deed and thought "अहिंसा परमोधर्म" is a humanitarian doctrine par excellence dating back to the third century a.c. Futhermore in Hinduism "वसुधैव कुटुम्बकम्" that the kinship of the whole world, elaborating thereby that human beings are all kith and kin of one family.

Whatever may be the definition of the terms 'refugees' and 'repatriates', it needs to be pointed out that the sufferings of such groups of persons are caused primarily due to serious disturbances in their normal habitat. These occur as a result of disasters that befall on them. Disaster, is a term that may be narrowly or widely defined. It is an event, concentrated in time and space, in which a group of persons or a relatively self-sufficient sub-division of a society, undergoes severe danger and incurs such loss to its members and such opportunities that the socio-economic structure of that group is severely disrupted and, therefore, the fulfilment of all or some of the important essential functions of living are disrupted.

Whether a refugee or a repatriate, the person suffers very many inconveniences, not at all caused by themselves, but by the act of others. A person in a normal abode in a country is all of a sudden turned into an unwelcome person in that country. In other words, he assumes the title of repatriate. Whether such an act on the part of the host country is a denial of a human right is a serious matter deserving consideration. Likewise, the term 'repatriate' presupposes that he will be take back unhesitatingly by his parent or original country when no longer wanted in host country.

I would like to briefly mention that, we in India have a long tradition of extending hospitality to many nationals of different countries who fled from their country as refugees. There is justification to assert that ever since the dawn of human civilization, humanism with all its humanitarian aspects has been upheld as the highest virtue in a person. The history of human civilization is woven around the fabric of human behaviour, whether in respect human rights or in violating them. It was the political philosophy generated by UN Charter affirming the dignity of human being and the futility of conflicts and wars that willy-nilly led to the formulation and enunciation of human rights. A legal obligation thus emerged, namely, the duty of every State to treat all persons under its jurisdiction with respect for human rights and fundamental freedoms without distinction as to race, sex, language or religion (Article 6 of the UN Charter). UNHCR, "Providing international protection ... and ... seeking prominent solutions for the problems of refugees" is in consonance with the above objectives. Our constitutional provisions and the setting up of the National Human Rights Commission in India bear resplendent testimony of the country's commitment to uphold human rights.

We have a liberal and humanitarian policy towards both refugees, rehabilitation and rehabilitation of repatriates. During the past few years, India has had repatriates from a large number of countries. These included Sri Lanka, Myanmar, Mozambique, Uganda, Zaire, Vietnam and Gulf countries. Without going into the details of repatriation, it can be asserted with authority that the Government of India and the State Governments have always rendered maximum facilities for their resettlement and rehabilitation in diverse fields like land, industry, service, trade and commerce, etc. Various incentives and concessions are provided to these repatriates, as the situation warrants.

There is a clear distinction between refugees and repatriates. As is well known, refugees flee the country "owing to well-founded fear of being persecuted for reasons of race, religion, nationality, membership of a particular social group or political opinion, is outside the country of his nationality .. and unable or unwilling to avail the protection of his country ..." Because of these reasons, they are complete aliens in the new country. It takes time for them to adjust to the new surroundings and it also takes time for the local population to receive in their midst the new set of people. In the case of repatriates, they are mostly non-residents for a shorter or longer duration, unable to adjust to the situation in the host country on account of political or economic compulsions, but not necessarily due to violence. They are able to adjust to the new situation in the country of origin more or less comfortably in due course. Hence, the psychological disturbances caused due to uprooting from normal place of residence is tolerably much less.

Whether refugees or repatriates, the women among them suffer most on all counts. The task of setting up of a family afresh in a new place is primarily that of women.

The children's education also suffers. There is also danger of sexual exploitation from own groups and outsiders. On account of these, all rehabilitation packages for repatriated, as well as refugees, women and children specific components must be included to facilitate smooth rehabilitation. In extending a helping hand, it must be remembered that repatriates are not a threat to their country. On the contrary, they are the threatened people, who, if given proper support could immensely contribute to the country's prosperity.

In conclusion, I would like to observe that much of the problems arising out of repatriation could be overcome by all countries, if the world leadership acknowledges that a healthy humane world order respecting human rights and endeavouring towards the well-being of human beings is all-pervasive and would ultimately be in the interest of everyone in this era of global economy.

Gender Equality—Key to New International Economic Order

On behalf of the National Commission for Women, the State Commissions for Women, NGOs, women activists, social scientists and millions of those women who are not assembled here but look towards NCW for wise counselling, support and activism, and on my own behalf, may I extend to you Hon'ble Prime Minister, a hearty and warm welcome. It was gracious of you to have accepted our request to be present with us today, on the International Women's Day and on the occasion of the Commission completing one and a half year of its second term of office to address this vast gathering.

UN Secy-General's message

I now read out from the message from Kofi A. Annan, UN Secretary-General on the occasion of International Women's Day: "International Women's Day is the day on which women on all continents bridge national, ethnic, cultural, economic and political divides to come together to celebrate their efforts towards the goals of equality, development and peace. It is the day on which we applaud the struggle of ordinary women." During this half century, the women's movement has become a truly global phenomenon. The Fourth World Conference on Women in Beijing in 1995 was the largest conference ever held by the United Nations, with some 17,000 participants representing 189 nations and more than 2,500 non-governmental organisations. The commitments made by governmental representatives in Beijing reflect the understanding that women's equality must be a central component of any attempt to solve the world's social, economic and political problems. Thus, where once women fought to put gender equality on the international agenda, gender equality is now one of the primary factors shaping that agenda.

Women are notably absent from the peace table, despite evidence suggesting that they bring a particular and positive perspective to preventive diplomacy, peace-making and peace-keeping. Those United Nations' peace and security missions which were characterized by gender balance in their management and staff clearly benefitted from the involvement of women.

International Women's Day is the story of ordinary women as makers of history; it is rooted in the centuries-old struggle of women to participate in society on an equal footing with men.

You are well aware of the circumstances and the objectives with which the National Commission for Women was set up.

NCW is just five years old and the Commission has been a ray of hope and inspiration to women at large. The National Commission for Women Act is the result of sustained and committed women's movement in our country. The Act was enacted during the Janata Dal Government regime. We recognise that our enlightened leadership is committed to uphold social justice and women can expect more than a fair deal to alleviate deprivation, injustice and inequality. The evidence is not far to seek. The introduction of the 81st Constitution Amendment Bill by the government, providing one-third reservation for women in Lok Sabha and State Legislatures speaks volumes of your concern, commitment and sincerity towards women's cause. We are confident that under your determined leadership this Bill will be passed and Presidential assent accorded before the conclusion of this present session of Parliament.

In order to perform its role as an autonomous statutory body and as a guardian of women's rights, to prevent as well as to make amends for injustices done to women, by definition it has to be independent both in its constitutional construction as well as in its operational details and process. The realisation of this objective would be possible only when it is vested with adequate powers and supported by suitable machinery for investigation, namely the powers of prosecution as a supportive mechanism to the existing justice delivery system.

We are passing through an important stage in the evolution of socio-political order in the country which makes it imperative for equal women's participation in governance and national development. The coalition government of regional and national parties provides the ideal opportunity for women's movement to come together and forge their identities as Indian women and not as merely belonging to one political party or the other, one religion or another, one caste or another. There is a strong bond amongst women which provides a natural platform for solidarity.

Esteemed Prime Minister, permit me to place before you some of the major concerns and responses that have emerged in our discussions with women's organisations. You have always highlighted the plight of the poor and drawn attention not only to poverty in this country but also to real deprivation. There are numerous habitations without safe drinking water, without shelter, without schools, without hospitals and so forth. We do not have to further explain to you how in the absence of these basic needs women suffer constantly and continuously. Allowing these basic minimum needs to remain unmet and out of the reach of women is a great loss to national development.

Besides, there are specific women's groups, widows, prostitutes and prisoners, as also those in custodial institutions and mental asylums. During the last one and half years we have visited 34 prisons and many red light areas, and met widows and destitutes. Hundreds of women pushed into prostitution want to be free from this mire. They demand their basic need to shelter and regular income.

Under the Indira Mahila Yojana, these unfortunate women can be offered shelter. NCW has had some success in approaching different school systems to provide 5 per cent seats for admission of their children in schools. If proper and timely rehabilitation packages are provided to them, large number of these oppressed women will voluntarily come out of the tortures of sexual exploitation on them by men and society at large. The anti arrack movement led by women of Andhra Pradesh, Kerala, Haryana and elsewhere have brought about partial or full prohibition in these States. This has to be sustained. The gains of prohibition have reached individuals, the family and the society, as a whole. Therefore, the accruing social cost benefit can never be overlooked in terms of better food, better health and family harmony. Prohibition has to be on the agenda of next NDC meeting of which you are the Chairman.

Authority of State Commissions cannot be doubted

Major States like Uttar Pradesh, Bihar, Madhya Pradesh, Rajasthan, Haryana, still have not set up the State Commissions for Women. On the other hand, Kerala Women's Commission which came into operation only this year is being dragged into litigation, questioning the authority of the statutory commission for probing into atrocities on women.

Questioning the authority of a statutory commission in the State or States is preposterous. The State Commissions for Women seek NCW's intervention and assistance. NCW will have to be fully equipped and empowered if need be by amendment of the NCW Act to render effective assistance to State Commissions which are our eyes and ears in the States.

To make the process of democratic decentralisation through Panchayats and urban local bodies a reality, there is urgent need for accelerated delivery of awareness and sensitisation programmes. This demands a policy shift in favour of promoting, encouraging and assisting NGOs to work in rural areas, in urban slums and peripheral townships. This alone will pave the way for grassroots democracy to establish itself for sustainable development.

NCW has studied in-depth the discriminatory provisions in the various laws affecting women and a number of recommendations by way of amendments and new Bills have been submitted to the government. Delay in accepting these will only perpetuate discrimination and injustice to women. An early decision on NCW's recommendations would benefit all and eliminate crimes against women. In addition, NCW has initiated a national debate on the need for codification of criminal laws pertaining to women. This would naturally entail a thorough overhaul of the criminal justice administration.

One of the most important issues of discimination against women is the wages that women receive, notwithstanding Equal Remunerations Act. Women in bonded labour, as contract labourers, domestic workers in agriculture and in the total unorganised sector still reel under economic and sexual exploitation and harassment at workplace. They must be provided adequate social security to meet the minimum needs for a life of dignity and honour. In short, the enforcement systems need a thorough revamping.

Judicial process comes to the rescue

Family disputes languishing in courts need urgent attention. The Parivarik Mahila Adalats, an innovative experiment in delivery of speedy justice has brought smiles to the suffering women. This cost-effective and no-cost experiment has been a roaring success with the active cooperation of the district level judiciary, including legal aid and the NGOs. Down south from the Andamans to Himachal up in the north, from Gujarat in the west to Assam in the east, we shall be completing a hundred PMLAs. The professional counsellors and social workers are working hard to make these adalats a grand success. We are covering all the districts in phases in the country.

The legal awareness programme launched by NCW in colleges with the sole aim of spreading knowledge of the rights and responsibilities of girls and lady teachers and through them to the public has been a success, too. In each State and from each district college, NGOs and counsellors are demanding for a legal awareness programmes for them also. Sensitisation of the judiciary and the police is our recent thrust area. Providing training to Panchayat women is not only a responsibility but a challenge. NCW has appealed to NGOs to extend their services to the grassroots and the villages for which adequate resources are required to be provided to NGOs by government funding for fulfilling this constitutional facility provided for Panchayat women to enter governance. A number of States visited by NCW have success stories to quote of women asserting their role as Panchayat Sarpanchas, Upsarpanchas and members, besides the elected women counsellors. They belie the apprehensions of many who wonder how these one million women are going to conduct themselves? These women feel the pulse of their people; they understand their needs, as assigned to them in the schedule. Villages will soon be safe and progressing under their care. They are the true rulers of tomorrow and the 21st century will be the century of women.

Women are aware and awake and it is heartening to watch the spontaneous demands of women coming up for literacy, vocational skills and employment. Informal and non-formal flexitiming packages are what is needed for them.

It is strange that at one end we have a large number of women cultivators and labourers in agriculture who need counsel and advice and at the other end there are sufficiently large number of highly educated women agricultural scientists without jobs. NCW recommends a study of the needs for creating definite linkages between the women farmers and available scientific support.

NCW has attended to cases of atrocities against Scheduled Caste women. In spite of the constitutional guarantees and reservations, women of Scheduled Castes and Scheduled Tribes are overlooked, subordinated, subjugated and oppressed not merely by their customs and practices, more so by patriarchal norms and values. Educational institutions must be empowered with enforcement powers to see that children/girls are compulsorily sent to school.

On the 1st of March, 1997, NCW launched a

programme of legal awareness for the visually handicapped and other disabled women because for they need public attention. Education and enlightened socialisation of children and girls of these categories are immediate imperatives before us. They need legal and social support, due attention, resources, and enforcement of laws.

We have prepared a few reports, the result of intensive consultations and interaction with women groups, experts, NGOs and government functionaries on various issues. We request you to be kind enough to release these.

Before I conclude, may we compliment your government for the profound initiatives and bold commitments made in the Annual Budget for the vast mass of our population, raising genuine hopes for a better future for the majority of our population.

---

*I destroy my enemies by making friends of them.

APPENDIX I

The National Commission for Women Act, 1990

(No. 20 of 1990)[1]

An Act to constitute a National Commission for Women and to provide for matters connected therewith or incidental thereto

Be it enacted by Parliament in the Forty-first Year of the Republic of India as follows:

CHAPTER I

Preliminary

1. **Short title, extent and commencement—** (1) This Act may be called the National Commission for Women Act, 1990.

(2) It extends to the whole of India except the State of Jammu and Kashmir.

(3) It shall come into force on such date[2] as the Central Government may, by notification in the Official Gazette, appoint.

2. **Definitions—** In this Act, unless the context otherwise requires, —

(a) "Commission" means the National Commission for Women constituted under section 3;

(b) "Member" means a Member of the Commission and includes the Member-Secretary;

(c) "prescribed" means prescribed by rules made under this Act.

CHAPTER II

The National Commission for Women

3. **Constitution of the National Commission for Women** — (1) The Central Government shall constitute[3] a body

to be known as the National Commission for Women to exercise the powers conferred on, and to perform the functions assigned to, it under this Act.

(2) The Commission shall consist of —

(a) a Chairperson, committed to the cause of women, to be nominated by the Central Government;

(b) five Members to be nominated by the Central Government from amongst persons of ability, integrity and standing who have had experience in law or legislation, trade unionism, management of an industry or organisation committed to increasing the employment potential of women, women's voluntary organisations (including women activists), administration, economic development, health, education or social welfare :

Provided that at least one Member each shall be from amongst persons belonging to the Scheduled Castes and Scheduled Tribes respectively;

(c) a Member-Secretary to be nominated by the Central Government, who shall be—

(i) an expert in the field of management, organisational structure or sociological movement, or

(ii) an officer who is a member of a civil service of the Union or of an all-India service or holds a civil post under the Union with appropriate experience.

4. **Term of office and conditions of service of Chairperson and Members**—(1) The Chairperson and every Member shall hold office for such period, not exceeding three years, as may be specified by the Central Government in this behalf.

2. The Chairperson or a Member (other than the Member-Secretary who is a member of a civil service of the Union

or of an all-India service or holds a civil post under the Union) may, by writing and addressed to the Central Government, resign from the office of Chairperson or, as the case may be, of the Member at any time.

(3) The Central Government shall remove a person from the office of Chairperson or a Member referred to in sub-section (2) if that person —

(a) becomes an undischarged insolvent;

(b) gets convicted and sentenced to imprisonment for an offence which in the opinion of the Central Government involves moral turpitude;

(c) becomes of unsound mind and stands so declared by a competent court;

(d) refuses to act or becomes incapable of acting;

(e) is, without obtaining leave of absence from the Commission, absent from three consecutive meetings of the Commission; or

(f) in the opinion of the Central Government has so abused the position of Chairperson or Member as to render that person's continuance in office detrimental to the public interest :

Provided that no person shall be removed under this clause until that person has been given a reasonable opportunity of being heard in the matter.

(4) A vacancy caused under sub-section (2) or otherwise shall be filled by fresh nomination.

(5) The salaries and allowances payable to, and the other terms and conditions of service of, the Chairperson and Members shall be such as may be prescribed.[4]

5. **Officers and other employees of the Commission**—(1) The Central Government shall provide the Commission with such officers and employees as may be necessary for the efficient performance of the functions of the Commission under this Act.

(2) The salaries and allowances payable to, and the other terms and conditions of service of, the officers and other employees appointed for the purpose of the Commission shall be such as may be prescribed.

6. **Salaries and allowances to be paid out of grants—** The salaries and allowances payable to the Chairperson and Members and administrative expenses, including salaries, allowances and pensions payable to the officers and other employees referred to in section 5, shall be paid out of the grants referred to in sub-section (1) of section 11.

7. **Vacancies, etc., not to invalidate proceedings of the Commission—** No act or proceeding of the Commission shall be questioned or shall be invalid on the ground merely of the existence of any vacancy or defect in the constitution of the Commission.

8. **Committees of the Commission—** (1) The Commission may appoint such committees as may be necessary for dealing with such special issues as may be taken up by the Commission from time to time.

(2) The Commission shall have the power to co-opt as members of any committee appointed under sub-section (1) such number of persons, who are not Members of the Commission, as it may think fit and the persons so co-opted shall have the right to attend the meetings of the committee and take part in its proceedings but shall not have the right to vote.

(3) The persons so co-opted shall be entitled to receive such allowances for attending the meetings of the committee as may be prescribed.[5]

9. **Procedure to be regulated by the Commission—**(1) The Commission or a Committee thereof shall meet as and when necessary and shall meet at such time and place as the Chairperson may think fit.

(2) The Commission shall regulate its own procedure and

the procedure of the Committees thereof.

(3) All orders and decisions of the Commission shall be authenticated by the Member-Secretary or any other officer of the Commission duly authorised by the Member-Secretary in this behalf.

CHAPTER III

Functions of the Commission

10. Functions of the Commission— (1) The Commission shall perform all or any of the following functions, namely, —

(a) investigate and examine all matters relating to the safeguards provided for women under the Constitution and other laws;

(b) present to the Central Government, annually and at such other times as the Commission may deem fit, reports upon the working of those safeguards;

(c) make in such reports recommendations for the effective implementation of those safeguards for improving the conditions of women by the Union or any State;

(d) review, from time to time, the existing provisions of the Constitution and other laws affecting women and recommend amendments thereto so as to suggest remedial legislative measures to meet any lacunae, inadequacies or shortcomings in such legislations;

(e) take up the cases of violation of the provisions of the Constitution and of other laws relating to women with the appropriate authorities;

(f) look into complaints and take *suo motu* notice of matters relating to, —

(i) deprivation of women's rights;

(ii) non-implementation of laws enacted to provide protection to women and also to achieve the objective of equality and development;

(iii) non-compliance of policy decisions, guidelines or instructions aimed at mitigating hardships and ensuring welfare and providing relief to women,

and take up the issues arising out of such matters with appropriate authorities;

(g) call for special studies or investigations into specific problems or situations arising out of discrimination and atrocities against women and identify the constraints so as to recommend strategies for their removal;

(h) undertake promotional and educational research so as to suggest ways of ensuring due representation of women in all spheres and identify factors responsible for impeding their advancement, such as, lack of access to housing and basic services, inadequate support services and technologies for reducing drudgery and occupational health hazards and for increasing their productivity;

(i) participate and advise on the planning process of socio-economic development of women;

(j) evaluate the progress of the development of women under the Union and any State;

(k) inspect or cause to be inspected a jail, remand home, women's institution or other place of custody where women are kept as prisoners or otherwise, and take up with the concerned authorities for remedial action, if found necessary;

(l) fund litigation involving issues affecting a large body of women;

(m) make periodical reports to the Government on any matter pertaining to women and in particular various difficulties under which women toil;

(n) any other matter which may be referred to it by Central Government.

(2) The Central Government shall cause all the reports referred to in clause (b) of sub-section (1) to be laid before each House of Parliament along with a memorandum explaining the action taken or proposed to be taken on the recommendations relating to the Union and the reasons for the non-acceptance, if any, of any of such recommendations.

(3) Where any such report or any part thereof relates to any matter with which any State Government is concerned, the Commission shall forward a copy of such report or part to such State Government who shall cause it to be laid before the Legislature of the State along with a memorandum explaining the action taken or proposed to be taken on the recommendations relating to the State and the reasons for the non-acceptance, if any, of any of such recommendations.

(4) The Commission shall, while investigating any matter referred to in clause (a) or sub-clause (i) of clause (f) of sub-section (l), have all the powers of a civil court trying a suit and, in particular in respect of the following matters, namely,—

(a) summoning and enforcing the attendance of any person from any part of India and examining him on oath;

(b) requiring the discovery and production of any document;

(c) receiving evidence on affidavits;

(d) requisitioning any public record or copy thereof from any court or office;

(e) issuing commissions for the examination of witnesses and documents; and

(f) any other matter which may be prescribed.

CHAPTER IV

Finance, Accounts and Audit

11. Grants by the Central Government— (1) The Central Government shall, after due appropriation made by Parliament by law in this behalf, pay to the Commission by way of grants such sums of money as the Central Government may think fit for being utilised for the purposes of this Act.

(2) The Commission may spend such sums as it thinks fit for performing the functions under this Act, and such sums shall be treated as expenditure payable out of the grants referred to in sub-section (1).

12. Accounts and audit— (1) The Commission shall maintain proper accounts and other relevant records and prepare an annual statement of accounts in such form as may be prescribed by the Central Government in consultation with the Comptroller and Auditor-General of India.

(2) The accounts of the Commission shall be audited by the Comptroller and Auditor-General at such intervals as may be specified by him and any expenditure incurred in connection with such audit shall be payable by the Commission to the Comptroller and Auditor-General.

(3) The Comptroller and Auditor-General and any person appointed by him in connection with the audit of the accounts of the Commission under this Act shall have the same rights and privileges and the authority in connection with such audit as the Comptroller and Auditor-General generally has in connection with the audit of Government accounts and, in particular, shall have the right to demand the production of books, accounts, connected vouchers and other documents and papers and to inspect any of the offices of the Commission.

(4) The accounts of the Commission, as certified by the Comptroller and Auditor-General or any other person appointed by him in this behalf, together with the audit report thereon shall be forwarded annually to the Central Government by the Commission.

13. **Annual report**— The Commission shall prepare in such form and at such time, for each financial year, as may be prescribed, its annual report, giving a full account of its activities during the previous financial year and forward a copy thereof to the Central Government.

14. **Annual report and audit report to be laid before Parliament**—The Central Government shall cause the annual report together with a memorandum of action taken on the recommendations contained therein, insofar as they relate to the Central Government and the reasons for the non-acceptance, if any, of any of such recommendations and the audit report to be laid as soon as may be after the reports are received, before each House of Parliament.

CHAPTER V
Miscellaneous

15. **Chairperson, Members and staff of the Commission to be public servants**— The Chairperson, the Members, officers and other employees of the Commission shall be deemed to be public servants within the meaning of section 21 of the Indian Penal Code (45 of 1860).

16. **Central Government to consult Commission**— The Central Government shall consult the Commission on all major policy matters affecting women.

17. **Power to make rules**— (1) The Central Government may, by notification in the Official Gazette, make rules for carrying out the provisions of this Act.

(2). In particular, and without prejudice to the generality of the foregoing power, such rules may provide for all or any of the following matters, namely,—

(a) salaries and allowances payable to, and the other terms and conditions of service of, the Chairperson and Members under sub-section (5) of section 4 and of officers and other employees under sub-section (2) of section 5;

(b) allowances for attending the meetings of the committee by the co-opted persons under sub-section (3) of section 8;

(c) other matters under clause (f) of sub-section (4) of section 10;

(d) the form in which the annual statement of accounts shall be maintained under sub-section (1) of section 12;

(e) the form in, and the time at, which the annual report shall be prepared under section 13;

(f) any other matter which is required to be, or may be prescribed.

(3) Every rule made under this Act shall be laid, as soon as may be after it is made, before each House of Parliament, while it is in session, for a total period of thirty days which may be comprised in one session or in two or more successive sessions, and if, before the expiry of the session immediately following the session or successive sessions aforesaid, both Houses agree in making any modification in the rule or both Houses agree that the rule should not be made, the rule shall thereafter have effect only in such modified form or be of no effect, as the case may be; so, however, that any such modification or annulment shall be without prejudice to the validity of anything previously done under that rule.

REFERENCES

1. The Act received the assent of the President on 30.8.1990.
2. The Act came into force on 31.1.1992, vide Notification No. S.O. 99 (E), dated 31.1.1992.
3. The National Commission for Women was constituted on 31.1.1992, vide Notification No. S.O. 100 (E), dated 31.1.1992.
4. The National Commission for Women (Salaries and Allowances of Chairperson and Members) Rules, 1992 vide G.S.R. 74 (E), dated 31.1.1992.
5. The National Commission for Women (Allowances Payable to Co-opted Members) Rules, 1992 vide G.S.R. 118(E), dated 21.2.1992.

APPENDIX II

Extracts from the Constitution (Seventy-third Amendment) Act, 1992

Part IX

The Panchayats

243D. (1) Seats shall be reserved for —

(a) the Scheduled Castes; and

(b) the Scheduled Tribes,

in every Panchayat and the number of seats so reserved shall bear, as nearly as may be, the same proportion, to the total number of seats to be filled by direct election in that Panchayat as the population of the Scheduled Castes in that Panchayat area or of the Scheduled Tribes in that Panchayat area bears to the total population of that area and such seats may be allotted by rotation to different constituencies in a Panchayat.

(2) Not less than one-third of the total number of seats reserved under clause (1) shall be reserved for women belonging to the Scheduled Castes or, as the case may be, the Scheduled Tribes.

(3) Not less than one-third (including the number of seats reserved for women belonging to the Scheduled Castes and the Scheduled Tribes) of the total number of seats to be filled by direct election in every Panchayat shall be reserved for women and such seats may be allotted by rotation to different constituencies in a Panchayat.

(4) The offices of the Chairpersons in the Panchayats at the village or any other level shall be reserved for the Scheduled Castes, the Scheduled Tribes and women in

such manner as the Legislature of a State may, by law, provide:

Provided that the number of offices of Chairpersons reserved for the Scheduled Castes and the Scheduled Tribes in the Panchayats at each level in any State shall bear, as nearly as may be, the same proportion to the total number of such offices in the Panchayats at each level as the population of the Scheduled Castes in the State or of the Scheduled Tribes in the State bears to the total population of the State :

Provided further that not less than one-third of the total number of offices of Chairpersons in the Panchayats at each level shall be reserved for women :

Provided also that the number of offices reserved under this clause shall be allotted by rotation to different Panchayats at each level.

(5) The reservation of seats under clauses (1) and (2) and the reservation of offices of Chairpersons (other than the reservation for women) under clause (4) shall cease to have effect on the expiration of the period specified in article 334.

(6) Nothing in this Part shall prevent the Legislature of a State from making any provision for reservation of seats in any Panchayat or offices or Chairpersons in the Panchayats at any level in favour of backward class of citizens.

APPENDIX III

List of State Commissions for Women

The Chairperson,
Assam State Commission for Women,
Bal Bhawan, Uzar Bazar,
Guwahati - 781 001

The Chairperson,
Delhi State Commission for Women,
G Block, IInd Floor,
I.P. Estate,
New Delhi - 110 002

The Chairperson,
Goa State Commission for Women,
Panaji

The Chairperson,
Himachal Pradesh State Commission for Women,
Shimla

The Chairperson,
Karnataka State Commission for Women,
Ist Floor, KHB Building,
Cauvery Bhawan, K.G. Road,
Bangalore - 560 009

The Chairperson,
Kerala State Commission for Women,
Poojappura,
Thiruvananthapuram - 695 012

The Chairperson,
Maharashtra State Commission for Women,
Griha Nirman Bhawan, Mezzanine Floor,
Bandra East,
Mumbai - 400 051

The Chairperson,
Orissa State Commission for Women,
10, Forest Park,
Bhubaneswar - 751 000

The Chairman,
Tamil Nadu State Commission for Women
19, Akbarabad Road,
First Street,
Chennai - 600 024

The Chairperson,
Tripura State Commission for Women,
Melarmath, Agartala,
Tripura

The Chairperson,
West Bengal State Commission for Women
Second Floor, 10 Rainey Park,
Calcutta - 700 019

The Chairperson,
Madhya Pradesh State Commission for Women,
Bhopal

APPENDIX IV

Constitutional Provisions Affecting Women

1. The Preamble to the Constitution of India resolves to secure to all its citizens:

JUSTICE, social, economic and political;

LIBERTY of thought, expression, belief, faith and worship;

EQUALITY of status and of opportunity; and to promote among them all;

FRATERNITY assuring the dignity of the individual and the unity and integrity of the nation.

To attain these national objectives, the Constitution guarantees certain Fundamental Rights to all its citizens. Again the Directive Principles of State Policy enunciated in the Constitution embody the major policy goals of a welfare state. They concretize together with the Fundamental Rights, the vision of a new India socio-political order. While the Fundamental Rights are justiciable and enforceable in courts of law, the Directive Principles are non-justiciable and non-enforceable in courts. But the Directive Principles are "nevertheless fundamental in the governance of the country" and the State is charged with a duty "to apply these principles in making laws." (Article 37 of the Constitution)

2. It will be noticed that while the Constitution guarantees certain Fundamental Rights and freedoms such as freedom of speech, protection of life and personal liberty, that may be termed positive rights, there are certain indirect rights such as prohibition of discrimination or denial of equal protection.

3. Indian women are the beneficiaries of these rights in the

same manner as Indian men. Article 14 ensures that the State shall not deny to any person equality before the law or the equal protection of the laws within the territory of India. Again Article 15 prohibits discrimination against any citizen on grounds only of religion, race, caste, sex, place of birth, or any of them. However, Article 15 (3) empowers the State to make any "special provision for women and children", even in violation of the fundamental obligation of non-discrimination among citizens, *inter alia* of sex. This provision has enabled the State to make special provisions for women, particularly in the field of labour legislation like the Factories Act, the Mines Act, etc. These special provisions in favour of women need not be restricted to measures which are beneficial in strict sense. Thus, it would support a provision like that in section 497 of the Indian Penal Code which says that in an offence of adultery, though the man is punishable for adultery, the woman is not punishable as an abettor. *(Yusuf vs. State of Bombay, AIR 1954 S.C.321)*. Restrictions upon the right of alienation of women have similarly been upheld. *(Kaur vs. Jaggar, AIR 1961 Punj. 489)*. Similarly, reservation of seats for women in local bodies or educational institutions has been held to be valid in view of the provisions of Article 15(3). *(Dattarya vs. State of Bombay, AIR 1953 Bom 311 and Sagar Vs. State AIR 1968 AP 1967)*

4. Article 16(1) guarantees that "there shall be equality of opportunity for all citizens in matters relating to employment or appointment to any office under the State." Again Article 16(2) guarantees that "no citizen shall, on grounds only of religion, race, caste, sex, descent, place of birth, residence or any of them be ineligible for, or discriminated against in respect of, any employment or office under the State." This obligation not to discriminate in matters relating to employment or appointment to any office under the State has thus ensured a significant position and status for Indian women.

5. Coming to the Directive Principles of State Policy, some of them concern women indirectly or by necessary implication. There are a few others which are specific to women. The ones which concern women directly and have a special bearing on their status are,—

—Article 39(a) which directs the State to frame its policy for ensuring that the citizens, men and women equally have the right to an adequate means of livelihood;

—Article 39(d) which directs the State to ensure that there is equal pay for equal work for both men and women;

—Article 39(e) which directs the State to ensure that the health and strength of workers — men and women and the tender age of children — are not abused and that citizens are not forced by economic necessity to enter avocations unsuited to their age or strength; and

—Article 42 which directs the State to make provision for ensuring just and humane conditions of work and maternity relief. Thus, the Fundamental Rights and the Directive Principles are the instruments for attaining our national objective of justice, liberty and equality. By adopting the principle of adult franchise, it seeks to establish a democratic republic by giving the adult population direct or indirect share in the Government. The special attention given to the needs of the women to enable them to enjoy and exercise their constitutional equality of status, along with other special provisions aimed at their participative role in society make the Indian Constitution a 'social' document embodying the objectives of a social revolution. It is clear that the Constitution contemplates attainment of an entirely new social order where all citizens are given equal opportunities and no discrimination takes place on the basis of race, religion, creed or sex.

—Article 51A. *Fundamental duties*—It shall be the duty of every citizen of India to promote harmony and the spirit of common brotherhood amongst all the people of India transcending religious, linguistic and regional or sectional diversities; to renounce practices derogatory to the dignity of women.

Source : Women Employees in Government, Monograph No. 3-86, Department of Personnel and Training, Government of India, New Delhi, pp 3-5 (as reproduced in ***Women in India—A Statistical Profile—1988).***

APPENDIX V

IN THE SUPREME COURT OF INDIA

Criminal Original Jurisdiction
Writ Petition (Criminal) Nos. 666-70 of 1992

Vishaka & Ors. (Petitioners)
Versus
State of Rajasthan & Ors. (Respondents)

Judgment

Verma, CJI

This Writ Petition has been filed for the *enforcement of the fundamental rights of working women under Articles 14, 19 and 21 of the Constitution of India* in view of the prevailing climate in which the violation of these rights is not uncommon. With the increasing awareness and emphasis on gender justice, there is increase in the effort to guard against such violations; and the resentment towards incidents of sexual harassment is also increasing. The present petition has been brought as a class action by certain social activists and NGOs with the aim of focussing attention towards this societal aberration and assisting in finding suitable methods for realisation of the true concept of 'gender equality'; and *to prevent sexual harassment of working women in all work places* through judicial process, to fill the vacuum in existing legislation.

The immediate cause for the filing of this writ petition is an incident of alleged brutal gang-rape of a social worker in a village of Rajasthan. That incident is the subject-matter of a separate criminal action and no further mention of it, by us, is necessary. The incident reveals the hazards to which a working woman may be exposed and the depravity to which sexual harassment can degenerate;

and the urgency for safeguards by an alternative mechanism in the absence of legislative measures.

In the absence of legislative measures, the need is to find an effective alternative mechanism to fulfil this felt and urgent social need.

Each such incident results in violation of the fundamental rights of 'Gender Equality' and the 'Right to Life and Liberty'. It is a clear *violation of the rights under Articles 14, 15 and 21 of the Constitution.* One of the logical consequences of such an incident is also the violation of the victim's fundamental right under Article 19(1)(g) *'to practise any profession or to carry out any occupation, trade or business.'* Such violations, therefore, attract the remedy under Article 32 for the enforcement of these fundamental rights of women. This class action under Article 32 of the Constitution is for this reason. A writ of mandamus in such a situation, if it is to be effective, needs to be accompanied by directions for prevention; as the violation of fundamental rights of this kind is a recurring phenomenon. The fundamental right to carry on any occupation, trade or profession depends on the availability of a 'safe' working environment. Right to life means life with dignity. The primary responsibility for ensuring such safety and dignity through suitable legislation, and the creation of a mechanism for its enforcement, is of the legislature and the executive. When, however, instances of sexual harassment resulting in violation of fundamental rights of women workers under Articles 14, 19 and 21 are brought before us for redress under Article 32, an effective redressal requires that some guidelines should be laid down for the protection of these rights to fill the legislative vacuum.

The notice of the petition was given to the State of Rajasthan and the Union of India. The learned Solicitor General appeared for the Union of India and rendered valuable assistance in the true spirit of a law officer to help us find a proper solution to this social problem of considerable magnitude. In addition to Ms. Meenakshi Arora and Ms. Naina Kapur who assisted the court with full commitment, Shri Fali S. Nariman appeared as amicus curiae and rendered great assistance. We place on record our great appreciation for every counsel who appeared in the case and rendered the needed assistance to the court which has enabled us to deal with this unusual matter in the manner considered appropriate for a cause of this nature.

Apart from Article 32 of the Constitution of India, we may refer to some other provisions which envisage judicial intervention for eradication of this social evil. Some provisions in the Constitution in addition to Articles 14, 19(1)(g) and 21, which have relevance are:

Article 15 :

"**15. Prohibition of discrimination on grounds of religion, race, caste, sex or place of birth**

(1) The State shall not discriminate against any citizen on the basis of religion, race, caste, sex, place of birth or any of them.

(2) xxx xxx xxx

(3) Nothing in this article shall prevent the State from making any special provision for women and children.

(4) xxx xxx xxx."

Article 42 :

"**42. Provision for just and humane conditions of work and maternity relief**—The State shall make provision for securing just and humane coditions of work and maternity relief."

"**51A. Fundamental duties** — It shall be the duty of every citizen of India —

(a) to abide by the Constitution and respect its ideals and institutions, ...

xxx xxx xxx

(e) to promote harmony and the spirit of common brotherhood amongst all the people of India transcending religious, linguistic and regional or sectional diversities; to renounce practices derogatory to the dignity of women;

xxx xxx xxx."

Before we refer to the international conventions and norms having relevance in this field and the manner in which they assume significance in application and judicial interpretation, we may advert to some other provisions in the Constitution which permit such use. These provisions are :

Article 51 :

"**51. Promotion of international peace and security** — The State shall endeavour to, —

xxx xxx xxx

(c) foster respect for international law and treaty obligations in the dealings of organised people with one another; and

xxx xxx xxx."

Article 253 :

"**253. Legislation for giving effect to international agreements** — Notwithstanding anything in the foregoing provisions of this Chapter, Parliament has power to make any law for the whole or any part of territory of India for implementing any treaty, agreement or convention with any other country or countries or any decision made at any international conference, association or other body."

Seventh Schedule :

"**List I — Union List :**

xxx xxx xxx

14. Entering into treaties and agreements with foreign

countries and implementing of treaties, agreements and conventions with foreign countries.

xxx xxx xxx."

In the absence of domestic law occupying the field, to formulate effective measures to check the evil of sexual harassment of working women at all work places, the contents of international conventions and norms are significant *for the purpose of interpretation of the guarantee of gender equality, right to work with human dignity* in Articles 14, 15, 19(1)(g) and 21 of the Constitution and *the safeguards against sexual harassment implicit therein.* Any international convention not inconsistent with the fundamental rights and in harmony and spirit must be read into these provisions to enlarge the scope and content thereof, to promote the object of the constitutional guarantee. This is implicit from Article 51(c) and the enabling power of the Parliament to enact laws for implementing the international conventions and norms by virtue of Article 253 read with Entry 14 of the Union List in Seventh Schedule of the Constitution. Article 73 also is relevant. It provides that the executive power of the Union shall extend to the matters with respect to which Parliament has power to make laws. The executive power of the Union is, therefore, available till the Parliament enacts legislation to expressly provide measures needed to curb the evil.

Thus, *the power of this court under Article 32 for enforcement of the fundamental rights and the executive power of the Union have to meet the challenge to protect the working women from sexual harassment and to make their fundamental rights meaningful.* Governance of the society by the rule of law mandates this requirement as a logical concomitant of the constitutional scheme. The exercise performed by the court in this matter is with this common perception shared with the learned Solicitor General and other members of the Bar who rendered valuable assistance in the performance of this difficult task in public interest.

The progress made at each hearing culminated in the formulation of guidelines to which the Union of India gave its consent through the learned Solicitor General, indicating that these should be the guidelines and norms declared by this court to govern the behaviour of the employers and all others at the work places to curb this social evil.

Gender equality includes protection from sexual harassment and right to work with dignity, which is a universally recognised basic human right. The common minimum requirement of this right has received global acceptance. The international conventions and norms are, therefore, of great significance in the formulation of the guidelines to achieve this purpose.

The obligation of this court under Article 32 of the Constitution for the enforcement of these fundamental rights in the absence of legislation must be viewed along with the role of judiciary envisaged in the Beijing Statement of Principles of the Independence of the Judiciary in the LAWASIA region. These principles were accepted by the Chief Justices of the Asia and the Pacific at Beijing in 1995 as those representing the minimum standards necessary to be observed in order to maintain the independence and effective, functioning of the judiciary. The objectives of the judiciary mentioned in the Beijing Statement are:

"Objectives of the Judiciary :

10. The objectives and functions of the Judiciary include the following :

(a) to ensure that all persons are able to live securely under the rule of law;

(b) to promote, within the proper limits of the judicial function, the observance and the attainment of human rights; and

(c) to administer the law impartially among persons and between persons and the State."

Some provisions in the 'Convention on the Elimination of All Forms of Discrimination against Women', of significance in the present context are :

Article 11 :

"1. State Parties shall take all appropriate measures to eliminate discrimination against women in the field of employment in order to ensure, on a basis of equality of men and women, the same rights, in particular, —

(a) the right to work as an inalienable right of all human beings;

xxx xxx xxx

(f) the right to protection of health and to safety in working conditions, including the safeguarding of the function of reproduction.

xxx xxx xxx."

Article 24 :

"States Parties undertake to adopt all necessary measures at the national level aimed at achieving the full realization of the rights recognised in the present convention."

The general recommendations of CEDAW in this context in respect of Article 11 are :

"Violence and equality in employment :

22. Equality in emplcyment can be seriously impaired when women are subjected to gender specific violence, such as sexual harassment in the work place.

23. Sexual harassment includes such unwelcome sexually determined behaviour as physical contacts and advances, sexually coloured remarks, showing pornography and sexual demands, whether by words or actions. Such conduct can be humiliating and may constitute a health and safety problem; it is discriminatory when the woman has reasonable grounds to believe that her objection would disadvantage her in connection with her employment, including recruiting or promotion, or when it creates a hostile working environment. Effective complaints procedures and remedies, including compensation, should be provided.

24. States should include in their reports information about sexual harassment, and on measures to protect women from sexual harassment and other forms of violence of coercion in the work place."

The Government of India has ratified the above Resolution on June 25, 1993 with some reservations which are not material in the present context. At the Fourth World Conference on Women in Beijing, the Government of India has also made an official commitment, *inter alia*, to formulate and operationalize a national policy on women which will continuously guide and inform action at every level and in every sector; to set up a Commission for Women's Rights to act as a public defender of women's human rights; to institutionalise a national level mechanism to monitor the implementation of the Platform for Action. We have, therefore, no hesitation in placing reliance on the above for the purpose of construing the nature and ambit of constitutional guarantee of gender equality in our Constitution.

The meaning and content of the fundamental rights guaranteed in the Constitution of India are of sufficient amplitude to encompass all the facets of gender equality including prevention of sexual harassment or abuse. Independence of judiciary forms a part of our constitutional scheme. The international conventions and norms are to be read into them in the absence of enacted domestic law occupying the field when there is no inconsistency between them. It is now an accepted rule of judicial construction that regard must be had to international conventions and norms for construing domestic law when there is no inconsistency between them and there is a void in the domestic law. The High

Court of Australia in *Minister for Immigration and Ethnic Affairs vs. Teoh, 128 ALR 353* has recognised the concept of legitimate expectation of its observance in the absence of a contrary legislative provision, even in the absence of a Bill of Rights in the Constitution of Australia.

In *Nilabati Behera Vs. State of Orissa, 1993(2)SCC 746*, a provision in the ICCPR was referred to support the view taken that 'an enforceable right to compensation is not alien to the concept of enforcement of a guaranteed right', as a public law remedy under Article 32, distinct from the private law remedy in torts. There is no reason why these international conventions and norms cannot, therefore, be used for construing the fundamental rights expressly guaranteed in the Constitution of India which embody the basic concept of gender equality in spheres of human activity.

In view of the above, and the absence of enacted law to provide for the effective enforcement of the basic human rights, gender equality and guarantee against sexual harassment abuse, more particularly against sexual harassment at work places, we lay down the guidelines and norms specified hereinafter for due observance at all work places or other institutions, until a legislation is enacted for the purpose. This is done in exercise of the power available under Article 32 of the Constitution for enforcement of the fundamental rights and it is further emphasised that this would be treated as the law declared by this court under Article 141 of the Constitution.

The guidelines and norms prescribed herein are as under :

Having regard to the definition of 'human rights' in section 2(d) of the Protection of Human Rights Act, 1993, taking note of the fact that the present civil and penal laws in India *do not adequately provide for specific protection of women from sexual harassment in work places* and that enactment of such legislation will take considerable time, it is necessary and expedient *for employers in work places as well as other responsible persons or institutions to observe certain guidelines to ensure the prevention of sexual harassment of women.*

1. Duty of the employer or other responsible persons in work places and other institutions

It shall be the duty of the employer or other responsible persons in work places or other institutions to prevent or deter the commission of acts of sexual harassment and to provide the procedures for the resolution, settlement or prosecution of acts of sexual harassment by taking all steps required.

2. Definition

For this purpose, sexual harassment includes such unwelcome sexually determined behaviour (whether directly or by implication) as —

a) physical contact and advances;

b) a demand or request for sexual favours;

c) sexually coloured remarks;

d) showing pornography;

e) any other unwelcome physical, verbal or non-verbal conduct of sexual nature.

Where any of these acts is committed in circumstances where-under the victim of such conduct has a reasonable apprehension that in relation to the victim's employment or work whether she is drawing salary, or honorarium or voluntary, whether in government, public or private enterprise such conduct can be humiliating and may constitute a health and safety problem. It is discriminatory for instance when the woman has reasonable grounds to believe that her objection would disadvantage her in connection with her employment or work including recruiting or promotion or when it creates a hostile work environment. Adverse consequences might be visited if the victim does not consent to the conduct in question or raises any objection thereto.

3. Preventive steps

All employers or persons in charge of work place whether in the public or private sector should take appropriate steps *to prevent sexual harassment. Without prejudice to the generality of this obligation they should take the following steps:*

(a) Express prohibition of sexual harassment as defined above at the work place should be notified, published and circulated in appropriate ways.

(b) The rules/regulations of Government and public sector bodies relating to conduct and discipline should include rules/ regulations prohibiting sexual harassment and provide for appropriate penalties in such rules against the offender.

(c) As regards private employers steps should be taken to include the aforesaid prohibitions in the standing orders under the Industrial Employment (Standing Orders) Act, 1946.

(d) Appropriate work conditions should be provided in respect of work, leisure, health and hygiene to further ensure that there is no hostile environment towards women at work places and no employee woman should have reasonable grounds to believe that she is disadvantaged in connection with her employment.

4. Criminal proceedings

Where such conduct amounts to a specific offence under the Indian Penal Code or under any other law, the employer shall initiate appropriate action in accordance with law by making a complaint with the appropriate authority.

In particular, it should ensure that victims, or witnesses are not victimized or discriminated against while dealing with complaints of sexual harassment. The victims of sexual harassment should have the option to seek transfer of the perpetrator or their own transfer.

5. Disciplinary action

Where such conduct amounts to misconduct in employment as defined by the relevant service rules, appropriate disciplinary action should be initiated by the employer in accordance with those rules.

6. Complaint mechanism

Whether or not such conduct constitutes an offence under law or a breach of the service rules, an appropriate complaint mechanism should be created in the employer's organization for redress of the complaint made by the victim. Such complaint mechanism should ensure time bound treatment of complaint.

7. Complaints Committee

The complaint mechanism, referred to in (6) above, should be adequate to provide, where necessary, a Complaints Committee, a special counsellor or other support service, including the maintenance of confidentiality.

The Complaints Committee should be headed by a woman and not less than half of its member should be women. Further, to prevent the possibility of any undue pressure or influence from senior levels, such Complaints Committee should involve a third party, either NGO or other body who is familiar with the issue of sexual harassment.

The Complaints Committee must make an annual report to the Government department concerned of the complaints and action taken by them. The employers and person in charge will also report on the compliance with the aforesaid guidelines including on the reports of the Complaints Committee to the Government department.

8. Workers' initiative

Employees should be allowed to raise issues of sexual harassment at workers' meeting and in other appropriate forum and it should be affirmatively discussed in employer-employee meetings.

9. Awareness

Awareness of the rights of female employees in this regard should be created in particular by prominently notifying the guidelines (and appropriate legislation when enacted on the subject) in a suitable manner.

10. Third party harassment

Where sexual harassment occurs as a result of an act or omission by any third party or outsider, the employer and person in charge will take all steps necessary and reasonable to assist the affected person in terms of support and preventive action.

11. The Central/State Governments are requested to consider adopting suitable measures including legislation to ensure that the guidelines laid down by this order are also observed by the employers in private sector.

12. These guidelines will not prejudice any rights available under the protection of Human Rights Act, 1993.

Accordingly, we direct that the above guidelines and norms would be strictly observed in all work places for the preservation and enforcement of the right to gender equality of the working women. These directions would be binding and enforceable in law until suitable legislation is enacted to occupy the field. These Writ Petitions are disposed of, accordingly.

New Delhi,
August 13, 1997

APPENDIX VI

Literacy and Education

Literacy Rates by Sex, India — 1901-91

Census Year	Percentage of literates to total population		
	Males	*Females*	*Persons*
(1)	(2)	(3)	(4)
1901	9.83	0.69	5.35
1911	10.56	1.05	5.92
1921	12.21	1.81	7.16
1931	15.59	2.93	9.50
1941	24.90	7.30	16.10
1951	27.16	8.86	18.33
1961	40.40	15.34	28.31
1971	45.95	21.97	34.45
1981	56.37	29.75	43.56
1991	64.13	39.29	52.21

Note : 1. For the years 1901 to 1941, figures relate to total population. For the years 1951 to 1971, the figures?

2. The 1981 figures exclude Assam where the 1981 census was not conducted and the 1991 figures exclude Jammu and Kashmir where the 1991 census was not conducted.

Source: 1. Census of India 1991. Paper 1 of 1981, Provisional Population Totals, Registrar General and Census Commissioner, India.

2. Census of India 1991, Series - 1 India, Paper 1 of 1991. Provisional Population Totals, Registrar General and Census Commissioner, India.

3. Census of India 1991, Series-1 India, Paper 2 of 1992. Final Population Totals: Brief Analysis of Primary Census Abstract, Registrar General and Census Commissioner, India.

Number of School Level Teachers by Sex, India — 1950-51 to 1995-96

(in .000)

	Number of teachers								
	Primary schools			*Middle schools*			*High/Higher Secondary Schools*		
Year	*Total*	*Male*	*Female*	*Total*	*Male*	*Female*	*Total*	*Male*	*Female*
(1)	*(2)*	*(3)*	*(4)*	*(5)*	*(6)*	*(7)*	*(8)*	*(9)*	*(10)*
1950-51	538	82	456	86	73	13	127	107	20
1955-56	691	574	117	151	132	19	190	155	35
1960-61	742	615	127	345	262	83	296	234	62
1965-66	944	764	180	528	389	139	479	368	111
1970-71	1060	835	225	638	463	175	629	474	155
1975-76	1248	955	342	778	554	224	759	559	200
1980-81	1363	1021	342	851	598	253	926	669	257
1985-86	1496	1094	402	968	663	305	1132	793	339
1990-91	1616	1143	473	1073	717	356	1334	917	417
1991-92	1636	1144	492	1079	714	365	1381	931	450
1992-93*	1682	1189	493	1082	736	346	1353	908	445
1993-94*	1703	1196	507	1080	710	370	1405	938	467
1994-95*	1714	1181	533	1122	732	390	1446	956	490
1995-96*	1740	1187	553	1165	756	409	1493	982	511

* Provisional

Source : Selected Educational Statistics, 1995-96, Department of Education, Ministry of Human Resource Development.

Percentage of Girls in School Enrolment by Stages, India — 1950-51 to 1995-96

Year I-V	*Primary VI-VIII*	*Middle 10+2/Inter*	*Sec/Hr. Sec. (Degree & above)*	*Hr. Education*
(1)	*(2)*	*(3)*	*(4)*	*(5)*
1950-51	28.1	16.1	13.3	10.0
1955-56	30.5	20.8	15.4	14.6
1960-61	32.6	23.9	20.5	16.0
1965-66	36.2	26.7	22.0	20.4
1970-71	37.4	29.3	25.0	20.0
1975-76	38.1	31.3	26.9	26.7
1980-81	38.6	32.9	29.6	26.7
1985-86	40.3	35.6	30.3	33.0
1990-91	41.5	36.7	32.9	33.3
1991-92*	42.6	38.8	33.9	33.2
1993-94*	42.7	39.1	34.3	33.5
1994-95*	42.8	38.9	34.4	34.0
1995-96*	43.2	39.0	35.3	35.8

*Provisional

Source : Selected Educational Statistics, 1995-96, Department of Education, Ministry of Human Resource Development, New Delhi.

Dropout Rates in Schools for General Education by Stages and Sex, India—1980-81 to 1994-95

		Primary Stage Classes (I-V)			Middle Stage Classes (I-VIII)			High School Stage Classes (I-X)		
No.	Year	Boys	Girls	Total	Boys	Girls	Total	Boys	Girls	Total
(1)	(2)	(3)	(4)	(5)	(6)	(7)	(8)	(9)	(10)	(11)
1.	1980-81	56.20	62.50	58.70	68.00	79.40	72.70	79.80	86.63	82.46
2.	1981-82	51.10	57.30	53.50	68.50	77.70	72.10	79.44	86.81	82.33
3.	1982-83	49.40	56.30	52.10	66.04	74.96	69.57	78.21	86.24	81.37
4.	1983-84	47.83	53.96	50.26	66.10	75.27	69.26	76.41	84.79	79.71
5.	1984-85	45.62	51.41	47.93	61.83	70.87	65.39	74.71	83.34	78.13
6.	1985-86	45.84	50.27	47.61	60.70	70.04	64.42	73.97	83.16	77.62
7.	1986-87	46.87	51.17	48.60	61.44	70.16	64.90	73.27	81.31	76.44
8.	1987-88	43.28	49.42	46.97	58.80	67.55	62.29	72.14	80.06	75.30
9.	1988-89	46.74	49.69	47.93	59.38	68.31	65.40	72.68	79.46	75.36
10.	1989-90	46.50	50.35	48.08	61.00	68.75	64.09	70.99	77.72	73.66
11.	1990-91	40.10	45.97	42.60	59.12	65.13	60.91	67.50	76.96	71.34
12.	1991-92*	41.03	45.17	42.78	54.30	62.04	57.48	68.55	75.87	71.51
13.	1992-93*	40.07	43.02	41.30	53.99	60.06	56.48	68.15	74.69	70.80
14.	1993-94*	36.07	39.05	37.32	49.55	56.78	52.80	68.41	74.54	70.90
15.	1994-95*	35.18	37.79	36.27	50.02	56.53	52.74	67.15	73.78	69.89

*Provisional

Source: Department of Education, Ministry of Human Resource Development, New Delhi.

Employment and Training

Total and Percentage Women Employees in Central Government — 1971 to 1991

Years	*No. of Employees* *Total (in lakhs)*	*Women*	*Percentage of Women to total employees*
(1)	*(2)*	*(3)*	*(4)*
1971	26.99	67369	2.51
1972	27.51	70874	2.58
1973	28.58	72879	2.55
1974	29.12	80371	2.76
1975	29.70	84051	2.83
1976	30.45	99272	3.26
1978	31.01	102321	3.30
1979	31.71	107172	3.38
1980	33.21	117139	3.53
1981	34.07	124032	3.64
1982	34.78	132010	3.80
1983	35.42	136598	3.86
1984	36.14	142011	3.93
1988	36.99	238984	6.46
1989	37.48	247158	6.60
1990	37.74	283380	7.52
1991	38.13	288999	7.58

Source : Census of Central Government Employees, Directorate General of Employment and Training. Ministry of Labour, New Delhi.

Personnel by Sex in All India and Central Services—1993-96

		Total			Scheduled Castes		Scheduled Tribes	
Central Service	*Year*	*Men*	*Women*	*Total*	*Men*	*Women*	*Men*	*Women*
(1)	(2)	(3)	(4)	(5)	(6)	(7)	(8)	(9)
Indian Administrative Service	1993	4427	455	4882	487	28	237	21
	1994	4427	483	4910	486	25	233	19
	1995	4473	492	4965	481	27	234	21
	1996	4546	501	5047	512	34	247	23
Indian Audit & Accounts Service	1993	483	90	573	93	4	29	—
	1994	488	89	577	96	4	28	—
	1995	439	95	534	99	4	28	—
Indian Customs & Central Excise Service	1993	1502	107	1609	192	11	85	10
	1994	1519	112	1631	202	11	93	12
	1995	1520	117	1637	222	11	86	12
	1996	1531	130	1661	228	11	89	12
Indian Economic Service	1993	311	72	383	NA	NA	NA	NA
	1994	326	76	402	NA	NA	NA	NA
	1995	341	82	423	NA	NA	NA	NA
(As on 31st Dec.)	1996	330	64	394	55	4	18	-
Indian Foreign Service								
(As on Ist April)	1993	507	57	564	70	2	29	4
(As on 15th April)	1994	489	59	548	75	2	34	4
(As on 15th April)	1995	481	66	547	81	2	31	4
Indian Forest Service	1993	2327	65	2392	NA	NA	NA	NA
	1994	2328	68	2396	NA	NA	NA	NA
(As on 31st Dec.)	1995	2390	73	2463	NA	NA	NA	NA
	1996	2387	78	2465	NA	NA	NA	NA
Indian Information Service	1994	424	80	504	48	15	4	3
	1995	417	76	493	52	18	4	4
(As on Ist January)	1996	400	74	474	51	15	4	4
Indian Police Service (As on 1st January)	1996	2883	64	2947	NA	NA	NA	NA
Indian Postal Service	1993	312	66	378	46	5	24	2
(As on Ist October)	1994	276	68	344	41	5	20	2
	1995	256	70	326	37	6	18	2
	1996	282	77	359	44	8	20	2

Central Service	*Year*	*Total* *Men*	*Total* *Women*	*Total* *Total*	*Scheduled Castes* *Men*	*Scheduled Castes* *Women*	*Scheduled Tribes* *Men*	*Scheduled Tribes* *Women*
(1)	*(2)*	*(3)*	*(4)*	*(5)*	*(6)*	*(7)*	*(8)*	*(9)*
Indian	1993	2032	224	2256	375	10	146	4
Revenue	1994	2022	246	2268	400	13	148	5
Service	1995	1980	276	2256	390	14	164	10
Indian	1993	570	35	605	59	3	6	1
Statistical	1994	550	35	585	69	3	5	1
Service	1995	481	35	516	66	3	8	1
Central	1993	—	—	742	—	—	—	—
Secretariat	1994	—	—	688	—	—	—	—
Service*	1995	—	—	678	—	—	—	—
(As on 1st January)	1996	657	51	708	86	1	12	1

Note : Figures relate to only Group A officers.

Source : Department of Personnel & Training, Ministry of Personnel, Public Grievances and Pensions, New Delhi.
Department of Revenue, Ministry of Finance, New Delhi.
Ministry of Information & Broadcasting, New Delhi.
Department of Economic Affairs, Ministry of Finance, New Delhi.
Ministry of External Affairs, New Delhi.
Department of Statistics, Ministry of Planning, New Delhi.
Ministry of Home Affairs, New Delhi.
Department of Posts, Ministry of Communications, New Delhi.
Ministry of Environment & Forests, New Delhi.
Office of the Comptroller and Auditor General of India, New Delhi.

Number of Judges by Sex in Supreme Court/High Courts — 1996*

Sl. No.	*Name of Court*	*Number of Judges*		
		Total	*Male*	*Female*
	Supreme Court	25	24	01
	High Court			
1.	Allahabad	63	62	01
2.	Andhra Pradesh	37	36	01
3.	Bombay	51	48	03
4.	Calcutta	40	39	01
5.	Delhi	28	27	01
6.	Guwahati	17	16	01
7.	Gujarat	29	28	01
8.	Himachal Pradesh	08	07	01
9.	Jammu & Kashmir	10	10	-
10.	Karnataka	30	30	-
11.	Kerala	23	22	01
12.	Madhya Pradesh	28	27	01
13.	Madras	23	23	-
14.	Orissa	14	14	-
15.	Patna	33	32	01
16.	Punjab & Haryana	33	32	01
17.	Rajasthan	32	31	01
18.	Sikkim	02	02	-
	Total	526	510	16

*Figures as on Ist October

Source : Department of Justice, Ministry of Law & Justice, New Delhi.

Total and Women Chartered Accountants by Region Registered with the Institute of Chartered Accountants of India—1995-96

Region	1995		1996	
	Total	Women	Total	Women
Western	23,036	1,652	23,911	1,883
Southern	18,270	1,020	19,240	1,214
Eastern	8,494	258	8,897	315
Central	7,600	173	8,023	199
Northern	13,563	594	14,281	699
Total	70,963	3,697	74,352	4,310

Note : As on Ist April each year

Source : Institute of Chartered Accountants of India, New Delhi.

Health, Family Welfare and Nutrition

Number of doctors by sex and qualification registered with State Medical Councils, India—1990-95

Year	Number of registered medical practitioners					
	Graduates		Licentiates		Total	
	Males	Females	Males	Females	Males	Females
(1)	(2)	(3)	(4)	(5)	(6)	(7)
1990	5,05,013	1,53,389	51,430	5,522	5,56,443	1,58,911
1991	4,08,529	1,12,647	41,887	3,831	4,50,416	1,16,478
1992	5,76,340	1,58,399	84,972	6,439	6,61,312	1,64,838
1993	6,06,011	1,70,490	87,319	6,470	6,93,330	1,76,960
1994	4,96,629	1,29,542	75,383	5,236	5,72,012	1,34,778
1995	4,36,287	1,27,496	65,590	4,342	5,01,877	1,31,836

Note : Refers to position as on 31st December of respective years

Source : Medical Council of India, New Delhi.

Number of qualified nurses, midwives, auxillary nurses and health visitors registered with State Nursing Councils, India — 1986-94

Year	Number of: Nurses/Midwives		Auxillary nurses midwives	Health visitors
	Males	Females		
(1)	(2)	(3)	(4)	(5)
1986	6,719	3,85,951	1,08,511	13,248
1987	6,838	3,73,107	1,10,016	12,741
1988	11,290	2,34,115	1,32,923	16,419
1989	14,071	2,50,433	1,41,191	16,635
1990	--3,11,235--		1,50,431	17,892
1991	16,320	3,23,888	1,50,658	17,302
1992	17,985	3,67,425	1,65,143	17,910
1993	18,762	4,30,589	2,03,451	22,144
1994	19,119	4,93,476	2,29,304	24,411

Note : 1. As at end of year
2. For 1990 separate figures for males and females are not available in respect of nurses/midwives

Source : Indian Nursing Council, New Delhi.

Social Defence

Incidence of crimes against women by crime head—1990-1994

Sl. No.	Crime Head	Year 1990	1991	1992	1993	1994	Percentage Variation in 1994 over 1990	1993
(1)	(2)	(3)	(4)	(5)	(6)	(7)	(8)	(9)
1.	Rape	9,518	9,793	11,112	11,242	12,351	29.8	9.9
2.	Kidnapping & abduction	11,699	12,300	12,077	11,837	12,998	11.1	-
3.	Dowry deaths	4,836	5,157	4,962	5,817	4,935	2.0	-15.2
4.	Torture	13,450	15,949,	19,750	22,064	25,946	92.9	17.6
5.	Molestation	20,194	20,611	20,385	20,985	24,117	19.4	14.9
6.	Sexual harassment	8,620	10,283	10,571	12,009	10,496	21.8	-12.6
7.	Importation of Girls*	-	-	-	-	167	-	-
8.	Sati Prevention Act*	-	-	-	-	2	-	-
9.	Immoral Traffic* (Prevention) Act	-	-	-	-	7,547	-	-
10.	Indecent Representation* of Women Act	-	-	-	-	389	-	-
	Total crimes against women	68,317	74,093	79,037	83,954	98,948	45.0	17.9
	Percentage to total IPC crimes	4.3	4.4	4.7	5.2	5.6	-	-

*Data collection under the crime head commenced in 1994.

Incidence and rate of cognizable crimes under IPC by crime head, India—1989-94

Crime Head	*Incidence and Rate*						*Quinquennial Avg. 1989-1993*	*Percentage change in 1994 over*	
	1989	*1990*	*1991*	*1992*	*1993*	*1994*	*(Q.A.)*	*1993*	*(Q.A.)*
(1)	*(2)*	*(3)*	*(4)*	*(5)*	*(6)*	*(7)*	*(8)*	*(9)*	*(10)*
Murder	31,222	35,045	39,174	40,105	38,240	38,577	36,757	0.9	5.0
	(3.8)	(4.2)	(4.6)	(4.6)	(4.3)	(4.3)	(4.3)		
Attempt to commit murder	23,748	27,095	29,778	31,202	29,725	30,020	28,310	1.0	6.0
	(2.9)	(3.3)	(3.5)	(3.6)	(3.4)	(3.3)	(3.3)		
Culpable homicide not amounting to murder	4,100	4,281	4,243	4,621	3,890	3,946	4,227	1.4	-6.6
	(0.5)	(0.5)	(0.5)	(0.5)	(0.4)	(0.4)	(0.5)		
Rape	9,752	10,068	10,410	11,708	12,218	13,208	10,831	8.1	21.9
	(1.2)	(1.2)	(1.2)	(1.3)	(1.4)	(1.5)	(1.3)		
Kidnapping and abduction	17,318	18,474	20,079	20,518	19,830	20,983	19,244	5.8	9.0
	(2.1)	(2.2)	(2.4)	(2.4)	(2.2)	(2.3)	(2.3)		
(i) Of women & girls	14,169	14,446	14,283	13,996	14,058	14,075	14,190	0.1	-0.8
	(1.7)	(1.7)	(1.7)	(1.6)	(1.6)	(1.6)	(1.7)		

(1)	(2)	(3)	(4)	(5)	(6)	(7)	(8)	(9)	(10)
(ii) Of others	3,149	4,028	5,796	6,522	5,772	6,908	5,053	19.7	36.7
	(0.4)	(0.5)	(0.7)	(0.8)	(0.7)	(0.8)	(0.6)		
Dacoity	9,896	11,089	10,831	11,308	9,357	9,271	10,496	-0.9	-11.7
	(1.2)	(1.3)	(1.3)	(1.3)	(1.1)	(1.0)	(1.2)		
Preparation and assembly for dacoity	1,015	1,286	1,393	1,297	1,102	946	1,219	-14.2	-22.4
	(0.1)	(0.2)	(0.2)	(0.1)	(0.1)	(0.1)	(0.1)		
Robbery	22,480	25,440	26,428	26,444	24,354	23,933	25,029	-1.7	-4.4
	(2.8)	(3.1)	(3.1)	(3.0)	(2.8)	(2.7)	(3.0)		
Burglary	1,29,020	1,31.331	1,32,087	1,27,281	1,23,020	1,21,536	1,28,548	1.2	-5.5
	(15.9)	(15.9)	(15.5)	(14.7)	(13.9)	(13.5)	(15.2)		
Theft	3,41,240	3,53.191	3,62,928	3,50,582	3,20,434	3,03,564	3,45,675	-5.3	-12.2
	(42.0)	(42.7)	(42.7)	(40.4)	(36.3)	(33.7)	(40.8)		
Riots	98,943	1,02.846	1,05,309	1,04,749	93,838	94,344	1,01,137	0.5	-6.7
	(12.2)	(12.4)	(12.4)	(12.1)	(10.6)	(10.5)	(11.9)		

Crime Head	*Incidence and Rate*						*Quinquennial Avg. 1989-1993*	*Percentage change in 1994 over*	
	1989	*1990*	*1991*	*1992*	*1993*	*1994*	*(Q.A.)*	*1993*	*(Q.A.)*
(1)	*(2)*	*(3)*	*(4)*	*(5)*	*(6)*	*(7)*	*(8)*	*(9)*	*(10)*
Criminal breach of trust	17,541 (2.2)	16,552 (2.0)	17,495 (2.1)	17,925 (2.1)	17,039 (1.9)	16,523 (1.8)	17,310 (2.0)	-3.0	-4.5
Cheating	23,691 (2.9)	24,466 (3.0)	27,466 (3.2)	29,397 (3.4)	30,079 (3.4)	31,207 (3.5)	27,020 (3.2)	3.8	15.5
Counterfeiting	2,075 (0.3)	2,576 (0.3)	4,467 (0.5)	5,133 (0.6)	3,728 (0.4)	2,851 (0.3)	3,596 (0.4)	-23.5	-20.7
Other IPC crimes	7,97,803 (98.3)	8,40,709 (101.7)	8,86,287 (104.3)	9,07,071 (104.5)	9,03,082 (102.2)	9,24,342 (102.7)	8,66,990 (102.2)	2.4	6.6
Total cognizable crimes under IPC	15,29,844 (188.5)	16,04,449 (194.0)	16,78,375 (197.5)	16,89,341 (194.7)	16,29,936 (184.4)	16,35,251 (181.7)	16,26,389 (191.8)	0.3	0.5

Note : Figures in brackets indicate rate of crime per lakh of population.

Source : Crime in India, 1994, National Crime Records Bureau.

DEMOGRAPHY

Population by sex, sex ratio and growth, India — 1901-91

Year	Population			Sex ratio (fameles) per 1000 males)	Decadal variation (per cent)	Annual average exponential growth rate (per cent)	Urban population as percentage to total population
	Persons	Males	Females				
(1)	(2)	(3)	(4)	(5)	(6)	(7)	(8)
1901	23,83,96,327	12,07,91,301	11,73,58,672	972	10.84		
1911	25,20,93,390	12,83,85,368	12,37,08,022	964	+5.75	0.56	10.29
1921	25,13,21,213	12,85,46,225	12,27,74,988	955	-0.31	-0.03	11.18
1931	27,89,77,238	14,29,29,689	13,57,88,921	950	+11.00	1.04	11.99
1941	31,86,60,580	16,36,85,302	15,46,90,267	945	+14.22	1.33	13.86
1951	36,10,88,090	18,55,28,462	17,55,59,628	946	+13.31	1.25	17.29
1961	43,92,34,771	28,62,93,201	21,29,41,570	941	+21.51	1.96	17.97
1971	54,81,59,692	28,40,49,276	26,41,10,378	930	+24.80	2.20	19.9
1981*	68,33,29,097	35,33,74,460	32,99,54,537	933	+24.66	2.22	23.31
1991**	84,63,02,688	43,92,30,458	40,70,72,230	927	+23.85	2.14	25.71

Note : The population figures exclude the area under illegal occupation of Pakistan and China.

* The 1981 Census was not held in Assam. The figures for 1981 include the interpolated population of Assam.

** The 1991 Census was not held in Jammu & Kashmir. The figures for 1991 include the population of Jammu & Kashmir as projected by the Standing Committee of Experts on Population Projections (October, 1989).

Source : i) Census of India 1991, Series-1 India, Paper-1 of 1991, Provisional Population Totals, Office of the Registrar General & Census Commissioner. India.

ii) Census of India 1991, Series-1 India, Paper-2 of 1992, Final Population Totals : Brief Analysis of Primary Census Abstract, Registrar General & Census Commissioner, India.

Percentage married among females by age group, India (rural, urban)—1961-91

Age Group	Rural				Urban			
	1961	*1971*	*1981*	*1991*	*1961*	*1971*	*1981*	*1991*
(1)	*(2)*	*(3)*	*(4)*	*(5)*	*(6)*	*(7)*	*(8)*	*(9)*
All ages	46.91	45.70	46.91	48.22	43.20	42.43	43.46	46.35
10-14	22.00	13.47	7.82	5.30	6.79	3.73	2.17	2.18
15-19	73.65	61.03	48.92	40.68	51.60	35.91	27.89	21.32
20-24	93.17	91.40	88.37	86.07	85.52	79.68	73.47	70.62
25-29	94.46	95.32	95.35	95.07	92.83	93.49	91.40	91.10
30-34	91.48	94.09	95.07	95.46	91.19	93.91	93.99	94.29
35-39	86.99	91.24	93.25	94.56	87.17	91.78	92.91	94.06
40-44	77.76	84.22	88.00	90.79	77.17	84.09	87.13	90.24
45-49	69.96	78.26	88.33	87.94	68.45	77.00	81.48	86.38
50-54	53.52	62.63	69.65	77.05	51.77	60.63	67.64	75.83
55-59	49.11	58.29	68.48	76.29	45.67	54.41	62.72	71.91
60-64	29.67	37.17	43.63	53.76	27.89	34.71	40.87	52.48
65-69	27.53	35.25	41.55	51.82	25.19	31.26	36.87	47.94
70 and above	15.08	19.47	22.11	30.21	13.11	16.73	20.13	22.34

Source : Census of India 1991, Series-1 India, Office of the Registrar General, India, New Delhi.

Vitals Statistics

Age-specific fertility rates, India (rural, urban, total)—1971-1993

Year Rate	Area	Total Fertility	Age-specific fertility rates						
			15-19	20-24	25-29	30-34	35-39	40-44	45-49
(1)	(2)	(3)	(4)	(5)	(6)	(7)	(8)	(9)	(10)
1971*	Total	5.2	100.8	150.8	254.8	202.2	137.8	62.2	24.4
	Rural	5.4	110.6	260.9	261.6	212.4	147.5	68.2	26.3
	Urban	4.1	64.9	213.9	227.9	158.0	96.5	34.9	15.4
1976*	Total	4.7	83.0	249.5	238.8	179.7	116.1	53.3	15.7
	Rural	5.0	87.0	260.2	250.8	190.9	126.3	58.9	17.3
	Urban	3.6	64.6	213.7	197.5	133.9	73.6	28.9	8.3
1981	Total	4.5	90.4	246.9	232.1	167.7	102.5	44.0	19.6
	Rural	4.8	98.2	261.3	244.9	180.4	112.6	48.4	22.0
	Urban	3.3	58.1	195.0	187.0	117.8	60.1	24.5	9.1
1986	Total	4.2	91.1	252.8	216.4	139.2	78.6	37.9	14.9
	Rural	4.5	100.3	264.6	229.4	153.6	89.3	43.5	17.8
	Urban	3.1	62.1	217.8	179.0	94.5	45.0	17.6	4.7
1990	Total	3.8	83.1	237.0	198.5	121.6	72.5	31.2	12.9
	Rural	4.1	92.6	249.8	209.7	135.0	82.2	36.0	14.7
	Urban	2.8	49.6	197.8	165.5	81.8	40.7	15.7	6.2
1991**	Total	3.6	76.1	234.0	191.3	117.0	66.8	30.6	12.1
	Rural	3.9	84.5	244.6	202.3	128.6	75.9	35.3	14.0
	Urban	2.7	46.1	200.7	158.7	81.6	37.4	14.9	5.3
1992**	Total	3.6	74.4	235.2	189.6	113.0	66.0	30.9	11.4
	Rural	3.9	83.3	249.4	200.8	125.1	75.3	35.2	13.0
	Urban	2.6	42.4	189.6	155.5	75.8	35.5	16.7	5.8
1993**	Total	3.5	236.1	307.9	207.6	121.3	65.7	31.8	12.0
	Rural	3.8	240.2	312.4	213.2	131.6	75.8	37.3	13.2
	Urban	2.8	213.1	292.8	194.1	95.3	41.1	16.0	8.5

*Excludes Jammu & Kashmir
**Excludes Bihar and West Bengal

Source: Sample Registration System. Fertility & Mortality Indicators. 1971, 1976, 1981, 1986, 1990 to 1993. Office of the Registrar General, India, New Delhi

Expectation of life at birth by sex, India (rural, urban, total) — 1970-93

Period	*Mid-year*	*Male*	*Female*	*Person*
		TOTAL		
1970-75	1973	50.5	49.0	49.7
1976-80	1978	52.5	52.1	52.3
1981-85	1983	55.4	55.7	55.4
1986-90	1988	57.7	58.1	57.7
1987-91*	1989	58.1	58.6	58.3
1988-92*	1990	58.6	59.0	58.7
1989-93*	1991	59.0	59.7	59.4
		RURAL		
1970-75	1973	48.9	47.1	48.0
1976-80	1978	51.0	50.3	50.6
1981-85	1983	54.0	53.6	53.7
1986-90	1988	56.1	56.2	56.1
1987-91*	1989	56.7	56.9	56.8
1988-92*	1990	57.2	57.4	57.4
1989-93*	1991	57.9	58.1	58.0
		URBAN		
1970-75	1973	58.8	59.2	58.9
1976-80	1978	59.6	60.8	60.1
1981-85	1983	61.6	64.1	62.8
1986-90	1988	62.0	64.9	63.4
1987-91*	1989	62.3	65.3	63.8
1988-92*	1990	62.8	65.5	64.1
1989-93*	1991	63.5	66.3	64.9

*Excludes Jammu & Kashmir

Source : SRS Based Life Tables. 1989-93, Office of the Registrar General, India, New Delhi.

Infant Mortality Rates by Sex, India and Major States (rural, urban, total) — 1992 and 1993

India / Major States	Total				Rural				Urban			
	1992		1993		1992		1993		1992		1993	
	Males	Females	Males	Females	Males	Females	Males	Females	Males	Females	Males	Females
(1)	(2)	(3)	(4)	(5)	(6)	(7)	(8)	(9)	(10)	(11)	(12)	(13)
India*	79	80	73	75	84	86	81	84	54	52	47	
Andhra Pradesh	73	68	70	57	80	75	76	64	43	40	53	38
Assam	86	78	81	81	90	79	84	83	40	61	53	66
Bihar	71	74	68	72	72	77	71	75	53	44	41	41
Gujarat	66	69	58	58	70	74	65	65	51	55	43	43
Haryana	73	78	60	73	78	80	64	77	47	67	49	57
Himachal Pradesh	67	66	72	53	70	67	74	54	22	45	35	37
Karnataka	77	67	69	66	89	75	82	75	40	43	38	46
Kerala	21	12	16	10	22	12	18	12	14	12	10	7
Madhya Pradesh	109	98	106	106	115	102	111	115	73	75	76	58
Maharashtra	61	57	50	50	68	67	66	60	45	34	28	36
Orissa	114	116	118	101	117	118	122	107	76	84	82	55
Punjab	54	60	49	62	56	68	52	70	46	34	40	38
Rajasthan	88	92	82	81	93	95	86	89	58	75	62	46
Tamil Nadu	58	59	57	56	65	68	66	56	45	38	38	38
Uttar Pradesh	92	105	87	100	94	110	91	107	79	77	67	65
West Bengal	67	62	57	59	74	67	63	66	34	41	34	31

*Excludes Jammu & Kashmir

Source : Sample Registration System, Fertility and Mortality Indicators, 1992 and 1993, Office of the Registrar General, India, New Delhi.

Percentage distribution of deaths by sex among major cause-groups, rural India — 1992-94

Major Cause Group		Percentage of Deaths								
		1992			1993			1994		
		Males	*Females*	*Persons*	*Males*	*Females*	*Persons*	*Males*	*Females*	*Persons*
	(1)	(2)	(3)	(4)	(5)	(6)	(7)	(8)	(9)	(10)
I	Accidents & Injuries	9.9	7.1	8.7	9.6	6.9	8.4	10.2	7.2	8.8
II	Childbirth and Pregnancy (Maternal mortality)	0.0	2.4	1.0	0.0	2.9	1.3	0.0	2.3	1.1
III	Fevers	7.0	8.5	7.7	6.1	7.4	6.7	6.6	8.1	7.3
IV	Digestive disorders	5.6	6.9	6.2	6.4	7.2	6.8	6.0	6.5	6.2
V	Cough (Disorders of respiratory system)	21.4	17.2	19.6	21.7	16.1	19.2	21.0	17.2	19.3
VI	Disorders of the central nervous system	4.7	4.3	4.5	4.2	4.3	4.2	5.1	5.0	5.0
VII	Diseases of circulatory system	11.9	9.3	10.8	11.4	9.7	10.6	11.8	10.5	11.2
VIII	Other clear symptoms	8.8	7.9	8.4	9.4	8.3	8.9	10.2	10.3	10.3
IX	Causes peculiar to infancy	9.2	10.2	9.6	10.4	11.7	11.0	9.2	10.1	9.6
X	Senility	21.4	26.2	23.5	20.7	25.6	22.9	19.9	22.9	21.2
Total		100.0	100.0	100.0	100.0	100.0	100.0	100.0	100.0	100.0

Source : Survey of Causes of Death (Rural), India, Annual Report 1993 and 1994, Office of the Registrar General, India, New Delhi.

INDEX

(SBS) Bill no 39266 8/12/07
Sl no 101

O/K